The First to Cry Down Injustice?

The First to Cry Down Injustice?

Western Jews and Japanese Removal during WWII

Ellen M. Eisenberg

LEXINGTON BOOKS

A division of
ROWMAN & LITTLEFIELD PUBLISHERS, INC.
Lanham • Boulder • New York • Toronto • Plymouth, UK

LEXINGTON BOOKS

A division of Rowman & Littlefield Publishers, Inc.
A wholly owned subsidiary of The Rowman & Littlefield Publishing Group, Inc.
4501 Forbes Boulevard, Suite 200
Lanham, MD 20706

Estover Road
Plymouth PL6 7PY
United Kingdom
United Kingdom

British Library Cataloguing in Publication Information Available

Library of Congress Cataloging-in-Publication Data

Eisenberg, Ellen.
    The first to cry down injustice : Western Jews and Japanese removal during
WWII / Ellen M. Eisenberg.
        p. cm.
    Includes bibliographical references and index.
    ISBN-13: 978-0-7391-1381-3 (hardcover : alk. paper)
    ISBN-10: 0-7391-1381-X (pbk. : alk. paper)
    ISBN-13: 978-0-7391-1382-0 (hardcover : alk. paper)
    ISBN-10: 0-7391-1382-8 (pbk. : alk. paper)
    1. Jews—West (U.S.)—History—20th century. 2. Jews—West (U.S.)—Politics and
government—20th century. 3. Jews—West (U.S.)—Societies, etc. 4. Japanese
Americans—Evacuation and relocation, 1942–1945. 5. World War, 1939–1945—
Japanese Americans. 6. Intergroup relations—West (U.S.)—Societies, etc. 7. West
(U.S.)—Ethnic relations. I. Title.
    F596.3.J5E57 2008
    940.53'1778089924—dc22   2008022018

    eISBN-13: 978-0-7391-3013-1
    eISBN-10: 0-7391-3013-7

Printed in the United States of America

⊗™The paper used in this publication meets the minimum requirements of
American National Standard for Information Sciences—Permanence of Paper for
Printed Library Materials, ANSI/NISO Z39.48–1992.

Contents

Acknowledgments

I began this project over a decade ago by looking at Jewish responses to wartime anti-Nikkei policies in Portland, Oregon. I had only recently reoriented my research focus to the American West, and I was interested in identifying promising local projects. Reading Cheryl Greenberg's article on national Jewish groups made me curious about whether her finding that these groups ignored the plight of the Nikkei would hold true in a western location. Familiar with the literature on Jewish work against prejudice, I expected to find some evidence of Jewish opposition to wartime Japanese American policy. I was taken aback by the Jewish silence in Portland and determined to understand it.

At that time, I would not have been in a position to make an argument based on regionalism. Despite the fact that I had moved to the West several years before, I knew little about the region's history, Jewish or otherwise. The West was barely mentioned in my undergraduate and graduate work in American studies and American history. Within the field of American Jewish history, with a few notable exceptions, the region was generally ignored. When I conducted my first research project on Jewish migration to Portland, I knew far more about the migrants than I did about the city.

I have spent much of the last decade becoming a western historian. Many projects, but most important, my collaboration with Ava Kahn and Bill Toll in writing an analytical history of Jews in the Pacific West, have provided me with new lenses for viewing the same historical questions that I first raised about Jewish responses to Japanese American incarceration a decade ago. I am grateful to both of them, not only for their outstanding work on our coauthored book but for the many, many ways that our joint exploration of western Jewish history has informed my thinking in this book.

This project has also been greatly informed by a larger conversation about regionalism in American Jewish history. It was my good fortune that the 2006 Scholars Conference on American Jewish History in Charleston, South Carolina, took place just as I began writing. The conference program included any number of sessions focusing on the theme of regionalism that helped shape the ways in which I have framed my analysis here. Many of my ideas about western Jewish history have developed through conversations with scholars I have come to know through the Western Jewish Studies Association. The WJSA annual conference, which I have attended faithfully for over a decade, has provided an extremely positive and encouraging forum for testing out new ideas.

My work on Jewish responses to the mass removal and incarceration policy has been encouraged by a number of colleagues. At Willamette, Linda Tamura of the School of Education, an accomplished historian of the Japanese American experience, first introduced me to the field when she invited me to plan a conference on the Japanese American experience in the Pacific Northwest. Ultimately, my dear friend and history department colleague Jennifer Jopp and I coordinated the conference, where I presented my first, very preliminary, paper on the responses of Portland Jews to the incarceration. Roger Daniels served as keynote speaker at that conference, and, in years since, has always been interested in talking about my findings and has consistently encouraged and supported this work.

Ava Kahn and Marc Dollinger invited me to expand this analysis—at that point focusing only on Oregon—to California and to contribute a chapter on the subject to their co-edited anthology, *California Jews*. Both of them have continued to encourage this project, as has Jonathan Sarna, who took notice of my work then and has continued to generously provide advice and encouragement in the years since. As I began my first work on California, Ava was particularly helpful in orienting me to various California collections, particularly those at the Bancroft Library and the Western Jewish History Center at the Magnes Museum. In southern California, Amy Hill Shevitz and Jodi Myers were excellent guides. Jodi's invitation to speak at California State University at Northridge, and Amy and Jodi's suggestion that the Urban Archives on CSUN's campus might hold useful materials, proved the turning point in my research, leading me to the papers of the Los Angeles Jewish Community Committee, which became the topic of chapter 4.

I am grateful to the archivists and librarians whose assistance proved invaluable at CSUN's Urban Archives Center, the Japanese American National Museum in Los Angeles, the Bancroft Library, the Western Jewish History Center, the Oregon Jewish Museum, the Oregon Historical Society, and the University of Washington Special Collections. Particular thanks to the Urban Archive Center's Robert Marshall and the OJM's Judy Margles and Anne LeVant Prahl. At Willamette's Hatfield Library, Rich Schmidt proved to be the interlibrary loan master, always pleasantly securing for me even the most obscure documents. My good friend and law librarian Galin Brown managed to produce in days a document that I had been trying to locate for months. Mary Plank, who serves as administrative assistant to the History Department, cheerfully helped with numerous tasks.

Late in the project, I discovered the work of the Kansha Project to create a record of individuals who supported and defended Japanese Americans during World War II. Shizue Seigel, editor of *In Good Conscience*, was generous in sharing the entire Kansha Project database with me and in passing along accounts that she thought would serve useful for my project. She put me in touch with Mrs. Pat (Yamakawa) Yamamoto, who provided me with an account of her family's experience and with copies of her parents' correspondence. I am thankful to both of them for sharing these materials with me.

Travel to archives and conferences requires financial support. I am incredibly grateful to Willamette University for supplying me with that support through the Dwight and Margaret Lear Chair in American History. Although it was originally the wish of the Lears that the chair be in western history, they ultimately agreed to a chair in American history. I'm sure that they would be pleased to know that the holder of the chair now sees herself as a western historian. In addition to providing my livelihood and supporting this project, Willamette University has for the past eighteen years been a wonderful community for me as a teacher and as a scholar. I am blessed to have such interesting and supportive colleagues throughout the entire College of Liberal Arts and especially in the History Department. I greatly value their daily encouragement, enthusiasm, and friendship.

At Lexington Books/Rowman & Littlefield, Brian Romer showed early interest in the project and provided much encouragement. Later, Julie Kirsch took over the editing and proved easy to work with, enthusiastic, and efficient. As the project approached completion, colleagues, students, friends, and relatives cheerfully read chapters. Willamette colleagues Cecily McCaffrey and Emily Drew and my sister, Julie Eisenberg, all provided useful comments on individual chapters. My work also benefited greatly from the insightful comments of Roger Daniels and Jonathan Sarna on chapter 4. My American Immigration History class in the spring semester of 2007 read chapter 1 and provided suggestions, as did my son Alex Korsunsky. The close reading of the entire manuscript by my parents, Meyer and Carolyn Eisenberg, my husband, Ami Korsunsky, and my friend and colleague Jennifer Jopp (twice!) was of tremendous help as I prepared to submit the manuscript.

Family and friends helped to keep things in perspective. Despite the crazi-ness of trying to write—and then trying to edit—both this and the coau-thored book at the same time, I have been able to maintain some sense of sanity and balance due to their support. Thanks are particularly due to my family—my sons Alex and Ben, and my husband Ami Korsunsky—for their patience (and sacrifice of their computer time) as I put in many weekend and summer hours on this project. I greatly appreciate their love and their support.

Introduction

On the Friday night following the attack on Pearl Harbor, several of the West Coast's most prominent rabbis chose to focus their sermons on local ramifications of the nation's recent entry into the Second World War. In Seattle, where nearly 7,000 Japanese Americans resided, Temple De Hirsch's Samuel Koch urged his congregants to remain calm and confident in their country's ability to prevail. He added,

> . . . one admonition seems necessary. There are many aliens on the coast—especially Japanese. The great majority of them are highly commended for their Americanism. They regret the folly of Japan as much as anyone. But they have had no part in it. They are anxious to remain good Americans. It is not unlikely that hotheads, here and there, will endeavor to embarrass them in various ways. But we should remind ourselves that the American way is tolerant, sympathetic, cooperative. Let's be on our guard to treat all Americans as Americans.[1]

On the same evening, Rabbi Irving Reichert of San Francisco's Temple Emanu-El expressed similar concerns in a sermon titled "The Price of Freedom," which was reprinted in the temple's newsletter the following week. Reichert emphasized the need for all racial groups to unite behind the war effort:

> I said all racial groups in our country. That brings up immediately the question of the groups of Axis extraction. There has already been an outcropping of hysteria in our country and community. . . . Already there have been unpardonable attacks and outrages upon American citizens of Japanese parentage whose loyalty to our country is as unyielding and assured as that of President Roo-

sevelt himself. While, to be sure, we must zealously be on our guard against 5th columnists and saboteurs and traitors, by the same token we must not commit the unpardonable offense of visiting upon the heads of the innocent the crimes of the guilty in lands from which they came but from which they have long since disassociated themselves. And we Jews, who have for 19 centuries suffered persecution because of the alleged conduct of some of our forbears in Judea 1900 years ago, ought to be among the first to cry down the unjust persecution of the foreign-born in our midst whose patriotism is equal to ours.[2]

Given the decades' long association of Jewish communities with a wide variety of civil rights and liberal causes, these powerful sermons seem, in retrospect, unsurprising. By the mid-twentieth century, rabbinical groups like the Reform Movement's Central Conference of American Rabbis (CCAR) and lay groups like the Anti-Defamation League of B'nai B'rith (ADL) had articulated a commitment to fighting anti-Semitism by speaking out broadly against discrimination in all its forms.[3] For people who came of age during the mid to late twentieth century, it seems natural that Jewish leaders would join other liberal spokespeople from secular groups like the ACLU in defending vulnerable minority groups.

Yet the sermons offered by Rabbis Koch and Reichert were not representative of the Jewish community's responses to efforts to impugn the loyalty of Japanese Americans after Pearl Harbor and, ultimately, to remove them from the West Coast and incarcerate them in concentration camps in the interior.[4] Nationally, as Cheryl Greenberg has demonstrated, the leading Jewish (and African American) civil rights organizations ignored the issue, failing to speak out against the policy as it unfolded in early 1942, due, in part, to their heavy investment in the war effort and their faith in the Roosevelt administration. Greenberg's analysis of such groups, including the National Urban League, the National Association for the Advancement of Colored People (NAACP), the National Council of Negro Women, the National Council of Jewish Women (NCJW), the Anti-Defamation League (ADL), the American Jewish Congress (AJCong) and the American Jewish Committee (AJC) finds that while all "knew of the Executive Order . . . [and] a few seemed to tacitly endorse the evacuation; most did not even discuss it." Among these Jewish and African American organizations, all of which, "came to recognize that their own persecution was part of a larger pattern of prejudice, and began working together on those larger issues," only two—the NAACP and the NCJW—"responded in any explicit or public way" in support of Japanese American evacuees, and even those two groups stopped short of an "unequivocally oppositional stance." Most of these groups, Greenberg argues, "did not even perceive the injustice of the racially based evacuation and incarceration."[5]

Individual Jewish leaders known as staunch supporters of civil liberties responded similarly. Felix Frankfurter, whose Sacco and Vanzetti defense is held up by historian Michael Alexander as emblematic of the American Jewish embrace of "outsider identification,"[6] not only failed to defend Japanese Americans but participated actively in constructing and upholding the incarceration policy. Thus, the man who had argued that Sacco and Vanzetti could not have gotten a fair trial "because an atmosphere of racial and political prejudice pervading America during the Red Scare of 1920 had created a condition of regular judicial bias"[7] apparently failed to see the prejudice contributing to wartime removal policy. Indeed, he provided advice on alien policy as an administration insider in 1942, and, later during the war, voted with the majority on the Supreme Court in affirming it.[8] While few American Jewish leaders played such an active role in supporting this policy, they were not prominent among the opponents either.[9] Most remained silent.

The silence of Jewish American groups mirrored that of secular organizations ordinarily known for their outspoken defense of minorities and the downtrodden. Although a disproportionate number of the *individual* activists who defended Japanese Americans came from progressive religious or politically liberal/leftist backgrounds,[10] they often broke with their organizations' official policies and with the majority of their comrades when they took this stance. For example, while one of the most moving speeches in defense of Japanese Americans before the Tolan Committee[11] came from a California CIO official, it was not the position of the CIO to oppose the removal and incarceration policy. As progressive Los Angeles lawyer Ben Margolis explained in a later oral history,

> Well, that was a kind of a unique period in American history because on many issues where there would have ordinarily been sharp breaks between the Left and the Right, they [sat] shoulder to shoulder. And around many of the issues relating to the conduct of the war that was so. The Communist Party at that time took the position that everything else had to yield to whatever was necessary in order to win the war. And that was the trade union position, both the AF of L and the CIO. It was, I suppose, the position of 95 percent of the people in organizations in this country, and I don't think I am exaggerating.
>
> I must say that I also supported this. And while I recognize in my career that I made many mistakes, this is the only one that occurs to me, at the moment, of which I am deeply ashamed. But I did wholeheartedly support the position of the CIO and—well, the position of almost everyone at that time.[12]

The country's leading civil liberties organization, the ACLU, shared this perspective. That organization's national executive board voted 2 to 1 to support the administration in its "internment" policy and kept legal efforts to test the "enemy alien" restrictions used against Japanese Americans at arm's length.[13] Although Socialist Party leader Norman Thomas "denounced incarceration in 1942," the party did not take a position on the issue.[14] The confidence that many leading civil rights and civil liberties groups had in Roosevelt and his administration and their close ties to that administration contributed to their trust that the government would be fair in its treatment of the Japanese American community. As ACLU historian Judy Kutulas explains, "Because liberals looked on Roosevelt as one of them, someone who believed as they did and could be trusted to do right, they excused his lapses or viewed them as necessary political compromises."[15]

This attitude was compounded by geography: based in eastern cities, far removed from Japanese American neighborhoods and the concentration camps, and unlikely to have personal relationships with Japanese Americans, the leaders of national civil rights and civil liberties groups had little personal experience to weigh against government arguments that Japanese Americans were inherently more loyal to their ancestral homeland than were other ethnic Americans, or that the camps were actually protecting Japanese Americans and fostering their integration in America. As Kutulas explains, "Virtually all persons of Japanese ancestry lived in California, Oregon or Washington. Most easterners had encountered them only as house servants or gardeners to their California friends. Having much trust in the Roosevelt administration's conduct of the war, they accepted that immediate internment 'based on Japanese ancestry' was reasonable."[16] Ultimately, she argues, "[ACLU] directors tended not to think much about Japanese Americans as people."[17]

For West Coast civil libertarians and others concerned with minority rights, however, the situation was not so easy to ignore. Residents of California, Oregon, and Washington had front row seats as the policy unfolded. Congress's Tolan Committee held open hearings on the issue in the major West Coast cities in February and March of 1942. Most of these cities were home to large communities of Japanese immigrants (Issei) and their children (Nisei), who were American citizens by birth. Stables at racetracks and fairgrounds in and near these cities became the temporary living quarters ("assembly centers") for Japanese Americans—120,000 individuals, two-thirds of whom were American citizens—until they were shipped to more permanent camps in the interior. The daily papers in these cities covered these developments extensively, particularly during the winter and spring of 1942.

Residents of California, Oregon, and Washington not only were witnesses to the removal and incarceration, but also were exposed to tremendous levels of anti-Nikkei[18] vitriol. Political leaders and a wide variety of organizations, ranging from Chambers of Commerce to American Legion posts to Granges, tapped into historic anti-Asian sentiment with their harshly worded accusations about the potential for Japanese American disloyalty and demands for strong actions against the entire community, alien and citizen alike. Newspaper coverage frequently conflated the Nikkei community, citizens and aliens, with the nation of Japan.[19] Although the mainstream press in the three Pacific states initially cautioned their readers that local Japanese Americans should not be blamed for the attack on Pearl Harbor, nearly all grew increasingly hostile in both their news coverage and editorial stances as the government formulated the incarceration policy. They reported unsubstantiated accounts of sabotage and subversion, despite the fact that no case of actual sabotage by Japanese Americans ever took place. Ultimately, they endorsed the government policy of forcibly removing Japanese Americans from the Western Defense Zone and incarcerating them in camps surrounded by barbed wire in remote and desolate locations in the interior West.[20]

The West Coast was home not only to the strongest and most widespread support for mass removal and incarceration but also to the small but active groups that tried to defend Japanese Americans. Individual ACLU activists on the West Coast who were familiar with the long history of racism against Japanese Americans and who had contacts in the Nikkei community ignored the instructions of their national office and took on test cases challenging the racially based restrictions and exclusions in court.[21] Students, faculty, and administrators at the University of Washington organized efforts to defend Nisei students and Japanese American Seattleites more generally against alien restrictions, acts of prejudice, and the relocation order. Similarly, the University of California at Berkeley became the center of organized activity to oppose mass incarceration by speaking out at the Tolan Committee Hearings and publicly opposing any policy based solely on race or ancestry. Faculty and administrators at several West Coast universities cooperated with colleagues farther east to enroll Nisei students in colleges and universities outside of the evacuation zone.[22]

The intensity of the debate on the West Coast left little middle ground. Yet, while there were individuals within each Jewish community who were active both as supporters and opponents of the government policy, the major organized Jewish communities of the West Coast chose not to take a position on this issue. As hearings took place, as the local secular press published countless stories, as public officials and citizens' groups made intolerant and racist statements, and as small groups of liberal activists spoke out sharply against the policy, Jewish organizations and newspapers maintained a near total silence on the issue.

This community silence is particularly striking when placed alongside the vocal support of the regional Jewish press and community organizations for civil rights causes in general. This contrast is what first drew me to this issue. How could newspapers that again and again published statements preaching tolerance and condemning prejudice in all of its forms ignore the injustice being committed on their doorstep? Why did the few Jewish leaders who did speak out publicly against the policy, like Rabbis Koch and Reichert, fail to generate any substantial support within the Jewish community or even within their own congregations? How could communities that saw the fight against discrimination as a central commitment appear to ignore these events, which were front-page news in their hometowns?

After studying the history of anti-Japanese sentiment on the West Coast and tracing the increasingly hysterical public discourse on the topic through the winter of 1942, I came to see the silence in a more nuanced way. Indeed, given the overwhelming anti-Nikkei sentiment, I began to see silence less as apathy and more as a conscious decision *not* to join the chorus. While Cheryl Greenberg argues that the Japanese issue "passed unnoticed" by national Jewish organizations like the ADL and Judy Kutulas found that the national ACLU directors "tended not to think much" about Japanese Americans, the local media coverage would have made it impossible for educated and engaged citizens in cities like Seattle, Portland, San Francisco, and Los Angeles to simply ignore the issue. Close analysis of the words surrounding the silence in the regional Jewish press suggested not ignorance but rather an acute awareness of the policy and some level of discomfort and disapproval. It became clear that there was something else going on. The silence could not be understood simply as part of the larger, national silence of Jews, civil libertarians, and liberals. Rather, it had to be studied in its local context.

Certainly, Jewish westerners, like Jews in general, were pulled in conflicting directions by their twin commitments to fighting discrimination and supporting the administration in its fight against Nazism. But for Californians, Oregonians, and Washingtonians, the fate of Japanese Americans was not the marginal, faraway issue that it was for the New Yorkers who filled the boards of organizations like the ADL and the ACLU but a real and local one. Jewish westerners were concentrated in the region's major cities, which were also home to substantial Japanese American communities. In Seattle's Central District and in Los Angeles's Boyle Heights, Jews and Japanese Americans shared residential districts and their children attended the same public schools. Unlike their eastern counterparts, who had little if any experience with Japanese Americans, these westerners resided in cities in which Japanese Americans were a very real presence.

Indeed, in all of these cities, Japanese Americans played an important role as the most visible minority ethnic group. In the early twentieth century, they had been the focus of vicious campaigns to restrict their rights and to end further immigration. Prominent "patriotic" organizations regularly assailed them as unassimilable, a threat to American workers and, potentially, to American democracy. Japanese Americans, as the region's most prominent nonwhite group, were, in many ways, those against whom whiteness was defined.

As many historians of this period have argued, the long history of anti-Asian sentiment is critical to understanding the racially based incarceration policy that targeted Japanese Americans in the West. But it is also central to understanding the responses of other ethnic minority groups in the West to that policy, for the identities of each group were bound up with perceptions of the others. For western Jews, whose long-standing acceptance as whites in the West was fostered in part by the rigid exclusion of Japanese and other Asian immigrants from "white" communities, responses to wartime policies directed at Japanese Americans reflect regionally specific ethnic group identities. Along with revealing the attitudes that they held toward Japanese Americans, Jewish responses reveal something about their own group identity within the western context.

That identity is critical to understanding the most surprising finding of my research: the secret participation of one Los Angeles Jewish civil rights organization in the campaign against Japanese Americans immediately before and after Pearl Harbor. As I demonstrate in chapter 4, the local context, in the form of the growing threat of pro-fascist and anti-Semitic groups in southern California, bred insecurity among community leaders. As they cooperated with government agencies to expose these enemies, their perception of what was "anti-American" expanded. Influenced by regional racist attitudes against Japanese Americans, the group contributed its resources to disseminating anti-Nikkei propaganda. Ultimately, their propaganda played a role in contributing to the case for mass removal and incarceration.

In her introduction to *In the Almost Promised Land*, a study of Jewish-Black relations, Hasia Diner explains, "I wanted to know how Jews saw American race relations and why they interpreted it the way they did. How did the confluence of their history and their circumstances in the United States cause them to develop a group-specific understanding of black Americans?" Although some have argued that Jewish association with liberal/progressive causes stems from "outsider identification" growing out of centuries of exclusion, Diner places emphasis on the particular context of early twentieth-century America and sees Jewish responses to African Americans as rooted in "their hopes and fears at that moment in time."[23] Similarly, I have approached the question of Jewish responses to Nikkei policy with an eye toward the specific environment in which these events unfolded. How did Jews in the West—a region with an ethnic landscape that sets it apart from other parts of the country—identify as Jews and as westerners, and how, in turn, did that identity affect their response to the plight of Japanese Americans? If western Jewish community leaders were, as many historians assert, particularly well integrated and acculturated as white westerners, why did they fail to more actively support a policy that was wildly popular among their white neighbors? On the other hand, if American Jews had developed by the early to mid-twentieth century what Michael Alexander has called an "outsider identification,"[24] a strong empathy with minorities and support for their rights, then why did most western Jews apparently not apply this ideology to the plight of the Japanese American community during World War II?

The responses of western Jews to measures taken against Japanese Americans, both during the war and in the decades leading up to it, are not the stuff of celebratory community history. This history reveals examples of individuals whose words and actions are commendable, but also cases of those who contributed to racially based fear mongering. The most common story is one of silence: of one community standing by as an injustice was done to another. In his seminal work on the anti-Asian movement in California, Roger Daniels writes,

> I have little sympathy with the basic assumptions of the California exclusionists whose chronicler I have chosen to become. I have tried to understand them. To a very great degree, I have let them tell their own story; its unfolding must tarnish several reputations. Yet in no sense have I attempted to evaluate the total careers of the leaders involved. Almost all of these men played many roles, and this study inspects only one facet—some would say flaw—of their public characters.[25]

A similar caveat is appropriate here. As much as I admire the personal courage of individuals of all faiths who had the courage to speak out in support of Japanese Americans, my purpose here is neither to celebrate them nor to condemn those who supported a policy that, while popular and deemed patriotic at the time, is now almost universally seen as racist and immoral. Rather, I hope to contribute to an understanding of the particular regional dynamics of ethnic identity that shaped all of these responses while remembering that the activities under examination here were, in Daniels's words, "only a small scene in a long public performance."

In exploring these issues, I begin by establishing the western context for the study. Chapter 1 explores the ethnic landscape of the West, beginning in the late nineteenth century. Here, I contrast the experience of the Jews as an ethnic minority in the West with the experience of the Japanese and argue that the two are linked, as the perception of each minority group is influenced by the particular combination of groups in any area. In addition to examining the status and acceptance of both the Jewish and Japanese American communities, I also discuss the attitudes of Jews toward Japanese, and other Asian, immigrants.

Chapter 2 examines silence as the predominant response of organized western Jewry to the events of early 1942. This chapter focuses on the Jewish press in several western cities, placing that coverage in the context of local and regional attitudes on the issue. Here, I highlight the tendency to avoid the issue, and I explore the community concerns that dominated press coverage. I argue that, when examined in context, the Jewish press silence on Japanese Americans suggests not ignorance but discomfort and tension over the issue of mass incarceration.

Chapter 3 focuses on the groups and individuals who took a stand against the Nikkei policies as they emerged, places the limited Jewish role in the context of the larger opposition movement, and examines the exceptional Jewish individuals who took a stand against the mass removal and incarceration. I argue that several factors, including the physical relationship of Jewish and Japanese American neighborhoods, the dynamics of local opposition groups, and Jewish political ideologies, shaped Jewish opposition.

Chapter 4 focuses on one organization, the Los Angeles Jewish Community Committee (LAJCC, later known as the Los Angeles Community Relations Council, or LACRC). Formed in the 1930s as a group whose mission was to stand against anti-Semitism and other forms of discrimination, the LAJCC cooperated enthusiastically with state and federal government efforts to expose and investigate the growing number of anti-Semitic and pro-fascist groups in southern California. Its focus on pro-Axis organizations led it to become involved in exposing groups and individuals who were supportive of Japan. These activities, in turn, led to active participation in the creation and dissemination of anti-Nikkei propaganda that played an important role in the lead-up to the incarceration program. This evidence of a significant Jewish community organization contributing to the case for mass removal and incarceration of Japanese Americans will, no doubt, be surprising if not shocking to many general readers as well as to historians of American Jewry. Chapter 4 aims to present this story within the context of local events and inter-group relations.

While studies of Jews and whiteness in recent years have made important contributions to our understanding of how Jews negotiated their racial/ethnic identity in settings like New York or Atlanta, the equation was necessarily different in the West where race relations are far more complicated than black and white.[26] In the West, historians are beginning to move beyond traditional studies, which have "isolated 'marginal' groups from each other and from a larger historical narrative," and toward analysis of the ways in which these groups have interacted with one another.[27] This examination of Jewish responses to the plight of the Nikkei aims to build upon this discussion by focusing on the response of one ethnic minority group to the persecution of another. The Jews who witnessed and responded to the mass removal and incarceration of Japanese Americans were not just American Jews whose yards happened to boast palm trees or Douglas fir instead of maples and walnuts, or who vacationed at Yosemite or Pacific City rather than the Jersey Shore or the Catskills. While they shared much with eastern Jews, their experiences and identities as Jews were shaped by their home region and particularly by its ethnic landscape. Their responses to the treatment of the Nikkei community must be understood within that context.

NOTES

1. *Temple Tidings,* Temple de Hirsch, Seattle, December 12, 1941.
2. *Temple Emanu-El Chronicle,* San Francisco, December 20, 1941.
3. Stuart Svonkin, *Jews against Prejudice: American Jews and the Fight for Civil Liberties* (New York: Columbia University Press, 1997), chap. 1; Marc Dollinger, *Quest for Inclusion: Jews and Liberalism in Modern America* (Princeton, N.J.: Princeton University Press, 2000), chap. 3.
4. Throughout this text, "removal and incarceration" will be used to describe what is commonly—but inappropriately—called the "internment" of Japanese Americans. Internment is a legal process under which *individuals* can be arrested and detained during wartime. During World War II, approximately 2,300 Germans, a few hundred Italians, and 8,000 Japanese—nearly all of them adult males—were interned due to suspicions based on their individual activities and affiliations. Internees had the right to appeal their detention. This is quite different from what happened to Japanese Americans on the Pacific Coast, who were detained indiscriminately based solely on their ancestry and regardless of age, gender, or status as citizen. They had no recourse to appeal their detention. See Roger Daniels, "Words Do Matter: A Note on Inappropriate Terminology and the Incarceration of the Japanese Americans," *Nikkei in the Pacific Northwest,* ed. Louis Fiset and Gail M. Nomura (Seattle: University of Washington Press, 2005), 190–214.
5. Cheryl Greenberg, "Black and Jewish Responses to Japanese Internment," *Journal of American Ethnic History* 14, no. 2 (Winter 1995): 4.
6. Michael Alexander, *Jazz Age Jews* (Princeton, N.J.: Princeton University Press, 2001), part II.
7. Alexander, *Jazz Age Jews,* 2–3.
8. Roger Daniels, "The Japanese American Cases, 1942–2004: A Social History," *Law and Contemporary Problems* 68, no. 159 (2005): 162. See also Peter Irons, *Justice at War: The Story of the Japanese American Internment Cases* (Oxford: Oxford University Press, 1983); and James Simon, *The Antagonists: Hugo Black, Felix Frankfurter and Civil Liberties in Modern America* (New York: Simon and Schuster, 1989), chap. 4.
9. The Kansha Project database lists individuals who defended and supported Japanese Americans in the face of wartime policies. Of several hundred individuals, only a handful are identified as Jewish (not all of the individuals are identified by religious and/or ethnic background). Shizue Seigel, *In Good Conscience: Supporting Japanese Americans During the Internment* (San Mateo, Calif.: AACP, 2006).
10. Robert Shaffer, "Cracks in the Consensus: Defending the Rights of Japanese Americans During World War II," *Radical History Review* 72 (1998): 84–120.
11. The Tolan Committee of the U.S. House of Representatives held hearings in several West Coast cities in early 1942 on the proposed removal policies.
12. Ben Margolis, "Law and Social Conscience" oral history interview by Michael Balter, 1984–85, University of California, Los Angeles, Oral History Program, Department of Special Collections, Charles E. Young Research Library, U.C. Los Angeles, p. 94.
13. Judy Kutulas, *The American Civil Liberties Union and the Making of Modern Liberalism, 1930–1960* (Chapel Hill: University of North Carolina Press, 2006), chap. 4. See also Judy Kutulas, "In Quest of Autonomy: The Northern California Affiliate

of the American Civil Liberties Union and World War II," *Pacific Historical Review* 67, no. 2 (1998): 201–31.

14. Daniels, "The Japanese American Cases," 164.

15. Kutulas, *The American Civil Liberties Union*, 92.

16. Kutulas, *The American Civil Liberties Union*, 98.

17. Kutulas, *The American Civil Liberties Union*, 99.

18. In referring to the Japanese American community, several terms will be used. *Issei* and *Nisei* are generation-specific terms. The former refers to members of the immigrant generation, and the latter to the children of immigrants. *Nikkei* is a general term that refers to the entire Japanese American community.

19. For example, it was common for newspapers in the region to use "Japanese" or "Japs," to refer to the Japanese government and army as well as to American-born members of the local communities.

20. For analysis of the press coverage in California, see Roger Daniels, *The Politics of Prejudice* (Berkeley: University of California Press, 1962), *Prisoners without Trial* (New York: Hill and Wang, 1993), and *Concentration Camps: North America Japanese in the US and Canada during World War II* (Malabar, Fla.: R.E. Krieger, 1981); Lloyd Chiasson, "Japanese American Relocation during World War II: A Study of California Editorial Reaction," *Journalism Quarterly* 68, nos. 1 & 2 (1991): 263–68; Gary Okihiro, "The Press, Japanese Americans, and the Concentration Camps," *Phylon* 44, no. 1 (1983): 66–83; and Morton Grodzins, *Americans Betrayed* (Chicago: University of Chicago Press, 1949). On Washington and Oregon, see Floyd McKay, "Pacific Northwest Newspapers and Executive Order 9066," presented at The Nikkei Experience in the Northwest conference, Seattle, 2000; Richard Berner, *Seattle Transformed: World War II to Cold War* (Seattle: Charles Press, 1999), 27–29; and Timothy Olmstead, "Nikkei Internment: The Perspective of Two Oregon Weekly Newspapers," *Oregon Historical Quarterly* (Spring 1984): 5–32.

21. Kutulas, "In Quest of Autonomy," 201–231. See also Kutulas, *The American Civil Liberties Union*, chap. 5.

22. These efforts to place Nisei students are examined in Allan W. Austin, *From Concentration Camp to Campus: Japanese American Students and World War II* (Urbana: University of Illinois Press, 2004).

23. Hasia Diner, *In the Almost Promised Land: American Jews and Blacks, 1915–1935* (Baltimore: Johns Hopkins, 1977, 1995), xii–xiii.

24. Alexander, *Jazz Age Jews*, 1.

25. Daniels, *The Politics of Prejudice*, vii.

26. Shana Bernstein, "Building Bridges at Home in a Time of Global Conflict: Interracial Cooperation and the Fight for Civil Rights in Los Angeles, 1933–1954," Ph.D. diss., Stanford University, 2003, 20.

27. Bernstein, *Building Bridges at Home*, 20. George Sanchez called for such studies during the plenary session "Roundtable on Regionalism: The Significance of Place in American Jewish Life," American Jewish History Biennial Scholars' Conference, Charleston, June 2006.

1

Western Jews, Whiteness, and the Asian "Other"

Western Jews, whether they opted to remain silent, to protest, or to support government policy with regard to the forcible removal and incarceration of Japanese Americans during World War II, were informed by their communal and individual identities and their histories of relationships with Japanese Americans. These were shaped by the racial landscape of a region in which Japanese Americans played a key role as the most prominent non-white group. To understand the responses of western Jews to the events of 1942, it is critical to examine them in light of this regional ethnic history.

Much of the work on American Jewish identity and intergroup relations reflects an eastern context. Because Jews have historically been concentrated in the Northeast, where the discourse about race has, until recently, focused primarily on black–white relations, analysis has concentrated on interactions between Jews and African Americans. Similarly, much of the recent literature on Jewish racial identity sets an emerging Jewish "whiteness" within the context of a racial landscape that became increasingly defined in the twentieth century by a black–white divide. According to this narrative, East European Jews, like other second-wave southern and eastern European immigrants who flooded into the cities of the Northeast and Midwest at the turn of the century, were regarded as "not-quite-white." While legally white (and, therefore, able to immigrate and naturalize), these groups faced considerable racialized prejudice based on their alleged biological inferiority to northern Europeans and they, therefore, were regarded as less than white, provisionally white, or, to use historian David Roediger's term, "inbetweens." However, by the mid-twentieth century, due to the virtual cessation of immigration, the growing proportion of American-born within these communities, the politics of labor and the New Deal, and the Great Migration of African Americans, Jews and

1

other "inbetweens" had "become white." Yet Jews' experience of "inbetween-ness"—along with their historic exclusion in Europe—created great empathy for similarly excluded groups, leading to strong Jewish support for the civil rights of African Americans and other minorities.[1]

As historian Eric Goldstein effectively demonstrates, Jews' "uncertain relationship to whiteness"[2] in the late nineteenth and early twentieth century was not simply a matter of prejudice on the part of native-born whites. Rather, Jews themselves were ambivalent about their racial identity, seeing themselves as whites but also empathizing with blacks as historical outsiders. Rather than framing the question as "how Jews *became* white," he argues that historians should explore "how Jews *negotiated* their place in a complex racial world where Jewishness, whiteness, and blackness have all made significant claims on them."[3] In exploring that "complex racial world," Goldstein makes clear that variations in the racial landscape led to regional differences in Jewish identity.

Thus, Jews in the late-nineteenth-century South faced a racial world that differed significantly from that found in other parts of the country. In the antebellum period, Jews were defined as white in a society in which the primary racial division was based on slavery. Jewish newcomers who joined in efforts to develop the New South in the aftermath of the Civil War had little stake in the traditional racial system and, for both ideological and economic reasons, often supported African American rights. According to Goldstein, they were able to do so and retain unquestioned white status until the final two decades of the nineteenth century, when their status as "whites" increasingly came to be questioned. First, economic depression and the failure of the New South economy led to a backlash against modernity and against Jews who were often associated with it. Second, the arrival of East European immigrants who "stood out as alien in dress and appearance," led some southerners to identify them as other than white. By the 1880s, as Jews began to be excluded from clubs and found their political bids untenable, it was becoming clear that southern Jews were "no longer seen as unambiguously white."[4]

Not surprisingly, their increasing anxiety about their own status strongly affected their responses to the racial discourse of the region. Thus, according to Goldstein, Jewish southerners "began to vehemently oppose any comparison between themselves and African Americans," leading them to denounce northern Jewish newspaper stories linking the persecution of blacks to the historic persecution of Jews.[5] Notably, while northern Jews facing social discrimination lobbied for civil rights legislation, southern Jews shied away from such efforts, because they "feared that a sustained public campaign against such exclusionary policies would do nothing more than underscore Jews' status as victims of 'racial discrimination' and lend credence to the comparison between Jews and African Americans."[6]

Western Jews were strongly connected to eastern communities and shared, through personal ties, national organizations, and wire services, a strong identity as *American* Jews. Still, like southern Jews, their understanding of their ethnic and racial identity was informed by regional factors that were distinctive. Jews had been prominent town founders, political leaders, and economic innovators from the beginning of white settlement in the region, stood firmly among the exalted western pioneers, and had been accepted as unequivocally white since the Gold Rush. Even after anti-Semitism began to increase in the late nineteenth- and early twentieth-century South, Northeast, and Midwest, western Jews—with the exception of those in Los Angeles, where anti-Semitism was more pronounced—were able to congratulate themselves on their continuing acceptance. Although western Jews did experience prejudice in the form of social and professional exclusions, they remained accepted as city fathers and continued to be elected to political office by overwhelmingly non-Jewish constituencies,[7] even in the 1920s and 1930s when anti-Semitism was at its peak nationally.

This is not to say that the rising tide of anti-Semitism, and the more general prejudice against the so-called new immigrants from southern and eastern Europe, were not expressed in the Pacific West. Such sentiments were strongest in southern California, where a large migration of white Protestants from the Midwest led to a purging of Jews from elite social clubs and prominent civic organizations.[8] In the Bay Area and in the Pacific Northwest, anti-Semitism was less pronounced but there were signs of the increasing popularity of scientific racism. During the 1910s, all of the Pacific Coast states developed state-sponsored eugenics programs. In Oregon, a short-lived State Immigration Commission worked to attract "desirable agricultural immigration from Northern European countries" and published guides for potential immigrants in German and Swedish.[9] Neighborhood covenants began to exclude Jews from upscale areas in Seattle and the Los Angeles area during this period as well.

Yet, the impact of this trend on the region's Jewish communities was less severe than in the East, due in part to their demographics. In contrast to eastern and midwestern Jewish communities, which were overwhelmed by the flood of East Europeans at the turn of the century, the migration to western cities was far smaller and later in arriving.[10] While there was an influx of both eastern and southern European Jews into western cities, they made up a proportionately smaller part of the Jewish community and, because they often had sojourned for extended periods in other parts of the country before arriving on the West Coast, they tended to be fairly acclimated by the time that they arrived. Only in Los Angeles was the flood of newcomers overwhelming and there the influx came late and, as elsewhere in the West, included many immigrants who already had years of experience in America. The relatively small number of "greenhorns" from the "undesirable"

East European countries meant that Jewish communities in the West were seldom specifically targeted by local eugenicists and restrictionists.

Local debates about eugenics and immigration played out in the context of a region with a long history of Jewish acceptance, even in organizations not generally known for tolerance. An interesting example is the prominence of Jews in the Native Sons organizations. In Native Sons of Oregon, Sol Blumauer served as a founding trustee and was elected president at the turn of the century. Blumauer, his wife Hattie Fleischner Blumauer, and at least six other Jewish Oregonians were named as native sons or daughters and honored with pictures and/or biographical profiles in the inaugural volume of the organization's publication *Oregon Native Son*.[11] Inclusion in Native Sons is vivid evidence of Jewish acceptance as whites—the organization and its magazine were largely dedicated to venerating white history in Oregon.[12] Inclusion of profiles of Jewish Oregonians, sometimes listing service to Jewish organizations along with the individual's other achievements, contrasts sharply with the publication's stereotype-laden treatment of groups that were perceived as nonwhite. The publication's frequent stories on Native Americans, for example, present a range of stereotypes, from romanticized versions of supposed Indian lore, to depictions of "savages," in both cases clearly situating them as the other, in contrast to white pioneers. On the rare occasion that African Americans were mentioned—even as "Negro pioneers"—they are often described in negative terms ("the sons of Ham") and their shortcomings highlighted ("truth was never a conscious ingredient of his character"). None of those mentioned as "Negro pioneers" was included as a member of the all-white organization. Asian immigrants are notable in *Native Son* for their absence. The one mention of the possibility of "the Chinaman a Pioneer" discusses an effort by the British to trick a group of Chinese men into settling in the area and helping to secure the British claim. The story explains that the group never landed and suggests that they have no place in pioneer history, for "what ultimately became of them has not been made a matter of history."[13]

Jews were, likewise, accepted in California's Native Sons and Daughters of the Golden West, organizations that, beginning in the 1920s, became known for their "increasingly strident nativism" and close cooperation with the Asiatic Exclusion League.[14] Indeed, brothers Meyer and Henry Lissner and David Edelman, son of Los Angeles's first rabbi, were among the mostly Jewish founding members of the Corona Parlor (number 196) of the Native Sons of the Golden West in 1896.[15] San Francisco native Henrietta Isaacs Weill was active in the Bakersfield Native Daughters.[16] Despite the growing practice of excluding Jews from social clubs in the 1920s, there is evidence that Jews retained their membership privileges in NSGW parlors.[17] For example, when Joseph Snow, son of an 1850 pioneer, died in 1926, the funeral service at the Masonic temple was conducted "under the auspices of Plac-erville Parlor No. 9, Native Sons of the Golden West," prior to his burial at the Jewish cemetery.[18] Indeed, according to one historian, in taking a strong stance against Asians, "the Native Sons played an important role between the world wars in helping various European-American ethnics, many new to California, to imagine themselves as 'white' pioneers."[19]

Even the Klan, an organization notorious for its anti-Semitism, avoided criticisms of Jews during its heyday in Oregon in the early 1920s, because there were "so many good and influential Jewish citizens in the city." Oregon Grand Dragon Gifford found it necessary to muzzle a traveling Klan lecturer "for expressing hatred of Jews and foreigners."[20] A Klan effort to use a boycott of the Meier and Frank department store to protest the appointment of Julius Meier to a state committee in 1925 failed after the *Oregon Voter*, the state's leading public affairs journal, condemned the action.[21] Just five years later, Oregonians overwhelmingly elected Meier governor. Running as an independent, he garnered more votes than his Republican and Democratic rivals combined.[22]

Such acceptance of Jews as pioneers and political leaders is indicative of the continuing inclusivity of whiteness in the West. In contrast to the late-nineteenth-century East and Midwest, where the influx of diverse Europeans led to stratification among whites, whiteness in the nineteenth-century West was defined against a diverse group of nonwhites including Native Americans, Hispanics, and, most often, Asians. Historians have argued that the unique racial diversity of the region led to the emergence of a broad, pan-ethnic white identity. As Patricia Limerick writes, "in race relations, the West could make the turn-of-the-century Northeastern urban confrontation between European immigrants and American nativists look like a family reunion."[23] Such shifting racial coalitions did not always lead to inclusive whiteness—Elizabeth Jameson found that the "white man's camp" of Cripple Creek, Colorado, excluded Chinese, Japanese, Slavs, Italians, Greeks, and Mexicans (but not African Americans).[24] More often, however, the distinctions among diverse whites mattered less than the distinction between them and people of non-European heritage. Matthew Frye Jacobson has argued that conflict with Native Americans tended to encourage a more inclusive white identity, not only for settlers on the frontier but also for Americans back East. Linda Gordon has shown how, as prejudice and discrimination against Mexican miners solidified, "Euro-Latins"—Spanish, Italian, and Jewish immigrants who in other parts of America might have been considered "not-quite-white"—became part of an Anglo mob that identified itself as the "citizenry" in early twentieth-century Clifton, Arizona. Historian Tomas Almaguer makes the case that "race and the racialization process in California became the central organizing principle of group life during the state's formative period of development" and contends that racialized identities "provided the basis upon which European immigrants differentiated themselves from the diverse populations they encountered during their expansion into the Far West."[25]

While nineteenth-century western "whites" unified against diverse nonwhites, as the century drew to a close Asian immigrants—first Chinese and later Japanese—increasingly came to be seen as the chief racial threat. In the Pacific states, with an African American population that remained extremely small until mobilization for World War II,[26] Hispanic communities that were sizable only in southern California,[27] and a Native American population that was decimated by contact and subsequently confined to reservations, Asian immigrants and their descendants were the largest, most visible, and most "problematic" population of racial "others." The intolerance and hostility expressed against Japanese Americans in 1942 had a long tradition in the region. Manifesting itself in the agitation for Asian exclusion, alien land laws, and, at times, violence against Asian immigrant communities, the focus on Asians served to diffuse prejudices against Jews and other southern and eastern European immigrants—and even against African Americans and other non-Europeans and reinforce the region's inclusive whiteness. Thus, in arguing for Oregon's 1923 Alien Land Law, a measure aimed directly at the Japanese, its chief proponent in the legislature explained, "The negro, who is permitted citizenship, makes a good citizen. He is peace-loving and harmless, and can be adapted into the white man's civilization. The Japanese can never be so adapted."[28]

As early as the 1870s, diverse groups of European immigrants banded together in San Francisco and other western cities to oppose the immigration of Chinese laborers and to defend "white labor." Beginning with the campaign for Chinese exclusion, and continuing through the early twentieth-century efforts to prohibit Asian land ownership and to eliminate Asian immigration entirely, Asians remained the primary target of western nativist and racist groups. In opposing Asians, nativists were notably *inclusive* with regard to European ethnics—even those from groups whose whiteness in other contexts was questioned. As the secretary of the Asiatic Exclusion League proclaimed in 1908,

> The sparsely settled, broad acres of California and the Western States do require immigration, but that immigration must be of the right kind, composed of the Caucasian race which soon assimilate with us. We can welcome the German, the French, the Italian, the Swiss, the English, the Slavs, and even the Turks, for although on their arrival they are generally uncouth and sometimes unclean, they in a few years pick up the American ideas and adopt American customs. Their children born in this country soon forget their ancestors' mother language and become some of the best citizens, always ready to serve their country with their lives when in need.

It is this kind of immigration which has in one hundred years transformed the deserts of America into the most prosperous, energetic and richest country on the face of the earth. These people must we continue to welcome with open arms, but if we want happiness and prosperity to be maintained in this fair country and handed down to our posterity, we must keep out of it people of the Mongolian race.[29]

Such examples support historian Fred Rosenbaum's observation that "it was the Asians who were abused during these years of turmoil; they and not the Jews became the scapegoats."[30]

For many westerners, the line between those eligible for citizenship and those ineligible—a line that was defined by federal courts as they determined which groups were "white" and therefore entitled to naturalize, and which were not—was the critical boundary. Such distinctions, according to historian David Yoo, "influenced access to public facilities, options for housing and employment, and movement within spatial boundaries."[31] Thus, Congressman Julius Kahn, a German Jewish immigrant and staunch opponent of measures aimed at limiting European immigration, supported exclusion of Asians, characterizing the Japanese worker as a "little brown man" whose physical constitution allowed him to "subsist on fare on which a Caucasian would starve." Japanese immigrants, he argued "will always remain loyal to the Mikado, and . . . the oath of naturalization would be to him but a hollow mockery, an empty formality signifying nothing."[32]

The formula that placed European immigrants of all stripes among those presumed to be assimilable and Asians among the "unassimilable" or "perpetual foreigners" was central to western attitudes during the early twentieth century and distinguished the discourse in the region from that in the East. As Frank Van Nuys explains in *Americanizing the West: Race, Immigration and Citizenship*, white residents of the western coastal states were far less concerned about southern and eastern European immigrants than they were about Asians, who, they believed, "menaced the very survival of western civilization" and whom they saw not as immigrants but as "invaders." The hostile tone of the anti-Asian movement's rhetoric is telling. At a meeting of the Asiatic Exclusion League in San Francisco in 1909, a report from the Building Trades Council, a union cooperating with the league, explained "While we, who have been placed as sentinels and guardians of the Caucasian civilization on the west coast of America, at times become apathetic and indifferent to our task, the brown and yellow races are coming like a swarm of maggots, worming and burrowing and eating the substance out of the land."[33] The perceived threat was cast as a fight across a "racial frontier," in which whites were called upon to defend the nation and Asians were "defined . . . as permanently outside of the American experience."[34] Such rhetoric illustrates Van Nuys's argument that in the West the concept of a racial frontier led to a "categorization of immigrants and minorities as either unassailably white and thus possessed of proper citizenship qualities, or decidedly nonwhite and therefore undesirable as possible citizens."[35]

The idea of a "racial frontier" was not limited to exclusionist political groups. Rather, in this era when "scientific racism" was common in the academy, such thinking was supported by social scientists. For example, in May 1900, Stanford sociologist Edward Ross addressed an anti-Japanese rally in San Francisco, warning that cheap and prolific Asian laborers would inundate California and overwhelm the white population. Local newspapers quoted him as warning, "And should the worst come to worst it'd be better for us to turn our guns on every vessel bringing Japanese to our shores rather than permit them to land."[36] Although Ross's speech drew criticism from a variety of California conservatives, "Ross's Populist position would be taken up in a few years by the Progressive movement of which he became an academic leader."[37] Such Progressives, romanticizing a lost "homogeneous community," "felt that America already possessed one such unassimilable group, whose presence warned eloquently against the addition of other ethnic groups."[38] Thus, Princeton scholar and progressive Democratic candidate Woodrow Wilson warned in 1912, "Democracy rests on the equality of the citizen. Oriental coolieism will give us another race problem to solve and surely we have learned our lesson."[39]

Even sociologists who rejected the notion of biological racism and hoped to mitigate racial tensions cautioned that a large population of Asians on the West Coast would generate racial tensions similar to those surrounding African Americans in other parts of the country. Leading Chicago School sociologist Robert Park believed that the Japanese were "quite as capable as the Italians, the Armenians, or the Slavs of acquiring our culture and sharing our national ideals." He argued, however, that their physical appearance set them apart and, as with African Americans, their distinctive features would continue to determine white responses to them: "The trouble is not with the Japanese mind but with the Japanese skin. The Jap is not the right color. The fact that the Japanese bears in his features a distinctive racial hallmark, that he wears, so to speak, a racial uniform, classifies him. He cannot become a mere individual indistinguishable in the cosmopolitan mass of the population."[40] Although Chicago School sociologists like Park rejected scientific racism in the 1920s and attempted to use their social science to counter western, anti-Asian race prejudice,[41] their work from the 1910s often reinforced the notion that such prejudice would be persistent. For example, sociologist Jesse Steiner, a student of Park's, also rejected the notion of Japanese mental incapacity and argued that, in fact, Japanese "if given a fair chance, might surpass other nationalities in their ability to acquire American culture."[42] Despite this, Steiner argued in his 1917 book *The Japanese Invasion* (for which Robert Park wrote an introduction) that their physical appearance would prevent their assimilation. "The fundamental difficulty is a difference of color and physical characteristics so marked that the Japanese cannot merge themselves unnoticed into American life. This makes inevitable the establishment of a color line between the East and the West, no less real than that between the White and the Black."[43]

That sociologists like Steiner found the situation of Asians in the West to be analogous to that of African Americans in the South is suggestive. Although the frontier that separated blacks and whites in the East, and especially in the South, is often perceived as the sharpest racial divide in America, the boundary between whites and Asians in the West was, in many ways, just as stark. In the immediate post-Reconstruction years, before the Jim Crow system had solidified, there was considerable uncertainty about the status of African Americans, and their citizenship under the 14th Amendment provided at least a semblance of legal standing. In contrast, during the same period Asian immigrants were found ineligible for naturalization by the courts. Like African Americans, they were barred from marrying whites and from residing in certain neighborhoods. But as residents who stood outside the bounds of citizenship, they could be legally restricted in ways that American citizens could not. Foreign miners' taxes and alien land laws are just two examples of the penalties that could be imposed on a group of immigrants defined as "aliens ineligible for citizenship."

The firmness of that boundary helped to shore up the citizenship status of those who were on the white side. Thus, it is interesting to note that in the South uncertainty about Jewish racial status emerged *after* the demise of the traditional racial system and the ratification of the 14th Amendment and during the period when the boundaries of race relations were being reestablished under the emerging Jim Crow system.[44] In the West, where the status of Asians as perpetual foreigners was essentially unchallenged, there was little uncertainty about where to draw the line.

The stark boundary between assimilable Europeans and unassimilable Asians was vividly demonstrated in a pair of acts passed by the California legislature in 1913.[45] On the one hand, California lawmakers acted to create a new Commission of Immigration and Housing (CCIH); on the other, they passed California's first Alien Land Law. The CCIH mission included "protecting immigrants from abuse and exploitation, distributing the immigrant population more widely, maintaining appropriate standards for health, sanitation, housing, education and justice, and offering programs to educate immigrants for citizenship."[46] While Asian immigrants and their children were sometimes able to benefit from its programs, they were not its primary targets.[47] Rather, the same governor and legislators, in passing the 1913 Alien Land Law, acted instead to prohibit Asians, as immigrants ineligible for naturalization, from participating in the act most closely associated with western development and Americanization: acquiring property.[48] Thus, the state of California simultaneously took measures to stigmatize and exclude Asians while fostering the absorption of European immigrants into the white citizenry.

The CCIH was a model of Progressive ideology, championed, designed and, ultimately, run by Simon Lubin, a Havard-educated economist who had been a resident in a Boston settlement house. That Lubin, a second-generation East European Jew,[49] stood at the helm of a state commission charged with Americanizing the immigrant is suggestive. Simon Lubin was a key advisor and confidant of Governor Hiram Johnson and, like his father David Lubin, who was a prominent California merchant, agriculturalist, economist, and member of the Grange, an example of the power of Americanization. Not surprisingly, given his own background, the younger Lubin was supportive of a variety of efforts to aid immigrants and served as a National Director of the Hebrew Sheltering and Immigrant Aid Society of America, a group that provided support to Jewish immigrants and actively lobbied against efforts to restrict immigration.[50] Lubin's version of Americanization was understanding of immigrant perspectives and cultures, and his CCIH saw Americanization as a two-way street: "it was strikingly anti-employer when employers' actions threatened industrial peace, and unusually careful in teaching immigrants their rights and duties as well as teaching native-born Americans their obligations to potential citizens."[51]

CCIH's creation of a Bureau of Immigrant Education, which was dedicated to teaching immigrants English and the other skills needed to become responsible citizens, is evidence of the commitment to immigrant absorption through education. In its annual report, the CCIH made the case for immigrant education, especially instruction in English, by emphasizing the costs of illiteracy to society, arguing that educated immigrants are better able to contribute to society and cautioning that, while an educated immigrant can become "a useful citizen," the uneducated have the potential to become "a menace."[52] Thus, the education advocated by the CCIH was closely linked to education for citizenship, and the commission pledged itself in 1916 to work in cooperation with local chapters of the Daughters of the American Revolution in order to disseminate "the propaganda of 'America First'" in an effort to encourage immigrants to naturalize.[53] Certainly, some of the educational programs initiated by the CCIH, including English classes, were beneficial to Japanese immigrants. The CCIH 1916 *Annual Report* includes a picture of a "class of Japanese immigrant mothers" with an accompanying report by their "home teacher," employed to educate groups of immigrants in neighborhood homes.[54] Yet, as aliens ineligible for naturalization, Japanese immigrants were not the primary audience of the "education for citizenship" program. Even for American-born Nisei, the Americanization efforts used in the public schools sent, at best, a mixed message. As historian David Yoo explains, Nisei students in California, whose public school experience was strongly shaped by CCIH Americanization programs, were acutely aware of the contradictions between a curriculum designed to bring immigrant children into the mainstream and the racial boundaries that prevented them from joining that mainstream.[55]

CCIH officials, believing that substandard living and working conditions ran counter to Americanization by creating resentments and fomenting radicalism, encouraged immigrants to report poor conditions in housing and at labor camps and exploitation by employers and landlords to its Complaint Department.[56] This department was, according to a CCIH report, "the most important," as it allowed the commission "not to theorize concerning the problems and difficulties met with by newly-arrived immigrants, but to find out from the immigrants themselves what these facts and problems are."[57] While some Asian immigrants may have indirectly benefited from the CCIH monitoring of housing and workplace conditions, their needs were not a primary concern. Thus, when the CCIH Complaint Department put up posters advertising its services in twelve languages, no Asian languages were included, despite the fact that the Japanese and the Chinese were two of the state's four largest immigrant groups. Indeed, complaints were sought in languages that likely had fewer than one thousand speakers in the state, while the nearly forty thousand Japanese residents were ignored.[58] In 1916, of the 2,906 complaints received by the department, only 6 came from Chinese immigrants and 3 from Japanese.[59] (See Figure 1.1)

The Americanization programs of the CCIH reflect the strong progressive spirit of the time. Such spirit dominated when the YMCA brought together a Pacific Coast Immigration Congress in San Francisco in 1913. There, Simon Lubin addressed the 327 delegates from the three coastal states in a congress described by the press in the most idealistic of terms. As historian Leslie Koepplin writes, "The overwhelming theme of the Congress was the deep, real humanitarian concern of those who attended for the problems of the uprooted, a concern which most often was based on a desire to avoid the problems of the East."[60] Along with ensuring that immigrants were properly housed, a key priority was their preparation for citizenship. San Francisco's Roman Catholic Bishop, Edward Hanna, urged the delegates to "see that they are prepared for citizenship. Try to see that these men might have power to vote in five years. Try to introduce into the night schools some sort of instruction in civics."[61] As western progressives worked to expand democracy through support for the direct election of senators, the direct primary, and the initiative process, their concern about the importance of an educated citizenry led them to strongly support both educational programs and efforts to enact a literacy requirement for immigration. Western progressives played a key role in the passage of the 1917 literacy requirement and in the successful effort to override President Wilson's veto of the bill.[62] They also, nearly universally, supported Asian exclusion.

Figure 1.1.   The California Commission of Immigration and Housing produced this multilingual poster, encouraging immigrants to report abuses. Asian languages are notably absent. CCIH Second Annual Report, January 2, 1916.

As Van Nuys demonstrates, the nationwide Americanization movement "collapsed" in the early 1920s, as native whites became increasingly pessimistic about the potential of southern and eastern Europeans to truly become Americans.[63] Scientific racism gained popularity, with restrictionists like Madison Grant arguing that inferior and prolific European immigrants would dilute the racial strains that made America great. According to this logic, "race suicide" could only be stemmed by stringent restrictions on immigration based on racial origins. This was the reasoning behind the National Origins system created in 1921 and strengthened in 1924, which severely limited the immigration of "undesirable" Europeans and completely excluded Asians.

Despite the turn away from Americanization programs nationally, California's programs survived and even expanded during the Red Scare that followed World War I. During this period, others who pushed a more nationalistic and coercive Americanization program challenged Lubin's tolerant attitude. Yet, even as the latter regarded southern and eastern European immigrants with suspicion or viewed them as substandard, they did embrace the idea that they had the potential to become true Americans—a possibility that, for Asians, was rejected out of hand.[64] As long as Lubin remained at the helm, the CCIH continued to embrace the possibility of Americanization. Indeed, under his continued leadership, the CCIH moved "considerably to the left of Liberal Americanizers,"[65] suggesting a continued belief in the possibility of assimilation even in the age of immigration restriction.[66] In comparison to the Americanization programs in eastern or midwestern states, the CCIH, writes one historian, was "more inclusive of Southeastern European immigrants than the tenor of the time encouraged."[67] Although the concerns about immigration that led to the creation of the CCIH suggest an increasing suspicion of foreigners, and particularly of the "less desirable" southern and eastern Europeans who, it was feared, would come in greater numbers once the Panama Canal opened in 1914, the contrast between the California program and those in the East suggests the continuing effect of the region's inclusive whiteness.

The virtually unanimous support of the western congressional delegation for the immigration acts of 1921 and 1924—the National Origins Acts, or Quota Acts—might, at first glance, seem a refutation of the ideas that whiteness in the West was broadly defined and that the regional attitude toward the "new" European immigrants was relatively accepting. The National Origins Acts, aimed primarily at severely reducing the influx of the allegedly inferior southern and eastern Europeans, found its greatest support in the West. Indeed, Representative Albert Johnson of Washington, who chaired the House Committee on Immigration and Naturalization and was an extreme restrictionist and "blatant anti-Semite," guided the legislation through Congress.[68] Yet, there is considerable evidence to suggest that what drove the strong western support for general restrictions on immigration was, first and foremost, the goal of Asian exclusion. Historian John Higham explains, "Far Western Congressmen repeatedly tried to attach anti-Japanese provisions to general immigration measures, and in doing so they became one of the foremost blocs in the whole restrictionist movement."[69] Johnson himself was motivated by the "hatred of the Japanese" that was so strong among his rural Washington constituency.[70]

Asian exclusion had long motivated western support for immigration restriction. Indeed, as early as 1900, Chester Rowell, editor of the Fresno *Republican* who would later emerge as a Progressive leader closely associated with Governor Hiram Johnson, wrote,

> Japanese coolie immigration is of the most undesirable class possible, and we are quite right in objecting to it and in demanding that something be done about it. The only question is what we can get done, and in this we must reckon with the cowardice and apathy of the rest of the country. Nothing is going to be done that is worth doing in regard to Japanese immigration unless the country can be aroused to the necessity of doing something in regard to immigration in general. . . .[71]

Rowell was early to come to the conclusion that the restriction of Asians would only come about as part of a more general immigration restriction. Gradually, according to Roger Daniels, "most of the California exclusionists eventually came to oppose all immigrants except those from the 'nordic homeland' of Northern Europe. Rowell was one of the first to lay down the prerequisites under which Japanese exclusion would be brought about."[72]

Thus, the desire for Asian exclusion was a major factor behind western support for the literacy requirement, which was repeatedly passed and vetoed before it was finally enacted over President Wilson's veto in 1917—with strong western support. While many western progressives supported the literacy restriction in part because they believed in the need for an educated citizenry, historian Leslie Koepplin argues that "the Congressional speeches and the individual acts of the far western progressives on the literacy bill and restriction in general are overwhelmingly concerned with the Oriental problem."[73] As Congress considered literacy and other general immigration restriction bills, western representatives repeatedly tried to "amend the bill so that 'aliens ineligible for citizenship' should be absolutely excluded from even entering the United States."[74] Despite the fact that Chinese were already barred from entering under the Chinese Exclusion Act and Japanese severely restricted under the Gentlemen's Agreement, western representatives in both the House and the Senate pushed repeatedly for exclusionary amendments to general immigration bills.[75] Thus, Koepplin concludes that the belief that the literacy bill "would aid in excluding Orientals" was a major reason for westerners' support.

The same is true for the major reform of immigration policy under the National Origins Act of 1924. In his analysis, Roger Daniels demonstrates that the relentless propaganda campaign by the western delegations—particularly California's—was key to the incorporation of an Asian exclusion within the larger immigration bill.[76] Despite the successful passage of anti-

Asian legislation on the state level, such as the 1920 Alien Land Law (designed to close loopholes in the 1913 law), California anti-Orientalists, newly reorganized after World War I, realized that their ultimate goal of total exclusion could only be reached through federal action.[77] During the period from 1921 to 1924, as the terms of the eventual immigration bill were negotiated, the leading anti-Asian activists made a strategic decision that "it would be unwise to make this an anti-Japanese campaign, but rather to conduct it . . . simply as a movement which no good American citizen can fail to endorse."[78] Even using this strategy, activists had a difficult time retaining the Asian exclusion as part of the bill—until a written comment from the Japanese ambassador suggesting that there would be "grave consequences" to its passage resulted in a backlash against this "veiled threat."[79] The passage of the Immigration Act of 1924, complete with a provision excluding all "aliens ineligible for citizenship," led California Senator Hiram Johnson to declare, "California's cherished policy is now the nation's maturely determined policy."[80]

Because Asian exclusion was so critical to western enthusiasm for general immigration restriction, it is difficult to gauge whether their support for such policies reflected any erosion in westerners' faith in the Europeans' potential to assimilate. Although rhetoric about the importance of "Anglo Saxon heritage" to the West was common, it was often surprisingly inclusive, and, whatever the concerns about "inferior" European immigrants, "those from across the Pacific presented an even greater menace."[81] This perspective is illustrated vividly in the rhetoric surrounding exclusionist measures. For example, in a 1910 letter California Progressive Chester Rowell wrote that an educated Japanese "would not be a welcomed suitor for the hand of any American's daughter [but] an Italian of the commonest standing and qualities would be a more welcomed suitor than the finest gentleman of Japan. So the line is biological, and we draw it at the biological point—at the propagation of the species."[82] A decade later, a popular, nationally serialized novel intended to expose the dangers of Japanese immigration had as a hero "a Californian of Spanish-Irish descent," whom the author referred to as "Anglo Saxon."[83]

The continuing inclusiveness of the western conception of whiteness suggested by these examples is also apparent in the 1920 (unsuccessful) election campaign of California Democratic Senator James D. Phelan. Phelan, a rabid anti-Orientalist who "personified California's forty year campaign to harass, dispossess, stereotype and otherwise bully its inhabitants of Japanese birth and descent,"[84] also championed the successful 1920 ballot measure aimed at closing loopholes in the 1913 Alien Land Law. The son of Irish immigrants, Phelan's political popularity as San Francisco's mayor at the turn of the century had been built on appeals to Irish workers and attacks on Asian immigrant labor.[85] Although he had been compelled to

mute his anti-Japanese agenda due to pressure from the Wilson administration during his successful run for the Senate in 1914, it became the central issue of his 1920 campaign. Despite Phelan's pronounced racism
against Asians, evidence suggests that his campaign slogan "Keep California
White!" aimed to connote an inclusive whiteness. Indeed, his campaign
published ads featuring that slogan in the state's Jewish newspapers. "East
and West recognize him as the leader of the fight for JAPANESE EXCLU-
SION," [emphasis in original] ran the text in San Francisco's *Emanu-El*. The
choice to place such ads in Jewish newspapers suggests that Phelan's campaign not only perceived Jews to be part of California's white citizenry, but
also believed they were likely to share his racial concerns. An endorsement
in *Emanu-El's* "Political Notes" column suggested a clear understanding of
what Phelan meant by "white" when it specifically mentioned his efforts to
exclude Japanese immigrants.[86] When Phelan held rallies in southern California, where there were more substantial numbers of Hispanic and African
American voters, he substituted the slogan, "Keep California American!"[87]
While Phelan, like many Democrats in 1920, failed in his reelection bid, his
defeat did not suggest any weakening of anti-Asian sentiment in California,
as the 1920 Alien Land Law passed by a three-to-one margin, winning a majority in every California county.[88]

Neither the 1920 land law nor the complete barring of further Asian migration fully satisfied western anti-Orientalists. Believing that Asian immigrants passed their alien stain on to subsequent generations, activists aimed
to pass a constitutional amendment that would deny citizenship to
American-born children of Asian immigrants.[89] This was one of the primary
goals of the Asiatic Exclusion League when it reconstituted as the California
Oriental Exclusion League in 1919. Senator Phelan, a leader in the group,
had been arguing for several years that Asian American children "could not
be transformed into real Americans."[90] After the passage of the 1920 land
law, exclusionists turned their attention to efforts to bar the Nisei from citizenship, especially when it became clear that Japanese immigrants could
avoid the consequences of the land laws by transferring land titles to their
American-born offspring. Exclusionist organizations also attacked the
Japanese language schools in an effort to expose the alleged loyalty of the
Nisei to Japan, sowing the seeds of accusations of disloyalty that would
come two decades later.[91] Arguing that Japanese language schools were
"teaching Mikadoism," anti-Asian groups succeeded in placing them under
the supervision of the California Department of Education. Sam Cohn, California's assistant superintendent of public instruction, charged with monitoring the schools, told a reporter that "state legislators believed that Japanese language schools threatened the very foundations of the United States
government because they taught American-born children imperialism and
loyalty to Japan. He argued that operation of these schools was equivalent

to another country forming inside the nation."[92] State supervision of language schools continued until 1927, when court rulings from other states suggested that this practice was invalid. After state supervision was discontinued, anti-Asian groups renewed their attacks on the schools.[93] It is interesting to note that, while Jewish communities also ran after-school language programs, including some that operated as either Hebrew or Yiddish language schools, they were never targeted in the same way.

The ethnic landscape of the Far West shaped Jewish responses to minority issues. Jewish westerners were influenced by their own identity as whites and the regional antipathy toward Asians as emphatically nonwhite. As in the South, where "the preservation of Jewish social status relied on their conformity to southern racial standards,"[94] the strength of anti-Asian sentiment and the centrality of Asian otherness to white self-definition in the West discouraged Jews from identifying with or publicly supporting Asians. Although there are certainly examples of individual Jews who defended Asians, the evidence suggests that many either accepted and embraced the prejudices common in the region or chose not to openly confront them.

During the height of the anti-Chinese movement in the late nineteenth century, it was not uncommon for Jewish spokespeople and the western Jewish press to express anti-Chinese sentiments, particularly in California. In the twentieth century, however, as national Jewish organizations and the Jewish press increasingly embraced the notion that Jews had a special responsibility to oppose discrimination, western Jews generally refrained from taking an active part in the strengthening anti-Japanese movement. That the most frequent Jewish response to anti-Japanese policies was silence provides a revealing model for their later response to the events of World War II. These silences are particularly striking when contrasted with the vocal stance taken by Jewish communities in countering discrimination against other groups. Indeed, the selective silences of western Jews suggest that, as in the South, where Jews avoided the harshest forms of racism, according to Goldstein, "there was a point at which their desire for social acceptance began to conflict with feelings of unease about adopting the mantle of white supremacy."[95]

In tracing the relationship between Jews and Chinese in the West, historian Rudolf Glanz notes that Jews were already well established in the West when Chinese immigrants began to arrive. The two groups most often met in the workplace, but not as equals or competitors. In San Francisco, many Chinese were employed in sectors of the economy, like garment and cigar manufacturing, that were dominated by Jewish owners; throughout the Pacific West, established Jews, like other established whites, frequently employed Chinese workers in their homes as cooks or houseboys.[96] Rabbi Isaac Wise reported sympathetically on the Chinese during his 1877 visit to

California and noted that some Jewish employers feared that anti-Chinese violence would harm their businesses.[97] Some Jewish employers defended Chinese labor, as when shoe and boot manufacturer Isaac Hecht testified before the Labor Bureau that Chinese workers in the industry were not displacing skilled white shoemakers.[98] Gradually, however, like other whites in the Pacific West, many Jews came to embrace the anti-Chinese movement as it gained strength in the 1870s.

Naturally, there were exceptions. San Diego's Simon Levi, as a leader in the Chamber of Commerce and secretary of the Committee of Public Safety, worked to protect Chinese from mob violence in 1877.[99] California Supreme Court Justice Solomon Heidenfeldt publicly praised Chinese contributions to the state. Analysis suggests that such activities to defend the Chinese were more common outside San Francisco, where the virulence of anti-Chinese sentiment was weaker.[100] In Portland, where members of the business community believed that cheap Chinese labor was essential to the economic development of the city, several Jews were among those who defended the Chinese community. David Solis-Cohen, a leading Oregon Republican, harshly criticized Jewish support for Chinese exclusion in Philadelphia's *Jewish Record* in 1879.[101] Jewish community leader and Republican politician Ben Selling joined other city leaders in fighting the efforts of outside agitators to violently drive Chinese from Portland in 1886.[102] However, most in the region eventually "fell for the anti-Chinese psychosis to a considerable extent, thereby earning bitter reproach from their brethren in all other regions of the country."[103]

The anti-Chinese sentiments of western Jews were carried to their coreligionists in the East through reports in the Jewish press. As early as 1879, Jewish newspapers in the East and from as far away as France criticized San Francisco's three leading rabbis, Elkan Cohn (Emanu-El), Henry Vidaver (Sherith Israel), and A.S. Bettelheim (Ohabai Shalome) when it was reported that they had "signed a telegram sent to President Hayes by some San Francisco clergymen asking him to sign the bill restricting Chinese immigration."[104] The *American Israelite*'s western correspondent, Isidor Choynski, who wrote under the pen name "Maftir" for nearly two decades, demonstrated to eastern readers the strength of anti-Chinese prejudice. Writing primarily from San Francisco, Choynski berated Chinese domestic laborers, ridiculed their traditions as "heathenish," denounced them as crafty, and linked them to illicit and illegal activities. In short, he "missed no opportunity to remind his readers of what was to him the Orientals' depravity."[105] While the strongest expressions of anti-Chinese sentiment came from San Francisco, they were echoed in other parts of the West. When Minnesota Rabbi Judah Wechsler visited Portland, his account, published in *The American Israelite*, demonstrated that he had absorbed local attitudes. He wrote of the Chinese community, "I consider this nationality an injury to the further development of any city, for they have no interest but their own and never identify themselves with our institutions. Their future emigration is, however, now wisely prohibited."[106] Such racial formulations informed discourse in the regional Jewish press.

The eastern Jewish press strongly castigated California's Jews for their anti-Chinese sentiments and for failing to oppose the Chinese exclusion movement in the early 1880s. In criticizing the Californians, eastern Jews argued that the Chinese were an unfairly persecuted minority, as Jews were in many places, and raised concern that discriminatory measures taken against the Chinese could, in the future, be aimed at Jews. According to Glanz, "The Jewish press of California was told bluntly that, by its anti-Chinese position, it had isolated itself not only from the Jews of most of America but also from the best spirits of the country generally, and that soon enough it would find itself morally isolated in California, too."[107] The *Jewish Messenger* accused its California counterparts of having an "un-Jewish but Californian attitude in the Chinese Question," and the *American Hebrew* warned in 1882, "Jews cannot afford to stand before the world in the character of oppressors. They have felt the rod too often, not to know the keenness of its application, and if there is any lesson for us in the last nineteen centuries of our history, it is that we must be liberal, talented, and catholic, that we may not be guilty of the crimes that have been practiced against us." The *Jewish Messenger* went so far as to compare the California papers to "Ignatieff's salaried journalists," a reference to the Russian Minister of the Interior believed responsible for the pogroms.[108]

Such criticism, according to historians Reva Clar and William Kramer, "had little or no effect on Jewish attitudes in the Far West."[109] Reporting in 1881 for *American Israelite*, a San Francisco correspondent rejected comparisons between Jews and Chinese writing,

> The Russian, Polish, German and all other Jews, and for the matter of that, all other immigrants, assimilate with the dominant race, settle down for good, raise families and take a deep and kindly interest in the body politic. The Chinese are as disgusting as the lowest type of the digger Indian, as treacherous as the greaser and as unprincipled as the Lazaroni. They do not come here to stay. They drive white labor out of cities, they monopolize every industry that requires physical labor, and contaminate the atmosphere where they are packed like sardines in tiers to the depth of thirty feet underground.[110]

Criticisms of their anti-Chinese position were met in the western Jewish press and western correspondents' reports with "lurid descriptions of Chinatowns' dirty streets, strange odors, opium dens, prostitutes, joss houses, noise and confusion . . . sent to the Eastern Jewish papers by Jewish residents of Western cities and by travelers."[111] While fear that the kinds of measures taken against the Chinese could also threaten immigrant Jews was potent in

eastern cities, where shiploads of East European immigrant Jews were arriving by the 1880s, in California, where the influx was far smaller, such concerns were more easily ignored.[112]

After the passage of the Chinese Exclusion Act, many California Jews continued to stand their ground on the issue and to try to convince their eastern coreligionists of the correctness of their position. Thus, in 1886 it was
reported that "during a recent visit to New York, en route to Europe, Mr. A.
Seligson of the San Francisco *Jewish Progress*, explained why the anti-
Chinese agitation exists in California. The fact that all classes united in the
resolve that the Chinese must go indicates that it is not narrow feeling but
one arising from the spirit of self-preservation. It is impossible to compete
with the Chinese."[113] Many prominent Jewish Californians shared these
sentiments. The *Jewish Progress* reported in 1886 that many San Francisco
Jewish merchants were participating in a boycott of Chinese labor by firing
employees.[114] Adolph Sutro, elected mayor of San Francisco in 1894,
bragged that he never employed Chinese workers and claimed that "The
very worst emigrants from Europe are a hundred times more desirable than
these Asiatics."[115] In 1896, Rabbi Voorsanger of San Francisco's elite congregation Emanu-El labeled the Chinese "a non-assimilative race," unable
to "mix with Caucasians."[116]

By the turn of the century, the Chinese Exclusion Act had been in effect
for nearly two decades, and, not surprisingly, anti-Chinese attitudes, while
still strong in the region, showed some signs of softening. Evidence of this
weakening can be seen in an 1899 editorial in San Francisco's *Emanu-El*.
Writing about a Fourth of July parade in which a "brigade" of U.S.-born
Chinese Americans marched, the editors walked a fine line, asserting their
fitness for citizenship, while affirming the significance of racial differences:

> There seems to be room herearound [sic] for John Chinaman. . . . *He is an
> American, but a Mongolian, and will be the latter unto the thousandth generation.*
> . . . Still it is a fact that *this Chinese population, separate and distinct, of different
> genus, religion, language and natural endowments,* can become a homogeneous
> element, in the sense that it can adapt itself to the laws of the land and assert,
> with intelligence, the rights of citizenship. That is a curious reduction of the
> facts that developed during the past fifty years, and incontrovertibly, have
> been registered as a part of the history of California. The law says that a Chi-
> naman born on American soil is a citizen and has the right to vote. If that were
> not the law it ought to be, for birth in the United States constitutes an inher-
> ent right to citizenship.[117] [emphasis added]

A controversy in Stockton over a local Fourth of July parade in the same
year, however, demonstrated that *Emanu-El*'s editors did not speak for all.
There, Benjamin Kohlberg, a synagogue board member, publicly objected
to participation in the parade by the "Oriental Annex," and threatened to

lead an alternative parade. His position was roundly criticized in the local (secular) press and the parade went on as planned.[118]

As hostility toward the Chinese began to soften at the end of the nineteenth century, attention quickly turned toward Japanese immigrants, who had begun to arrive in large numbers in the 1880s. Soon, Japanese immigrants came to be viewed as a greater threat than the Chinese, in part due to the military strength of Japan. More importantly, many westerners resented the success of Japanese farmers and feared they were intent on buying up land and establishing Japanese colonies.[119] That antipathy toward Japanese immigrants centered on opposition to their acquisition of agricultural land is ironic, given that well into the twentieth century western states worked to *recruit* potential farmers from other states and from foreign countries.[120] When Japanese immigration was limited through the Gentlemen's Agreement, exclusionists were outraged at its provision allowing the continued entrance of Japanese immigrants' wives, including "picture brides." As Japanese couples settled on farms and began to raise large numbers of American-born children, anti-Orientalists' fears multiplied.

Many who had been active in the anti-Chinese movement shifted seamlessly into the anti-Japanese movement. Among them was Congressman Julius Kahn, certainly the most prominent Jew to be actively involved in anti-Asian agitation. Kahn, who had cosponsored the 1902 renewal of the Chinese Exclusion Act, went on to sponsor anti-Japanese legislation in 1906–1907[121] and continued to voice anti-Japanese sentiments throughout his long career as a congressman from San Francisco.[122] Interestingly, Kahn was a staunch opponent of general immigration restrictions, setting him against many of his comrades in the exclusion movement, who supported the literacy measure in the hope that any immigration restriction would help facilitate Asian exclusion. Indeed, he was the only member of the western delegation to oppose the literacy requirement during the Progressive Era, and he repeatedly took the floor to argue in favor of "the unrestricted entrance of immigrants in the traditional manner, with safeguards only against those of bad character."[123] Despite his opposition to general immigration restrictions, he was a leader in the Asiatic Exclusion League, which focused its attention on the "Japanese problem." Kahn served as a member of the organization's speakers' bureau and was attacked for his position in the eastern Jewish press.[124]

Despite Kahn's prominence in the movement, during the first decade of the twentieth century western Jewish sympathy for the anti-Japanese movement was far less visible than had been their support for the earlier anti-Chinese movement. In contrast to nineteenth-century expressions of enthusiasm for the exclusion acts in the regional Jewish press, San Francisco's most prominent Jewish newspaper, *Emanu-El*, did not engage in or report on the debate over the Alien Land Law that was on the fall ballot in 1920.

In trying to understand the reasons for this shift, it is useful to examine the newspapers' words as well as its silences.

In the 1920 election, the focus of anti-Asianists in California was on property ownership. The movement had consolidated in 1919 and begun to focus its efforts on eliminating loopholes in the earlier 1913 Alien Land Law. Despite the tremendous attention to this issue in the 1920 election, there was no direct mention of it in *Emanu-El*. It was, however, indirectly referenced in an editorial on October 1. Under the headline "The Japanese Demand for Racial Equality," the editors of *Emanu-El* drew their readers' attention not to the anti-Japanese ballot measure but to Japan's "demand for racial equality, before the League of Nations." "Doubtless," the editors argued, "such a demand is meant to offset the anti-Japanese agitation in California."[125] The issue grew out the negotiations over the 1919 Covenant of the League of Nations. In response to President Wilson's proposal at the Paris Peace Conference that all member nations be obliged to uphold religious freedom and "refrain from discrimination on the basis of religion," Japan had introduced a proposal to add a prohibition of discrimination based on race or nationality against foreign residents. The United States and the United Kingdom balked at this proposal; the result was that neither the prohibition against religious discrimination nor that against racial and national discrimination was included in the covenant.[126] Rather than sympathizing with Japan's concerns about discrimination against her nationals, *Emanu-El* chose instead to blame Japan for the failure of the anti-discrimination measure, editorializing, "From all that we have read, we judge that the [1919] conference was on the very verge of granting general Jewish rights when the Japanese claim threw everything into disorder. The Jew, as usual, was the sufferer."[127]

The newspaper's failure to mention the land proposition that was at the center of the "anti-Japanese agitation" was not the result of an editorial decision to avoid California politics. In advance of both the August 31 primary and the November general election, *Emanu-El* published political advertisements for candidates and against a prohibitionist ballot measure, and featured a column titled "Political Notes," which made endorsements.[128] While the paper did not express an opinion on every race or ballot measure, it appears to have made a conscious effort to avoid the land law, as it was the obvious referent not only in the October editorial on the League of Nations but also in both the advertisements and the column endorsing Senator Phelan. "Save our State; Keep California White!" ran the ad for Phelan. "East and West recognize him as the leader of the fight for JAPANESE EXCLUSION. . . . LET HIM FINISH HIS WORK" [emphasis in original]. The "Political Notes" column, headlined "Senator Phelan's Reelection a Certainty," ran an enthusiastic endorsement of the notoriously anti-Asianist Senator:

Without detracting one jot or tittle from the merits of his opponent, observations free from bias, political or otherwise, leads to the conclusion that through the length and breadth of California, people regardless of political affiliation and in every walk of life believe that Senator James D. Phelan's splendid merits entitle him to re-election.

Those who have watched his career for more than thirty years know him to be a man of culture, experience, and of the broadest sympathies. To be helpful, to render service, to promote the wellbeing of his fellow man has been his aim in life. His fine record as the first mayor of San Francisco under the new charter which he helped to frame has endeared him to the people of his native city. He is a Californian in the fullest sense of the term and whether as mayor or as exposition commissioner or as United States Senator the one great all absorbing motive of his official acts has been to render the best possible service he was capable of to his fellow citizens.

Senator Phelan's opposition to the Japanese immigration does not spring from race prejudice but because their standard of living is at variance with the hopes and aspirations of the white people.

Senator Phelan's supporters in the dominant parties ask that his candidacy be judged by his record and that he be returned to Washington to continue the work for the State he has served so long and well, to be in future as he has been in the past a Senator for all California and for all its people.[129]

Although it did not take a position on the alien land law on California's ballot in 1920, *Emanu-El*'s election coverage is quite revealing. The decision to run an editorial focusing on the harm done to Jews by Japan's demands at the League of Nations, rather than on the anti-Japanese prejudice to which Japan was responding, suggests little sympathy for the plight of California's Nikkei community. Indeed, the paper's endorsement of Phelan strongly implies support for the land law, since that was the central issue in his campaign. Yet instead of proudly endorsing the land law, as did many publications in California, *Emanu-El*'s editors instead tried to disassociate support for the Senator from support for prejudice by characterizing the senator as a man with the "broadest sympathies," emphasizing his concern for the "wellbeing of his fellow man," and claiming that his anti-immigration position was not rooted in racism. This seems a striking contrast with the nineteenth-century anti-Chinese sentiment openly expressed in the California Jewish press. Why, in 1920, did the paper attempt to distance itself from this issue?

Attention to the broader themes of the paper in this period is instructive. Study of the coverage in *Emanu-El*, beginning in the summer of 1920, shows considerable attention to international and domestic (although not local) manifestations of anti-Semitism. For example, in the June 25, 1920, issue, *Emanu-El* led with a story on Henry Ford's anti-Semitism, linking it to the increase in international anti-Semitism. The same edition included stories with the headlines "Terrible Troubles of the Hungarian Jews," "Algerian Jews

Ask Equal Civil Rights," "Expulsion of German Jews Demanded," and "The White Terror in Hungary," among others.[130] The focus on anti-Semitism, with particular attention to Henry Ford, continued through the summer months and into the fall, with much of the material, including opinion pieces and columns, originating in the eastern Jewish press. Columns stressing the importance of responding to Ford and arguing that his attacks should not be ignored suggest the emergence of a new, more assertive American Jewish anti-defamation strategy.[131] Another response can be seen in a series of articles focusing on efforts to Americanize Jewish immigrants.[132]

In its attention to domestic anti-Semitism, *Emanu-El* reflected growing national Jewish concern over the issue. In May of 1920, Henry Ford's *Dearborn Independent* had begun publishing a long series of accounts of an alleged international Jewish conspiracy based on the infamous forgery *The Protocols of the Elders of Zion*. This came at a time when, according to the Central Conference of American Rabbis, "there was perhaps more antisemitic [sic] literature published and distributed in the United States than in any previous period of its history."[133] The inclusion of Jews among the alleged "undesirables" whom immigration reformers wanted to bar from entry, the resurgence of the KKK, and the marked increase in the exclusion of Jews from social clubs, firms, universities, and neighborhoods all "shook the Jewish community's confidence and strengthened its sense of unease and apartness."[134]

Increased concern about anti-Semitism focused attention on Jewish defense efforts. By the 1920s, several major Jewish defense groups were operating as national organizations with local chapters in Jewish communities throughout the country, including the major cities of the West. These organizations included the American Jewish Committee (founded in 1906), the Anti-Defamation League of B'nai B'rith (1913) and the American Jewish Congress (1918). While each of these groups had a different constituency, character, and approach, all "expressed their mission in the universal rhetoric of liberty and equality."[135] Many of the most prominent leaders of these groups also participated actively in founding and supporting organizations like the NAACP and the National Urban League, which defended the civil rights of others, particularly African Americans.[136] The linking of Jewish defense work with the broader civil rights movement was a prominent theme in the Jewish press and informed the mission of synagogues and community groups across the country. In her study of the national Jewish press (both Yiddish and English), Hasia Diner argues that during the decades following 1915, "no organ of Jewish public opinion failed to express some degree of sympathy and commiseration with the plight of black people."[137]

The linking of Jewish defense work with civil rights work clearly informed western Jewish organizations and the western Jewish press. The settlement houses established by National Council of Jewish Women sections on the West Coast, for example, prided themselves on serving the diverse constituencies in their neighborhoods and spoke of that service in universal terms. Gladys Trachtenberg, a volunteer at Portland's Neighborhood House and the niece of its director, emphasized that the settlement house "would admit to membership anyone, regardless of race, creed, color or ethnic background," stressing that "anyone was welcome and we did have several black members."[138] Similarly, western Jewish newspapers carried news of national organizations' civil rights agendas and frequently published condemnations of racism and endorsements of civil rights work. For example, when the Central Conference of American Rabbis (CCAR), the professional body of Reform rabbis, adopted its Social Justice Program in 1920, Portland's *Scribe* prominently featured its call for industrial peace, its opposition to immigration restriction, and its condemnation of lynching.[139]

During the 1920s and 1930s, the leading Reform rabbis of the West Coast's most prominent congregations became known as civic leaders who championed civil rights. Rabbi Samuel Koch, for example, who served Seattle's Temple de Hirsch from 1906 to 1941, made social justice a centerpiece of his tenure. As early as the mid-1910s, he was "on the board of nearly every social welfare organization and worthy civic cause in Seattle." In these efforts, he worked closely with civic and religious leaders in the city. He also was one of the founding members of the CCAR's Commission on Social Justice, and he spoke out against prejudice from the pulpit.[140] Los Angeles's Rabbi Edgar Magnin was known for his efforts to rid motion pictures of anti-Semitic images and also crusaded against anti-black stereotypes. Indeed, one of his first public campaigns was against D. W. Griffith's notoriously racist depiction of the Civil War and Reconstruction in *Birth of a Nation*.[141] Similarly, Irving Reichert, rabbi at San Francisco's Emanu-El beginning in 1930, was an ACLU activist whose "passion for liberal causes seemed insatiable." He actively championed the causes of the Scottsboro Boys and of local farm workers, among others.[142]

The strong embrace of an anti-discrimination, pro-civil rights agenda likely inhibited the open expression of anti-Japanese sentiments among those western Jews who were otherwise inclined to support measures like the alien land laws. On the other hand, the strength of regional anti-Asian sentiment likely gave pause to those who might otherwise seek to apply their civil rights sensibilities to the Asian situation. The result was a tendency in the regional Jewish press to avoid the issue. When forced to confront it, the press reacted with uncertainty. In 1920, for example, Portland's *Scribe* reported that a Stockton rabbi, Emanuel Jack, "preached a sermon taking to task the anti-Japanese measures before the California people on the basis of preferring to be right than white." Observing that "the race question makes the matter a very delicate one," the *Scribe* praised the rabbi

*assoc.
w|
government*

for his courage in speaking out. Yet its editors refused to take a position on the substance of the issue, instead explaining, "Whether or not Rabbi Jack is right is a matter for a wider range of discussion than this paragraph," and noting further, "he may be wrong."[143]

More often, the Jewish press opted for silence. An interesting example is the response to the 1923 U.S. Supreme Court case *Frick v. Webb*, which challenged the 1920 California Alien Land Law. Despite the California Jewish press's tendency to avoid this issue, the fact that Louis Marshall, one of the most prominent Jews in America, was the lawyer for the appellant would normally have placed the case firmly within their purview. Marshall was nationally known among Jews as a founder and the sitting president of the American Jewish Committee, a staunch opponent of literacy and other immigration restrictions, the lawyer for Leo Frank (whose 1913 lynching in Georgia sparked the formation of the ADL), and a key supporter of minority rights at the post–World War I Paris Peace Conference. While it was common for these newspapers to report on the activities of nationally prominent Jewish lawyers, even when their cases had no particular relevance to Jews or to the region,[144] neither San Francisco's *Emanu-El* nor Los Angeles's *B'nai B'rith Messenger* covered Marshall's argument before the Court in April 1923 or the Court's decision the following November. In its April 27, 1923, issue, the first issue after the case was heard, the *B'nai B'rith Messenger* had no comment on the case or on Marshall's participation, but the paper did run editorials denouncing anti-Semitic discrimination in hiring and anti-Catholic prejudice. "Now we hold no brief to defend the Catholic Church," explained the editors, "but we stand Americanly for justice and equality. . . . The country needs to be saved from THESE BIGOTS."[145] Such outrage, frequently expressed in response to varied forms of prejudice, never appeared in response to the anti-Asian measures.

This pattern is similar to that described by Eric Goldstein with regard to southern Jews and anti-black racism. There, Goldstein argues, Jews were caught between the increasing calls by national Jewish leaders and organizations to oppose racism and the intense social pressure to conform to local racial norms. The result was that most Jews avoided the harshest expressions of racism without actually challenging racial norms: "The tendency of southern Jews to uphold social and cultural distinctions between blacks and whites while generally shying away from strong support of racial violence or disenfranchisement indicates that there was a point at which their desire for social acceptance began to conflict with feelings of unease about adopting the mantle of white supremacy."[146]

In the West, unlike the South, it was quite easy for Jews to laud the efforts of Julius Rosenwald to improve the lives of African Americans.[147] Even in the Northwest, which had never been hospitable to African Americans, their numbers were tiny until the mobilization for World War II be-

Louis Marshall of NY for appellants   Frick v. Webb (1923)   appellees

gan. To take a similar stand for Asian Americans, however, would require westerners to free themselves of the pervasive prejudice in the region and stand up, virtually alone, against local norms that even the region's most prominent progressives had difficulty countering. The result was that, while the organized western Jewish community embraced the national pro-civil rights agenda, they did not apply that agenda to the most volatile racial issues in their region.

For example, although Portland's *Scribe* had publicly endorsed the Social Justice Program adopted by the Central Conference of American Rabbis in 1920,[148] it applied its precepts quite selectively as it negotiated the tumultuous years that followed. Occasional evidence of anti-Asian sentiments appeared in the pages of the *Scribe*, but these were seldom directly connected to local issues. Thus, in a 1920 discussion of the religious underpinnings of morality, Oregon's *Scribe* made the case that "the history of the white man's struggle for rights is involved with his religion" and identified Hebraism and the Old Testament as the sources of justice and humanitarianism. It continued, "civilization has not progressed thru Asian mysticism but thru moral directness and honesty akin to that lived and preached by prophets of Israel [sic]."[149]

On the real issues of Asian exclusions and restrictions, the paper maintained silence. The political events of 1922–1923 provide an excellent opportunity to study one Jewish community's selective silence on Asian issues and to contrast it with the community's active engagement in defending other minorities. In November of 1922, the rapidly expanding Oregon Ku Klux Klan claimed victories at the polls, succeeding in electing a majority of the state legislature and the governor. In the same election, voters endorsed the Klan-supported anti-Catholic compulsory public school initiative, known as the Oregon Schools Bill; and just after the new legislative session began in 1923 the newly seated legislature passed Oregon's Alien Land Law. Although the organized Jewish community spoke out strongly against the Klan and the School Bill, it was silent on the Alien Land Law.

As early as the spring 1922 primary season, Oregon's Jewish *Scribe* published editorials and paid advertisements that sharply criticized the Klan. The first of these appeared on May 12, in a full-page advertisement announcing the existence of the Klan locally and describing it as an "insidious poison" that was "un-American." It urged readers to vote against Klan candidates, explaining that the KKK aimed "to assume the sole ownership of the title 'American'," that it characterized "Catholics, Jews, Negroes and all naturalized citizens as being incapable of loyalty to the Government," and that it created "prejudices and enmities."[150] The following week, an editorial warned that the Klan would create a "division of American life into bitter race and religious factions."[151] After the primary, the paper expressed its disappointment with the results, claiming that Oregon had been "set back

twenty years by the events of the last six months."[152] In the following
months, stories about Klan activity in the state were frequent and critical.

The discussion of the Klan merged with coverage of the School Bill in the
fall, as the paper relentlessly editorialized against the bill from July until the
November election. Although the initiative's supporters—including the
Scottish Rite Masons who were the primary sponsors—portrayed it as an effort to foster Americanization and break down barriers between groups, the
Scribe consistently painted it as a bigoted, KKK-sponsored attack on
Catholics.[153] Since the overwhelming majority of Jewish children attended
public school, the bill did not threaten the Jewish community directly.
Rather, Jews—including a number of Jewish Masons—publicly opposed the
bill as an attack on their inclusive vision of America. In addition to its own
editorials, the paper also reprinted anti–School Bill and anti-Klan articles
that had appeared in local and national publications.[154] While a few paid
advertisements appeared endorsing the School Bill, editorial opinion and
the majority of paid advertisements were strongly critical. In the final edition before the election, the paper's lead editorial, titled "Vote No" began,
"The time has come for every man and woman to defend Oregon from an
invasion of bigotry. No Attila sweeping across the plains of Europe was
more threatening than the sinister policy suggested in the Compulsory Education Bill. To vote for it is to support reaction and tyranny; not to vote at
all is to stand idly by the destruction of one's own house."

Along with this strongly worded editorial, three full-page advertisements
against the bill appeared, including one signed by Jesse Winburn, identified
as a member of B'nai B'rith and a Mason, and one signed by five of Portland's most prominent Jewish leaders.[155]

Jewish Oregonians did not confine their campaigning to the Jewish
press, but actively engaged in the public debate about the bill. For example, several Jewish doctors were among the fifty-eight "non-Catholic physicians" who signed a full-page advertisement opposing the school bill in
Oregon Voter.[156] Similarly, a key opposition group, representing "the cream
of the Portland elite," included Mrs. Sol Hirsch, a member of one of the
state's most prominent Jewish families.[157] Indeed, a recent analysis of the
opposition to the bill lists "the Jewish community" as a key player.[158] A
group calling itself the Jewish League for the Preservation of American
Ideals took out a full-page advertisement in the *Portland Telegram* calling
the bill "a measure as oppressive to mankind as any promulgated by czaris-
tic tyranny when at its worst." Jonah Wise, Portland's best-known rabbi,
preached a sermon against the bill that was quoted in the *Oregonian.*[159]
Ben Selling, who had an extensive career in state and city politics and was
a prominent lay leader in the Jewish community, served on the speakers'
bureau for the Protestant and Non-Sectarian Schools Committee, formed
to combat the bill.[160]

The vigorous Jewish opposition to the School Bill and to the election of Klan-endorsed candidates stood in stark contrast to the community's silence on the Alien Land Bill, which quickly emerged out of the newly elected Klan-dominated legislature in February of 1923. In contrast with the School Bill, which supporters portrayed as an inclusive measure to assist in the Americanization of children from diverse backgrounds, the land bill was framed in explicitly racist terms. For example, the *Oregon Voter*, the state's leading public affairs journal, referred to the measure as an "anti-Jap bill" and quoted its supporters as stating "we want to see the state remain white and American."[161] The weak opposition to the bill argued principally in terms of the damage it might do to trade with Japan, while supporters stated baldly that Japanese immigrants were racially unfit for citizenship. This debate clearly defined the boundaries of whiteness. When asked why the law would target only Asians and not Greeks, one of the bill's supporters explained on the floor of the legislature, "the Greeks are a white race and can become citizens." William Woodward, who was also a key proponent of both the Alien Land Law and the Public School Bill, argued, "the nation is engaged in the task of assimilating many races of men, and past experience has proven that the yellow race cannot be assimilated."[162]

This demarcation between inclusive conceptions of whiteness on the one hand and Asian-ness on the other, played a critical role in determining the extent of opposition to the various nativist measures debated by the Oregon legislature during the 1923 session. For example, HB 205, a measure requiring *all* foreign business owners to "post conspicuously" their nationality, generated spirited opposition.[163] Even Woodward hedged his support for HB 205 by conceding, "possibly it is unfair, and possibly it is unjust." The *Oregon Voter* called HB 205 "perhaps the most drastic of the anti-alien measures" of the session.[164] The concerns expressed about this measure, aimed at aliens in general, were not echoed in the debate over the Alien Land Bill, aimed solely at Asian (primarily Japanese) immigrants, whom the federal courts had determined were racially ineligible for naturalization. The Alien Land Bill passed the state senate unanimously, and the house with only one vote in opposition. Even the *Oregon Voter*, which opposed other, more general, measures against aliens, failed to editorialize against the land law.[165]

The Jewish press similarly discriminated between more generally prejudiced initiatives, like the School Bill, and the more focused anti-Japanese Land Bill. Although the Jewish community had not hesitated to play a prominent role in the fight against the intolerance championed by the School Bill and by Klan candidates, it took no position on the land bill. Indeed, the *Scribe's* active coverage of state politics, evident throughout the Klan/School Bill crisis of late 1922, vanished as the Alien Land Bill debate took place in early 1923. The *Scribe* not only ignored the bill but also failed to mention Asians or Japanese immigrants at all during this period.

After the passage of the alien land laws and immigration restrictions in the early 1920s, there was a period of legislative calm in this arena in the late 1920s and through the 1930s. Groups like the KKK, which had gained such prominence in the early 1920s, were less visible by mid-decade and concerns about immigrants in general and Asians in particular were less pronounced after the passage of the 1924 national immigration law. Historians have argued that, with immigration no longer a pressing political issue, the "new" immigrants and their children were able to solidify their position as white Americans during this period. This was particularly true during the 1930s, when Roosevelt and the Democratic Party actively reached out to urban, ethnic communities.[166] Even as war with Germany and Italy seemed imminent, efforts were made to include the Italian and German American communities due to their electoral clout.

Historians like Eric Goldstein have argued that Jewish American support for minority rights was fostered by their increasing acceptance as whites by the late 1930s. Although anti-Semitism was loudly voiced by prominent national figures like Henry Ford, Charles Lindbergh, and Father Coughlin in the period, the increasing political acceptance and support by the Roosevelt administration reinforced Jewish confidence in speaking up for their own rights and for those of other minorities, particularly African Americans. Whereas the social sanctions—the "price of whiteness"—attached to speaking out against anti-black racism had earlier been an inhibiting factor, the relative liberalism of the New Deal coalition on race questions reinforced Jewish support for civil rights.[167] During the war, there was even more inducement to speak out in favor of civil rights, as racism and actions disruptive to racial harmony were cast as unpatriotic and undermining of the unity so critical to the war effort. Thus, in supporting administration civil rights initiatives, such as the desegregation of defense industries (forced on the administration by a threatened march on Washington), American Jews were not only standing up for their own employment rights but also standing with the administration in support of what was both "right" and good for the war effort.[168]

Yet few of these changes were relevant to the relationships between Jews and Japanese in the West. For Japanese Americans, the late 1920s and the 1930s were the calm before the storm. With immigration ended, Japanese American families became more established and their American born children began to come of age and create a subculture that allowed them to take steps toward defining a place for themselves in the West.[169] Yet there remained few sanctions against anti-Asian prejudice. Japanese American communities were not a force to be reckoned with in terms of electoral politics—they were small in number, the immigrants were ineligible for citizenship, and their children were only beginning to reach voting age. As the war approached, and particularly after Pearl Harbor, there was no countervailing force to weigh against traditional stereotypes of the Japanese. Accusations that had been voiced by groups like the Asiatic Exclusion League and embraced by organizations such as the Native Sons, local granges, and the American Legion since early in the century were unleashed. Once it became clear that the government was embarking on a policy of mass exclusion, the administration and the army had branded the Japanese American community—both immigrants and the native born—as potential enemies. While fighting prejudice against African Americans was a patriotic activity that aided the war effort, fighting the prejudice that led to the exclusion order for Japanese Americans was a potentially subversive activity.

The absence of major anti-Asian initiatives during the decade and a half prior to World War II makes it difficult to definitively trace the attitudes of Jewish westerners toward Japanese Americans during this period. After the passage of the land laws and the provisions in the 1924 immigration legislation that barred further entry to all Asians, the issue receded from the public eye, and, in any event, the "Japanese problem," had never received much attention in the Jewish press. When the issue made an explosive reentry in the wake of Pearl Harbor, western Jewish communities experienced the same tension between their commitments to civil rights and to supporting all aspects of the war effort that was shared by their coreligionists nationally.

Yet, locally, responses reflected the peculiarities of a western ethnic landscape in which Jews were part of an "Anglo" world that was defined, in part, by contrast with Japanese Americans, the region's most conspicuous non-white group. While the "price of whiteness" was no longer a major factor inhibiting American Jews (at least those outside the South) from speaking out against anti-black racism, the vehement anti-Japanese sentiment in the West made it clear that support for the Nikkei community still carried a heavy cost. Western Jewish responses to the anti-Asian efforts of the early 1920s reveal a precedent for negotiating such a situation. These communities had a history of acting selectively on their commitment to support tolerance and to fight bigotry by avoiding engagement in an issue that was locally volatile.

NOTES

1. For excellent discussions of Jews and whiteness, see Matthew Frye Jacobson, *Whiteness of a Different Color* (Cambridge, Mass.: Harvard University Press, 1988) and David Roedigger, *Working toward Whiteness* (New York: Basic Books, 2005). Hasia Diner explores Jewish fascination with and identification with African Americans in the early twentieth century in *In the Almost Promised Land: American Jews and Blacks, 1915–1935* (Baltimore: Johns Hopkins University Press, 1977, 1995). More recently Michael Alexander has argued that the long history of Jewish exclusions led to an "outsider identification" that led Jews to identify with and defend "marginal

Americans." See Alexander, *Jazz Age Jews* (Princeton, N.J.: Princeton University Press, 2001).

2. Eric Goldstein, *The Price of Whiteness: Jews, Race and American Identity* (Princeton, N.J.: Princeton University Press, 2006), 1.

3. Goldstein, *Price of Whiteness*, 5.

4. Goldstein, *Price of Whiteness*, 52–55. See also Leonard Rogoff, "Is the Jew White? The Racial Place of the Southern Jew," *American Jewish History*, special issue on Directions in Southern Jewish History 85, no. 3 (September 1997): 195–230.

5. Goldstein, *Price of Whiteness*, 55.

6. Goldstein, *Price of Whiteness*, 57.

7. There was a long tradition of Jews being elected to political office in the West. To take Oregon as an example, elected officials there included many Jewish mayors, among them Bernard Goldsmith (Portland, 1869–1871), Philip Wasserman (Portland, 1871–1873), Joseph Simon (Portland, 1877 and 1909–1911), and the mayors of at least nine other Oregon cities prior to World War II. Simon also served in the U.S. Senate from 1898–1903, and he and Solomon Hirsch both served as president of the senate (Simon for five terms) during the late nineteenth century. Ben Selling served as both president of the Oregon Senate and speaker of the house in the 1910s, and won nomination as a Republican for the U.S. Senate (although he lost the general election). Edward Hirsch and Louis Fleischer both served as state treasurer, the former from 1878–1887 and the latter from 1870–1874. Julius Meier served as governor 1930–1934. Steven Lowenstein, *The Jews of Oregon* (Portland: Jewish Historical Society of Oregon, 1987), 60–61.

8. Mike Davis, *City of Quartz: Excavating the Future in Los Angeles* (New York: Verso, 1990), 116. Anti-Semitism in Los Angeles will be discussed in greater detail in chap. 4.

9. Oregon State Immigration Commission, *Biennial Report*, 1913–1914.

10. Ellen Eisenberg, Ava F. Kahn, and Bill Toll, *Jews of the Pacific West: Creating a Regional Society* (Tentative title) (Seattle: University of Washington Press, forthcoming), chap. 3.

11. *Oregon Native Son*, volume I, May 1899: 3; July, 1899: 138, 175.

12. On the role of the Native Sons organizations in defining "white space," see David Glassberg, "Making Places in California" in *Sense of History: The Place of the Past in American Life* (Amherst: University of Massachusetts Press, 2001), 167–202.

13. *Oregon Native Son*, volume I. On Native Americans, see recurring stories on "Indian War Recollections," for example, August 1899: 210–11; examples of romanticized Native American lore are also frequent. See, for example, October 1899: 305. One story recalls the first "neck tie party" (lynching) in the region, recalling in celebratory tones the way a white trader acted as "judge, jury, and executioner," and "Mr. Indian dangled to the music of the breeze," October 1899: 337. On African Americans, see "Negro Pioneers; Their Page in History": 432–433; on Chinese, "Chinamen a Pioneer": 530.

14. Frank Van Nuys, "Sowing the Seeds of Internment: James D. Phelan's Anti-Japanese Crusade, 1919–1920" in *Remembering Heart Mountain: Essays on Japanese American Internment in Wyoming*, ed. Mike Mackey (Powell, Wyo.: Western History Publications, 1998), 7.

15. Laurence Stuppy, "Henry H. Lissner, M.D., Los Angeles Physician," *Western States Jewish Historical Quarterly* 8, no. 3 (1976): 212.

16. Irma Weill "Alphonse Weill of Bakersfield," *Western States Jewish Historical Quarterly* 4, no. 1 (1971): 1.

17. This trend led one historian to wonder whether, particularly in Los Angeles, the exclusions of Jews from social clubs and downtown institutions in the 1920s might also have been "paralleled by an effort to purge Jews from the Pioneer rosters?" Glassberg, "Making Places in California," 258n50.

18. Reva Clar, "Samuel Sussman Snow: A Pioneer Finds El Dorado," *Western States Jewish Historical Quarterly* 3, no. 1 (1970): 23.

19. David Glassberg, posting on H-California, July 15, 2002.

20. Lawrence J. Saalfeld, *Forces of Prejudice in Oregon, 1920–1925* (Portland, Ore.: Archdiocesan Historical Commission, 1984), 30.

21. Lowenstein, *The Jews of Oregon*, 171.

22. Meier won 54.5 percent of the vote, and more than twice the number (135,608) of his nearest competitor, the Democratic candidate (62,434). "Julius L. Meier, 1931–1935" Oregon State Library, http: //www.osl.state.or.us/home/lib/governors/jlm.htm.

23. Patricia Limerick, *Legacy of Conquest* (New York: Norton, 1987), 27.

24. Elizabeth Jameson, *All That Glitters: Class, Conflict and Community in Cripple Creek* (Urbana: University of Illinois, 1998), 153.

25. Jacobson, *Whiteness of a Different Color*; Linda Gordon, *The Great Arizona Orphan Abduction* (Cambridge, Mass.: Harvard University Press, 2001); Tomas Almaguer, *Racial Fault Lines: The Historical Origins of White Supremacy in California* (Berkeley: University of California Press, 1994), 7. In contrast to these accounts, Allison Varzally categorizes Jews, along with Asians, Mexicans, and African Americans, as "non-whites" in California during the 1930s and 1940s. Her analysis focuses on notably diverse areas like Los Angeles's Boyle Heights and San Francisco's Fillmore, where Jews intermingled with other ethnic and racial minority groups. The mixing that occurred in these areas—and its impact on the ethnic identity of those who resided there—is important to consider, but must be placed in the larger context of the historic Jewish acceptance as whites in the West and their relative integration in other residential areas. The impact of the mixing in areas like Boyle Heights on Jewish responses to Japanese Americans will be explored in chap. 3. See Allison Varzally, "Ethnic Crossings: The Making of a Non-White America in the Second Quarter of Twentieth Century California," Ph.D. diss., University of California, Los Angeles, 2002.

26. It is notable that the Oregon Territory and later the state of Oregon prohibited both slavery and the settlement of free blacks. While the 14th Amendment of the Constitution rendered the prohibition on black settlement in the state null, the Northwest had a strong reputation as a region inhospitable to blacks, and a significant African American migration to this region did not occur until World War II.

27. The situation of Hispanics and Mexican immigrants began to change in the 1910s and 1920s. As their numbers grew, these groups attracted more attention from nativist and eugenicist groups. On the California eugenics program, for example, see Alexandra Minna Stern, *Eugenic Nation: Faults and Frontiers of Better Breeding in America* (Berkeley: University of California Press, 2005).

28. "Debate on the anti-Jap Bill" *Oregon Voter*, February 10, 1923: 19. This statement is particularly striking, given Oregon's notorious record of prejudice against blacks.

29. "Proceedings of the Asiatic Exclusion League" (1908) in *Proceedings of the Asiatic Exclusion League, 1907–1913* (New York, Arno Press, 1977), 16.

30. Fred Rosenbaum, *Visions of Reform: Congregation Emanu-El and the Jews of San Francisco, 1849–1999* (Berkeley: Judah L. Magnus Museum, 2000), 108.

31. David Yoo, *Growing Up Nisei: Race, Generation and Culture among Japanese Americans of California, 1924–1949* (Urbana: University of Illinois Press, 2000), 9.

32. "Lone Japanese Hears His Nation Assailed" *New York Times*, December 12, 1906: 6. On Julius Kahn's position on general immigration restrictions, such as literacy requirements, see Leslie Koepplin, *A Relationship of Reform: Immigrants and Progressives in the Far West* (New York: Garland Press, 1990), 36–37.

33. "Proceedings of the Asiatic Exclusion League" (January 1909) in *Proceedings of the Asiatic Exclusion League, 1907–1913* (New York: Arno Press, 1977), 12.

34. Frank Van Nuys, *Americanizing the West: Race, Immigrants, and Citizenship, 1890–1930* (Lawrence: University Press of Kansas, 2002), 18–19, 24.

35. Van Nuys, *Americanizing the West*, 15.

36. Fred H. Matthews, "White Community and 'Yellow Peril'," *The Mississippi Valley Historical Review* 50, no. 4 (March 1964): 614–15.

37. Matthews, "White Community and 'Yellow Peril'," 615.

38. Matthews, "White Community and 'Yellow Peril'," 619.

39. Quoted in Matthews, "White Community and 'Yellow Peril'," 620.

40. Quoted in Jesse F. Steiner, *The Japanese Invasion* (Chicago: A.C. McClurg, 1917; reprint, New York: Arno Press, 1978), 178.

41. Most notable among these efforts were the *Survey of Race Relations on the Pacific Coast*. See Eckard Toy, "Whose Frontier? The Survey of Race Relations on the Pacific Coast in the 1920s," *Oregon Historical Quarterly* 107, no. 1 (Spring 2006): 36–63.

42. Steiner, *The Japanese Invasion*, 179.

43. Steiner, *The Japanese Invasion*, v–vi. Steiner would later join the faculty at the University of Washington and devote himself to the defense of Nisei against wartime restrictions.

44. Goldstein demonstrates that the status of southern Jews as white began to be questioned in the 1880s. This was precisely the period when the legal status of African Americans was redefined as the Jim Crow system emerged in the years following the demise of Reconstruction.

45. This contrast was examined in Spencer C. Olin, Jr., "European Immigrant and Oriental Alien: Acceptance and Rejection by the California Legislature of 1913," *Pacific Historical Review* 35 (1966): 303–15.

46. Van Nuys, *Americanizing the West*, 39.

47. Olin, "European Immigrant and Oriental Alien," 303–15. There is evidence that some of the CCIH services were extended to Asians; see Anne Woo-Sam, "Americanizing Californians: Americanization in California from the Progressive Era through the Red Scare," *PART* (CUNY, 2003) http://dsc.gc.cuny.edu/part/part9/identities/articles/woosa.html.

48. Olin, "European Immigrant and Oriental Alien," 303–15. Governor Johnson played a less open role in the passage of the Alien Land Law than he did in the CCIH. However, Roger Daniels has demonstrated that Johnson was "the behind-the-

scenes manager of the alien land bill." See Daniels, *The Politics of Prejudice* (Berkeley: University of California Press, 1962), 59.

49. The story of Simon's father's immigration and career is told in Olivia Rossett Agresti, *David Lubin: A Study in Practical Idealism* (Berkeley: University of California Press, 1922).

50. *The Jewish Immigration Bulletin*, Report of the 6th annual meeting of the Hebrew Sheltering and Immigrant Aid Society of America 5, no. 30 (March 1915): 50. Lubin is listed as a National Director.

51. Anne Woo-Sam, "Americanizing Californians."

52. California Commission on Immigration (CCIH), *Second Annual Report*, January 1916: 131.

53. CCIH, *Second Annual Report*, January 1916: 135–36.

54. CCIH, *Second Annual Report*, January 1916: 140,142–44.

55. David Yoo, *Growing Up Nisei: Race, Generation, and Culture among Japanese Americans of California, 1924–1949* (Urbana: University of Illinois Press, 2000), chap. 1.

56. Woo-Sam, "Americanizing Californians."

57. CCIH, *Second Annual Report*, January 1916: 95.

58. CCIH, *Second Annual Report*, 97. The poster appears in the report, and includes text in English, Spanish, Hungarian, Italian, Portuguese, Greek, Russian, Polish, Bohemian, Yiddish, Croatian, and French. It is difficult to determine the exact number of speakers of some languages, such as Croatian, since they did not make up a national group distinguishable in the census, yet it is clear that many of these languages were far less widely spoken than Japanese or Chinese. To take a few extreme examples, the 1910 census lists only a total of 345 California residents as immigrants from Bohemia or Slovakia and only 974 Hungarians. All of those listed as Austrian, Hungarian, and as immigrants from other nations that were part of the Austro-Hungarian Empire—for whom translations into several different languages were provided—together total about 22,000, compared to over 38,000 Japanese and over 27,000 Chinese.

59. CCIH, *Second Annual Report*, 177.

60. Leslie Koepplin, *A Relationship of Reform: Immigrants and Progressives in the Far West* (New York: Garland Press, 1990), 124.

61. Quoted in Koepplin, *A Relationship of Reform*, 125. Clearly, Hanna's remarks did not apply to Asian immigrants, who were permanently barred from citizenship.

62. For a discussion of western progressives' support for a literacy requirement, see Koepplin, *A Relationship of Reform*, chap. 6. The 1917 immigration act not only introduced a literacy test but also formalized an "Asiatic Barred Zone," which eliminated Asian immigration not already covered by a previous restriction. Since Chinese immigration came under the Exclusion Acts and Japanese immigration was regulated through the terms of the Gentlemen's Agreement, the Asiatic Barred Zone provision had no real effect on Chinese and Japanese immigration. See Roger Daniels, *Guarding the Golden Door: American Immigration Policy and Immigrants Since 1882* (New York: Hill and Wang, 2004), 46; Desmond King, *Making Americans: Immigration, Race and the Origins of the Diverse Democracy* (Cambridge, Mass.: Harvard University Press, 2000), 79.

63. Van Nuys, *Americanizing the West*, 172.

64. Van Nuys, *Americanizing the West*, chap. 2.

65. Woo-Sam, "Americanizing Californians."

66. Van Nuys, *Americanizing the West*, 180.

67. Woo-Sam, "Americanizing Californians."

68. Daniels, *The Politics of Prejudice*, 94–95; Roger Daniels, *Not Like Us: Immigrants and Minorities in America, 1890–1924* (Chicago: Ivan R. Dee, 1997), 132–33; Van Nuys, *Americanizing the West*, 184.

69. John Higham, *Strangers in the Land: Patterns of American Nativism, 1860–1925* (New York: Atheneum, 1985 [original edition, 1963]), 166.

70. Higham, *Strangers in the Land*, 307.

71. Quoted in Daniels, *The Politics of Prejudice*, 23–24.

72. Daniels, *The Politics of Prejudice*, 24.

73. Koepplin, *A Relationship of Reform*, 151.

74. Koepplin, *A Relationship of Reform*, 151.

75. Koepplin, *A Relationship of Reform*, 152.

76. Daniels, *The Politics of Prejudice*, chap. 6.

77. For a discussion of this campaign, see Daniels, *The Politics of Prejudice*, chaps. 6–7.

78. Daniels, *The Politics of Prejudice*, 97.

79. Daniels, *The Politics of Prejudice*, 101–2.

80. Van Nuys, *Americanizing the West*, 188.

81. Van Nuys, *Americanizing the West*, 185.

82. Quoted in Daniels, *The Politics of Prejudice*, 49.

83. Daniels, *The Politics of Prejudice*, 92.

84. Van Nuys, "Sowing the Seeds," 1.

85. Van Nuys, "Sowing the Seeds," 2.

86. *Emanu-El*, October 29, 1920: 15, 16.

87. Van Nuys, "Sowing the Seeds," 9.

88. Daniels, *The Politics of Prejudice*, 90.

89. Van Nuys, "Sowing the Seeds," 7.

90. Van Nuys, *Americanizing the West*, 186.

91. Van Nuys, "Sowing the Seeds."

92. Noriko Asato, *Teaching Mikadoism: The Attack on Japanese Language Schools in Hawaii, California, and Washington, 1919–1927* (Honolulu: University of Hawaii Press, 2006), 69.

93. U.S. Department of the Interior, *Wartime Exile: The Exclusion of the Japanese Americans from the West Coast* (originally published 1946; reprint, New York: AMS Press, 1975), 44.

94. Goldstein, *The Price of Whiteness*, 57.

95. Goldstein, *The Price of Whiteness*, 59.

96. Rudolph Glanz, "Jews and Chinese in America," *Jewish Social Studies* 16, no. 3 (1954): 220–21.

97. Reva Clar and William Kramer, "Chinese-Jewish Relations in the Far West: 1850–1950," *Western States Jewish History* 21, no. 1 (1988): part I: 30.

98. Clar and Kramer, "Chinese-Jewish Relations in the Far West," part 1: 33.

99. Clar and Kramer, "Chinese-Jewish Relations in the Far West," part II: 139.

100. Clar and Kramer, "Chinese-Jewish Relations in the Far West," part II: 135–40.

101. Clar and Kramer, "Chinese-Jewish Relations in the Far West," part I: 25–26. David Solis-Cohen was a member of the well-known Philadelphia family.

102. For a discussion of this incident, see Marie Rose Wong, *Sweet Cakes, Long Journey: The Chinatowns of Portland Oregon* (Seattle: University of Washington Press, 2004), 45. On Selling's participation, see letter from Ben Selling, March 23, 1886, Selling Papers, Oregon Historical Society.

103. Glanz, "Jews and Chinese," 222, 224. A separate article provides additional examples of positive relations between individual Jews and Chinese, particularly in the early years. See Clar and Kramer, "Chinese-Jewish Relations in the Far West," part I: 12–35.

104. Clar and Kramer, "Chinese-Jewish Relations in the Far West," part 1: 24.

105. Clar and Kramer, "Chinese-Jewish Relations in the Far West," part 1: 32–33.

106. Clar and Kramer, "Chinese-Jewish Relations in the Far West," part II: 135.

107. Glanz, "Jews and Chinese," 229.

108. Glanz, "Jews and Chinese," 230, 231.

109. Clar and Kramer, "Chinese-Jewish Relations in the Far West," part II: 134.

110. Glanz, "Jews and Chinese," 226.

111. Clar and Kramer, "Chinese-Jewish Relations in the Far West," part I: 24.

112. Glanz, "Jews and Chinese," 231–32.

113. Glanz, "Jews and Chinese," 231.

114. Clar and Kramer, "Chinese-Jewish Relations in the Far West," part I: 34.

115. Glanz, *The Jews of California*, quoted in Clar and Kramer, "Chinese-Jewish Relations in the Far West," part I: 25.

116. Rosenbaum, *Visions of Reform*, 89.

117. Clar and Kramer, "Chinese-Jewish Relations in the Far West," part II: 147.

118. Clar and Kramer, "Chinese-Jewish Relations in the Far West," part II: 147–48.

119. Secretary's message, *Proceedings of the Asiatic Exclusion League*, September 1908: 16.

120. Both Washington and Oregon had Immigration Commissions that, particularly during the 1910s, worked to promote the immigration of farmers from other parts of the United States, from Canada, and from Europe. Koepplin, *A Relationship of Reform*, chap. 5. See, for example, *Biennial Report of Oregon State Immigration Commission, 1913–1914*.

121. Clar and Kramer, "Chinese-Jewish Relations in the Far West," part II: 149.

122. Alan Boxerman, "Kahn of California," *California Historical Quarterly* 55, no. 4 (1976): 349.

123. Koepplin, *Relationship of Reform*, 36–37, 134.

124. *Proceedings of the Asiatic Exclusion League* show Kahn's active involvement. On his censuring in the press see Clar and Kramer, "Chinese-Jewish Relations in the Far West," part II: 149.

125. *Emanu-El*, October 1, 1920.

126. Jan Herman Burgers, "The Road to San Francisco: The Revival of the Human Rights Idea in the Twentieth Century," *Human Rights Quarterly* 14, no. 4 (November 1992): 449.

127. *Emanu-El*, October 1, 1920.

128. *Emanu-El*. "Political Notes" began to appear in the month before the August primary, then disappeared, and reappeared on October 22, in advance of the general

election. Advertisements for candidates appeared throughout August and again in late October. In late October several advertisements opposing the Harris Bill, a pro-prohibition ballot measure, were published.

129. *Emanu-El*, October 29, 1920.

130. *Emanu-El*, June 25, 1920.

131. On the increased Jewish defense activity in this era, see Stuart Svonkin, *Jews against Prejudice: American Jews and the Fight for Civil Liberties* (New York: Columbia University Press, 1993), chap. 1; and Marc Dollinger, *Quest for Inclusion: Jews and Liberalism in Modern America* (Princeton, N.J.: Princeton University Press, 2000).

132. For example, several articles on Americanization appear in the Rosh Hashanah edition, *Emanu-El*, September 10, 1920.

133. Quoted in Jonathan Sarna, *American Judaism: A History* (New Haven, Conn.: Yale University Press, 2004), 217.

134. Sarna, *American Judaism*, 216.

135. Svonkin, *Jews against Prejudice*, 11.

136. Svonkin, *Jews against Prejudice*, 13.

137. Diner, *In the Almost Promised Land*, 20.

138. Gladys Trachtenberg oral history, Portland Jewish Oral History Project Oregon Jewish Museum (1): 6.

139. See, for example, Portland's *Scribe*, August 6, 1920: 4.

140. Molly Cone, Howard Droker, and Jacqueline Williams, *Family of Strangers: Building a Jewish Community in Washington State* (Seattle: University of Washington Press/Washington State Jewish Historical Society, 2003), 108–9. Writings and sermons in which the rabbi spoke out against prejudice are available in the Rabbi Samuel Koch Papers, University of Washington Archives, accession #1759. See for example, clipping from May 14, 1917, titled "Prejudice Is Blind to Justice, Says Rabbi" covering a sermon in which the Rabbi preached that "prejudice is unfair, unfair to those who harbor it, unfair to the victims of it. . . ."

141. Felicia Herman, "Jewish Leaders and the Motion Picture Industry," in *California Jews*, ed. Ava Kahn and Marc Dollinger (Hanover, N.H.: Brandeis University Press/University Press of New England, 2003), 98.

142. Rosenbaum, *Visions of Reform*, 186–87.

143. *Scribe*, December 3, 1920: 3.

144. For example, in the week following the arguing of *Frick v. Webb* before the Supreme Court, *Emanu-El* noted that Felix Levy, "distinguished member of the New York bar," had won an important case in federal appeals court, reversing a Federal Trade Commission order. *Emanu-El*, May 24, 1923.

145. Editorial, *Emanu-El*, April 27, 1923.

146. Goldstein, *The Price of Whiteness*, 59

147. See, for example, an article on Julius Rosenwald's efforts to establish fellowships for "negro graduates for advanced medical studies," *Emanu-El*, June 25, 1920.

148. *Scribe*, August 6, 1920: 4.

149. *Scribe*, April 16, 1920: 3.

150. *Scribe*, May 12, 1922: 7.

151. *Scribe*, May 19, 1922: 3.

152. *Scribe*, May 26, 1922: 3.

153. For example, *Scribe*, July 21, 1922: 3.

154. For example, a lengthy expose on the Klan from *The Nation* ran in the July 21, 1922, edition; and an editorial from the Catholic publication *The Spectator* ran in the August 11, 1922, edition.

155. *Scribe*, November 3, 1922. Ben Selling, Nathan Strauss, Rabbi Jonah Wise, David Solis Cohen, and Roscoe Nelson signed the latter ad.

156. *Oregon Voter*, October 22, 1922: 13.

157. Robert Johnston, *The Radical Middle Class* (Princeton, N.J.: Princeton University Press, 2003), 242.

158. Benjamin Morris, "True American: The Media Battle on Private Schools and the Oregon Compulsory Education Bill, 1922–1925," unpublished thesis, University of Portland, December 2005, 13–14.

159. Morris, "True American," 13–14. The ad appeared in the *Telegram* on November 3, 1922; coverage of Rabbi Wise's lecture was in the *Oregonian*, October 21, 1922: 15. See also Saalfeld, *Forces of Prejudice in Oregon*, 75.

160. Saalfeld, *Forces of Prejudice in Oregon*, 78.

161. *Oregon Voter*, "Ousting the Japanese," January 27, 1923: 37; "Debate on the Anti-Jap Bill," February 10, 1923: 18–21.

162. *Oregon Voter*, "Debate on the Anti-Jap Bill," February 10, 1923: 19–21.

163. The House vote on the measure was 35 in favor and 10 opposed.

164. *Oregon Voter*, February 17, 1928: 10.

165. It should be noted that the *Oregonian* published a lengthy piece critical of the Alien Land Bill on February 11, 1923—after it had passed the state house and was moving to the senate. Headlined "Anti-Japanese Legislation in Oregon Held to be Menacing," the opinion piece made a strong case against the bill but was signed "An American Citizen," and not claimed as the position of the newspaper's editorial board. *Oregonian*, February 11, 1923, section 5: 3.

166. Goldstein, *The Price of Whiteness*, 190. Roedigger, *Working toward Whiteness*, chap. 7.

167. Goldstein, *The Price of Whiteness*, 191. See also Svonkin, *Jews against Prejudice*, 23.

168. Goldstein, *The Price of Whiteness*, 194–96.

169. Lauren Kessler's biographical account of Hood River's Yasui family paints this period as one in which the family became more established and, to some degree, accepted. Kessler, *Stubborn Twig* (New York: Penguin, 1993), 104–6. On the emerging Nisei subculture in the interwar period, see Yoo, *Growing Up Nisei*, chaps. 1–3.

2

A Studious Silence: Western Jewish Responses to Japanese Removal

On February 19, 1942, President Franklin D. Roosevelt issued Executive Order 9066, providing the Secretary of War with the legal authority for the internment of the Japanese American community of the West Coast. The next day, Portland's Jewish newspaper, the *Scribe*, ran a statement by Wendell Wilkie under the headline "Americans All." Wilkie said:

> this country's strength is the composite of persons of all descents—Irish, English, German, Italian and a myriad of other races, colors and creeds. No American has the right to impugn the patriotism or loyalty of any other American because of the accident of his birth or descent or religion. In times of war unthinking persons sometimes forget the basic concepts of freedom for which America fights. Prejudices arise and persecutions are practiced.
>
> They must be protected in their rights and their liberty for they are the very marrow of the bone of America.[1]

Such proclamations of equality were staples in the West Coast Jewish press in this period, reflecting the strong commitment of the American Jewish community to fighting prejudice and discrimination. That commitment, and the publication of Wilkie's statement, would seem to suggest opposition to discriminatory practices like those carried out under Executive Order 9066. Yet, while expressions of concern about discrimination and assertions of equality appeared regularly in the pages of western Jewish newspapers, this concern was almost never extended to the Japanese American community. Indeed, the western Jewish press and the large organized Jewish communities that they served scrupulously avoided the issue. Only one of the major West Coast Jewish newspapers endorsed the government's relocation policy, and only one opposed "mass evacuation"—and both took these positions in brief, one-time statements and with little fanfare. The others did not endorse or condemn the decision. Indeed, they did not mention it at all. The failure of the western Jewish press to speak out on the issue of Japanese removal reflects these communities' silence, a silence that is particularly striking when contrasted with their vocal stance on other civil liberties questions at the time.

Nationally, the silence of Jewish (and other) civil rights groups in the face of the federal policy of removal and incarceration has been explained, in part, by the considerable investment of these groups in the Roosevelt administration and the war effort.[2] Their inclusion in the Roosevelt coalition, their stake in administration policies such as the Fair Employment Practices initiative, and their enormous investment in defeating Nazi Germany and saving their European brethren led the American Jewish community to make support of the administration and the war effort a top priority. These communities were unlikely to publicly question or protest a policy that the administration and the army claimed was essential to that effort.

Indeed, in her study of the responses of national Jewish groups to the removal and incarceration policy, Cheryl Greenberg found that security concerns thwarted the only attempt of such a group to question the policy. The National Council of Jewish Women (NCJW) was well known for its strong progressive views and stance against prejudice. The organization's social legislation committee immediately expressed concerns about E09066, drafting a statement in March that the committee "recognize the need to take every precaution to safeguard our country from sabotage but believe that the wholesale evacuation of the Japanese without regard to their citizenship creates a 'second class citizenship' which disregards Article 14 of the Constitution of the United States of America." Although the NCJW executive committee "agreed that the evacuation presented a 'civil liberties' problem," President Blanche Goldman balked at the idea of questioning "publicly any decision the military believed 'absolutely necessary for the safety of our war effort.'" Goldman also expressed fear that such a statement might be seen as influenced by "subversive elements."[3] Apprehensions about national security clearly gave pause to groups and individuals who might otherwise have questioned these policies. Such concerns were strongest in the West, where residents feared a potential Japanese invasion on the American mainland.

Yet the national silence has also been attributed to the remoteness of many national Jewish (and other civil rights/civil liberties) leaders from the process. Greenberg found that there was no record of the issue being discussed by major, East Coast–based groups, including the American Jewish Congress, the American Jewish Committee, and the Anti-Defamation League of B'nai B'rith, even in private meetings. This led her to conclude that the issue "passed unnoticed."[4] The proximity of western Jewish communities to Japanese American communities and to the livestock pavilions and racetracks that served as the initial incarceration sites in the spring of 1942 placed these issues squarely in their line of vision. In addition, western Jews, like all residents of the Pacific states, were exposed to a flood of anti-Nikkei propaganda. Their responses—and their silences—occurred against a backdrop of intense public attention to the issue by local and state governmental bodies and civic organizations and saturation coverage in the press. These events simply could not "pass unnoticed" by western Jews as they did for their counterparts in the East.

Therefore, despite the fact that the silence of western Jewish communities echoed that of Jewish communities nationwide, it cannot be viewed as simply a local example of a national trend. While Japanese American removal and incarceration may have been off the radar screen of Jews in other parts of the country, this was not the case for western Jews. Their silence resulted not from ignorance but from the tension between their commitment to fighting intolerance and prejudice, on the one hand, and a combination of their support for the war effort and the overwhelming regional anti-Japanese sentiment on the other. This tension, evident in community newspapers, seems to have paralyzed these communities: they failed to protest and they also refrained from jumping onto the wildly popular pro-removal bandwagon.

These communities' silence must be understood in the context of the prominence of the issue in public consciousness and the strong anti-Nikkei sentiment throughout the region. In the aftermath of Pearl Harbor, public attention in the West quickly came to focus on the perceived threat posed by the large, local Japanese American population. While government officials and the press tried at first to call for calm and emphasize the loyalty of most Japanese Americans,[5] anti-Nikkei sentiment increased rapidly in January and February as false allegations of fifth-column activity were spread by interest groups, the mainstream press, and politicians. By February, the momentum for mass removal of Japanese Americans—both aliens and citizens by birth—was growing rapidly.

As the policy unfolded, residents of the major West Coast cities had front-row seats. The region's major Jewish communities were concentrated in the same cities that served as sites for hearings held by the House Select Committee on National Defense Migration, known as the Tolan Committee. As removal got underway, most Japanese Americans subject to the relocation order were first brought to "assembly centers" in or near these same cities— at locations such as the livestock pavilions in Portland or the Tanforan racetrack near San Francisco—before being sent on to more permanent camps in the interior. Several of the major cases challenging alien restrictions—cases that would ultimately reach the Supreme Court—were initiated in these cities, such as the Minoru Yasui case in Portland, the Gordon Hirabayashi case in Seattle, and the Fred Korematsu case in the Bay Area. These developments generated intense coverage in the mainstream press in these cities.

Several studies of the mainstream western press have concluded that coverage became increasingly hostile to Japanese Americans and supportive of mass removal and incarceration during the winter of 1942, as the government policy took shape against a backdrop of American and Allied reverses in the war in the Pacific that included the fall of the Philippines and the Japanese advance that threatened Australia. Morton Grodzins found in his study of more than one hundred California newspapers that editorials expressed generally favorable opinions of Japanese Americans for the first month after Pearl Harbor but that opinion began to shift in January and became overwhelmingly unfavorable thereafter.[6] Similarly, in his examination of editorial responses in California, Lloyd Chiasson found that the press served more as "a government publicist," than as a "watchdog," shifting from a more sympathetic view to a pro-removal one as government policy was formulated.[7] Floyd McKay has demonstrated that all of the Seattle dailies followed this pattern, moving from "supporting Nikkei rights and calling for tolerance" to supporting mass removal. This shift was accompanied by an increasing propensity to use the term "Jap" to refer to Japanese Americans as well as to the Japanese enemy.[8]

Reporting in Portland's *Oregonian* was typical and exemplifies the patterns in the press coverage to which westerners were exposed. In the wake of Pearl Harbor, the *Oregonian* turned its attention almost immediately to the state's Japanese American community, which in 1941 numbered approximately four thousand, by far the smallest of the three West Coast states.[9] During the first four months of the war, the *Oregonian* ran an average of ten items per week, including articles, op-ed pieces, and letters to the editor, focused specifically on Japanese Americans. Portlanders regularly woke up to front-page stories on the restrictions imposed on aliens. In one two-week period, the paper published forty-three separate items on this story, including twelve front-page stories.[10]

While the daily coverage to which Oregonians were exposed became ever more hostile to the Nikkei community in February and March, earlier reporting on the issue in December and January was quite mixed, with the paper publishing both sympathetic and pro-restrictionist articles. For example, immediately after Pearl Harbor the *Oregonian* featured a story headlined "Nisei are Placed in a Tough Spot."[11] Later in the month, the paper made "An Appeal for Fair Play," in an editorial speaking out against prejudice toward Japanese Americans.[12] As late as February 12, 1942, the paper reported that while 80 percent of Portlanders surveyed favored evacuation of "all enemy aliens," only 36 percent believed "native born children (including adults) of enemy aliens," should be evacuated.[13] Despite such sympathetic stories, the *Oregonian* used the terms "aliens," "Japanese," and "Japs" interchangeably to refer to both Japanese immigrant aliens and their American born offspring.

Beginning in February, the *Oregonian*, like other western newspapers, took an increasingly pro-removal position, officially endorsing a mass removal and incarceration policy in an editorial on February 26, 1942: "As we see it, it is absolutely essential that the aliens be evacuated, and that they be transferred inland beyond the Pacific coast forest belt."[14] An April editorial headlined "Protecting the Refugees" asserted that American treatment of Japanese Americans was "democratic" and compared favorably to treatment of "refugees" by Nazi Germany.[15] A front-page story on the arrival of Japanese Americans forced to report to the North Portland assembly center failed to mention that the accommodations were the stockyards and stables that had recently housed livestock at the Pacific International Livestock Exposition Center. The article implied a more civilized form of housing when it noted that the internees were "bringing homey things to tidy up their new apartments or dormitory quarters."[16] An article about Minoru Yasui's case challenging the constitutionality of alien restrictions repeatedly referred to the Hood River, Oregon, native and University of Oregon graduate as "the Japanese."[17] Similarly, in response to a letter to the editor from a Japanese American questioning his "alien" classification, the editor wrote of the impossibility of separating the loyal from the disloyal and argued that all, therefore, had to be "moved in the interests of national security."[18]

The increasing hostility of the press toward the Nikkei community and support for strong measures against Japanese Americans, both citizens and aliens, reflected the emerging governmental policy.[19] On February 13, the West Coast congressional delegation urged President Roosevelt toward a relocation policy for "all persons of Japanese lineage . . . aliens and citizens alike, from the strategic areas of California, Oregon and Washington."[20] Six days later, President Roosevelt signed Executive Order 9066, which authorized the Secretary of War to designate military areas from which "any or all persons" could be excluded. Two days later, the Tolan Committee opened its West Coast hearings in San Francisco. In sessions held over several weeks in five West Coast cities, a wide variety of city, state, and federal officials, as well as representatives of various citizens' and veterans' groups, testified to the necessity of mass removal of Japanese Americans. Several groups and individuals testified to Nikkei loyalty and argued for selective programs based on an assessment of individual loyalty, and some testified only to the practical aspects of a potential relocation policy.[21] However, of those who expressed a position on the central question of whether mass removal was necessary, most argued in support of the idea. Many of these witnesses stressed the urgency of the situation, imploring committee members to take immediate steps to initiate the removal of all Japanese American citizens and aliens.

The Portland hearings were the most one-sided, with only one individual, a Methodist missionary, explicitly opposing mass removal. At those hearings, many community groups, including the American Legion, the Portland City Council, and several Chambers of Commerce, enthusiastically endorsed the concept of mass removal and incarceration. Portland Mayor Earl Riley presented a statement urging quick "evacuation" of both Japanese aliens and Japanese American citizens, explaining, "I would like to have them [orders] today, if possible—to evacuate all Axis aliens and second generation Japanese from this area as soon as possible. We feel—and I think that I am speaking the sentiment of the great majority of our people—that they are definitely a hazard."[22] The Portland City Council shared with the committee its resolution, urging the immediate removal of "all Japanese nationals and persons of Japanese descent irrespective of American citizenship . . . for the duration of the war."[23] The *Oregonian*'s publisher, Palmer Hoyt, expressed his concern about the potential for sabotage and presented his paper's editorial, claiming that removal of Japanese Americans was "absolutely essential."[24] The strongest pro-internment statement at the Portland hearings was that of the American Legion. Joseph K. Carson Jr., a former mayor of Portland and representative of the American Legion in Oregon, claimed, "it is practically unanimous [among Oregon Legion posts] that Japanese nationals should be interned for the duration of the emergency."[25] Members of American Legion Post 97 of Portland cautioned the committee that sabotage was probable, claiming that the lack of such attacks to date demonstrated that they had been "held in leash until a critical moment for most telling effect," and presented its resolution that

> This is no time for namby-pamby pussyfooting, fear of hurting the feelings of our enemies; that it is not the time for consideration of minute constitutional rights of those enemies but that it is time for vigorous, whole-hearted, and concerted action . . . toward removal of all enemy aliens and citizens of enemy alien extraction from all areas along the coast. . . .[26]

Although the Portland hearings were notable for the near absence of opposition, similar sentiments were expressed up and down the West Coast. Certainly, within the American Legion the Oregon chapters were by no means exceptional. Legion posts in all three Pacific states presented pro-restrictionist resolutions to the Tolan Committee—twenty from Washington alone, although it is notable that a number of these advocated selective, rather than mass, removal of the Nisei.[27] Nor was the American Legion alone in its views. In the San Francisco, Los Angeles, and Seattle hearings, as in Portland, politicians, newspaper editors, and businessmen joined the chorus advocating removal of all Japanese Americans, aliens and citizens. Local governments and a wide variety of civic groups presented the Tolan Committee with their resolutions urging the removal of Japanese Americans. Several localities passed their own restrictions on the Nikkei community. For example, Los Angeles County dismissed Nikkei workers, as did the Seattle school district.[28] The mayors of San Francisco, Los Angeles, and Seattle, along with representatives from many smaller cities, joined Portland's Earl Riley testifying in favor of mass removal.[29] Los Angeles's Fletcher Bowron, elected as a liberal with support from the Nikkei community, quickly shifted from a "friendly" position in December to a vigorously pro-evacuation position.[30] Seattle's mayor Earl Millikin testified that "the sentiment of the people of Seattle is overwhelmingly in favor of evacuation," explaining, "They think that it is a danger. . . . They know that we can't take the chance of leaving them here and having another Pearl Harbor or something worse right here in Seattle or in the Pacific Northwest."[31] Using the same reasoning as the Oregon Legion, Millikin conjectured that the lack of sabotage since Pearl Harbor indicated not that Japanese saboteurs were not in the area, but that they were waiting for the perfect moment to strike.

Central to the argument for the removal of the Nikkei was a belief that the Japanese, unlike the Germans and the Italians, were likely to retain their ancestral ties—often cast in racial or biological terms—and that it was impossible to distinguish the loyal from the disloyal among them. Millikin explained in his testimony that while there were "citizen Japanese" who were loyal and would like to assist the U.S. government in arresting subversives, the nature of the Nikkei community made this impossible: "There is this difference in the Japanese trait and the Italian: the Japanese don't inform."[32] California Attorney General Earl Warren, in testimony that historian Morton Grodzins characterized as making "one of the most extensive arguments in favor of evacuation," made exactly the same claim—despite the fact that he had indicated only a few weeks before that Japanese Americans *had* provided useful information to authorities.[33] California Governor Culbert Olson, who had earlier argued against such a plan, urged the mass evacuation of Japanese but not German and Italian immigrants. He explained that the issue was that Japanese Americans "all look alike," making it impossible to distinguish between the loyal and the disloyal. As the governor testified, "The distinction between the Japanese and the Italian and German is the difficulty of telling who is who among the Japanese."[34] While Olson's statement was particularly crass, his sentiments were not atypical. Grodzins argues in his analysis of the opinions of political leaders that "there prevailed a basic distrust of the Japanese population as a group. Virtually every statement made by state and local officials reflected a special fear of resident Japanese because of the alleged difficulty of 'separating the good from the bad' or the alleged impossibilities of 'trusting any Jap.' This was asserted by officials of all degrees of importance and from each of the three western states."[35] This sentiment was clearly expressed by General DeWitt, the commander of the Western Defense Zone, who wrote in his 1943 *Final Report*, "In the war in which we are now engaged racial affinities are not severed by migration. The Japanese race is an enemy race and while many second and third generation Japanese born on United States soil, possessed of United States citizenship, have become 'Americanized,' the racial strains are undiluted."[36] Earlier, DeWitt had been more succinct, explaining, "A Jap is a Jap."

It was against this backdrop that the Jewish communities of the West Coast responded to the issue. They differed little in their public reactions from one another and from Jewish communities nationally: all maintained a near total silence on the issue, despite the fact that the issue dovetailed well with several of their community priorities. On the one hand, their tremendous focus on support for the war effort to defeat Nazi Germany might have led them to join other westerners in endorsing the removal as an essential defense measure. On the other, their commitment to fighting prejudice might have encouraged them to oppose a measure that threatened to incarcerate Americans based on race or ancestry. Questioning restrictions that military authorities deemed necessary smacked of undermining the war effort, but supporting measures that were based on race had the potential to undermine deep commitments to equality and the fight against prejudice. As the policy of Japanese removal and incarceration emerged, western Jewish communities maintained silence not because the issue was outside of their purview but because any impulse to defend Japanese Americans based on their commitment to fighting prejudice was balanced against their desire to fully support the war effort and the overwhelming nature of local anti-Nikkei sentiment.

Thus, understanding the western Jewish response to Japanese removal requires an examination of these communities' central goals. Prewar and wartime coverage in these major West Coast Jewish newspapers, San Francisco's *Emanu-El*, Los Angeles's *B'nai B'rith Messenger*, Portland's *Scribe*, and the *Seattle Jewish Transcript*, makes clear that support of the war in order to defeat Nazism and save European Jewry was—not surprisingly—these communities' most important priority. The destruction of European Jewry was a frequent focus of all four newspapers, and all presented the war effort as vital to their readers, both as Americans and as Jews.

Throughout the years leading up to World War II, all of these papers had focused intense attention on the plight of the Jewish communities of Europe. In virtually any week's edition during the five years before the American entry into the war, a reader would have encountered numerous articles reporting the disasters befalling European Jewry. After Pearl Harbor, while the mainstream media in the West focused primarily on Japan and the war in the Pacific, the western Jewish press continued to emphasize the European theater and the impact of the war on European Jews. For example, *Emanu-El*'s first edition after Pearl Harbor included many war-related stories on topics including achieving unity, the Nazis, the situation in France, Palestine and Zionism as solutions to the plight of Jews in Europe, local Jews serving in the armed forces, and Russian war relief.[37] As weekly papers, these publications generally did not report on the day-to-day progress of the war covered in the mainstream press. Instead, they tended to focus on news about European Jewish communities and the postwar prospects for those communities—particularly in Palestine.[38] They also reported with great frequency on steps that readers could take to aid the war effort. In a mid-December issue of Seattle's *Transcript*, for example, one front-page story focused on the need to aid the Red Cross Disaster Relief Commission, reprinting President Roosevelt's plea for support for the organization.[39]

Although stories like that on the Red Cross addressed general wartime issues, editors frequently inserted specific appeals based on Jewish ties. In this case, the editors added in boldfaced type, **"Beyond all possible question, the Jews of Seattle may be confidently called upon to do their full share and do it now."** Next to this story ran one headlined "B'nai B'rith Offers Full Power to War Effort," documenting the efforts of the national Jewish organization to contribute to the war effort. Later in the month, the paper's editorial "The Citizenship of the Jew," provided readers a list of ten things that "American Jews must do **not distinctively as Jews**, but as patriotic members of the general society of a nation at war," [emphasis in original].[40] Similarly, in its December 12 edition, San Francisco's *Emanu-El* ran twin editorials rallying support for the war effort under the headlines "Americans Unite!" and "Jews Unite!"[41] And in just one December issue, the *Scribe* carried a story on the American Jewish Congress's pledge of support, an op-ed piece discussing Jewish deaths at Pearl Harbor and the numbers of Jewish servicemen in all branches of the armed forces, the text of a B'nai B'rith pledge to support the war effort, and an article headlined "Jews in the World War" documenting proof of Jewish "patriotism and heroism" in World War I.[42] Stories of local organizations' contributions, through efforts ranging from bandage rolling to providing social and athletic outlets for soldiers, ran frequently in all of these papers.

Given the obvious Jewish interest in the defeat of Nazi Germany, calls for and documentation of Jewish support for the war effort might have seemed unnecessary. Yet they were prominent in these papers throughout the period, beginning immediately after Pearl Harbor. Although the *Transcript's* editors admonished their readers that "it is a lamentable thing to think of but there are people in this country and they are not confined to any race or class who are very much worried over, 'whether or not they will get the credit they deserve for their war efforts,'"[43] coverage by the *Transcript* and its sister papers suggests exactly this concern. Jews, like African Americans—and Japanese Americans—hoped that their contributions to the war effort could be used as a counterweight to existing popular prejudices.[44] While Jews enthusiastically supported the war as patriotic Americans and as Jews hoping to defeat Nazism and save their European brethren, their contributions to the national effort were also viewed as a means of fighting anti-Semitism at home.

While the West had a remarkable record of tolerance and acceptance toward Jews in the nineteenth and early twentieth centuries, the rise of vocal anti-Semites like Henry Ford and Father Coughlin on the national scene in the 1920s and 1930s led to increased concern among national Jewish leaders about anti-Semitism, concerns that were clearly shared by western Jews.[45] Indeed, anxiety about local anti-Semitism grew dramatically in the West in the two decades preceding World War II. This was particularly true in southern California, where vocal pro-fascist and anti-Semitic groups like the Silver Shirts and the German American Bund gained a stronghold in this period. Anti-Semitism fueled by the significant presence of Jews in Hollywood's motion picture industry was also a key local concern.

By 1940, national Jewish groups fighting anti-Semitism and their regional branches had developed a strategy of countering anti-Semitism by working with non-Jewish groups to condemn all forms of discrimination. Defending the rights of other minority groups was seen as a defense of the rights of all. This strategy was reinforced during the war by a federal public relations campaign aimed at unifying Americans behind the fight.[46] Thus, on February 6, 1942, Seattle's *Transcript* was able to reinforce one of its favorite themes by quoting President Roosevelt in a front page article headlined "Cooperation Vital as Army, Says President Roosevelt." "In every time of danger in the past," the president's message explained, "the good sense and loyalty of our people has repudiated the counsel of those who sought to divide and confuse them by arousing suspicion and hatred." As if to affirm the message, the *Transcript* reported on the same page that William Dudley Pelley, the virulently anti-Semitic leader of the Silver Shirts, had been sentenced for violation of security laws.[47]

The following week, the *B'nai B'rith Messenger* in Los Angeles invoked Roosevelt's words to support its editorial, calling for support for National Brotherhood Week activities. The editorial emphasized that "toleration of difference" was essential to democracy and praised Mayor Bowron's pairing of brotherhood with patriotism, calling for local celebration of "War-Time Americanism Week" together with National Brotherhood Week. This editorial appeared alongside another titled "Unity and Sacrifice," which emphasized Jewish support for the war effort through both civil defense and efforts to stand against anti-Semitism. Here, the *Messenger*'s editors made the case that, in uniting against anti-Semitism, Jewish groups were participating in a civil defense activity, as "anti-Semitism, if permitted to become strong, would be a serious national menace."[48]

Indeed, western Jews had embraced the strategy of working with non-Jews to counter prejudice in all of its forms. The San Francisco Survey Committee—a local branch of an American Jewish Committee defense organization—"produced offshoots that supported African American, Asian, and Mexican American civil rights during and after World War II."[49] At Portland's Neighborhood House, when the question of "the Negro Problem in relation to Neighborhood House" was raised at a November 1942 meeting, it was resolved that "Negro service men be welcome to all Neighborhood House facilities and be given full privileges except where Oregon Laws interfere."[50] Such policies reflected the new consciousness of an emerging leadership group that saw their "demand for the protection of the civil rights of Jews as the basis of support of the same rights for other minorities."[51] Jewish organizations and leaders joined in city-wide efforts to combat discrimination such as the Tri-County Community Council's Group Work and Recreation Division in Portland or the Bay Area Council against Discrimination in San Francisco.

The same agenda was clearly expressed in the regional Jewish press, whose editorial boards included many men who were active in civil rights and interfaith networks. The *Scribe's* editorial board, for example, included David Robinson, the founder of the local ADL chapter, who would ultimately serve as the first chair of the Mayor's Commission on Human Rights, president of the Urban League and the City Club of Portland, and chair of the Civil Rights Division of the Oregon Labor Bureau.[52] Likewise, the *Messenger's* board included Rabbi Magnin, well known for his interfaith and anti-prejudice work, David Coleman of the Los Angeles Anti-Defamation League, and several leaders of the Los Angeles Jewish Community Committee, an organization dedicated to fighting anti-Semitism and other forms of prejudice.[53]

In this spirit, during the period from the bombing of Pearl Harbor through the removal of the Japanese population in the summer of 1942, the western Jewish press ran numerous articles and opinion pieces asserting the equality of all Americans. Some of these focused specifically on the rights of Jews. Thus, reports on the Fair Employment Practices Commission often made specific reference to discrimination against Jews as they covered the commission's actions to stem bias in defense industries.[54] Yet others discussed equality in general terms or the civil rights of specific minority groups outside the Jewish community, reflecting the new urgency for unity in the face of war. In its first edition after Pearl Harbor, the *Transcript* published a wire service story headlined "Race Hatreds End Democracy," quoting a leader of the Jewish War Veterans as saying "If Americans begin to hate each other because of race or religion, the end of democracy is in sight."[55] A week later, the paper ran an opinion piece by Theodore Lewis, the associate editor of *The Reconstructionist*, titled "Justice to the Negro." The editors preceded it with their own appeal "to the Jewish people and all other good citizens to fully recognize the rights of the American Negro and to contribute a full measure of support to a proper and just solution of the problem."[56]

These papers not only exposed prejudice as an injustice and a danger to democracy and to the war effort but also made the case that Jews had a special responsibility to fight discrimination. This perspective was particularly clear in articles focusing on African Americans. As one *Scribe* article noted, Jews should support African Americans in their fight for justice because "we Jews, who ourselves have been victims of injustice should be especially sensitive to this."[57] Similarly, in response to a violent effort to prevent African Americans from moving into a Detroit housing project, a *Messenger* editorial headlined "Defend the Negro" argued that "Jews who say that the American way of life is their shield should be the first to recognize the crucial issue involved in the riot which took place in Detroit" and made the case that racial and religious prejudice were linked. "The burning crosses that dotted the landscape before and after the bloody encounters symbolized the all-consuming anger of racial and religious hatred, which recognizes no barriers once its flames have been fanned."[58] More generally, readers of all of these newspapers were enjoined to teach tolerance to their children.[59]

Despite the frequent emphasis on this theme, these expressions of concern for minority rights were not extended to the Japanese American community, the largest minority community in Portland and Seattle and one of the largest in Los Angeles and San Francisco.[60] Indeed, given the events unfolding in the West, the absence of Japanese Americans from the papers' frequent pleas for tolerance is striking, particularly when read alongside a chronology of events leading up to their removal. For example, on December 19, 1941, an *Emanu-El* editorial titled "Risks of Repression" reminded readers of the intolerance of the World War I era and urged them to avoid this danger. Similarly, several stories in early January relayed statements made by Catholic leaders against intolerance. While the stated message of these stories is well captured in the January 16 headline "Social Stability Demands End of Race Hate," no mention was made of Japanese Americans who were the objects of increasingly vitriolic attacks in the regional press at this time.

On February 27, just days after the first Tolan Committee hearings in San Francisco and following a week of extensive coverage of the Japanese question in the mainstream press, *Emanu-El* published two brief admonitions on the editorial page. The first emphasized the need to cooperate with all defense efforts. The second was a statement characterizing discrimination as a "fifth column" activity that aided the enemy.[61] With removal and incarceration being presented in the public arena as a key defense measure because of the alleged danger of fifth-column activity among Japanese Amer-

icans, it is difficult to imagine the editors publishing—or the public reading—these side-by-side editorials without referencing the Nikkei question,
despite the failure of either editorial to mention it.

Similarly, Portland's Jewish *Scribe* never mentioned the evacuation program even as it continued to preach tolerance by publishing a series of statements in the winter of 1942. Viewed against the backdrop of the unfolding
policy and the enthusiastic local support for that policy, these statements
are suggestive. For example, on February 20, the day after President Roosevelt signed Executive Order 9066 and the Portland City Council passed its
resolution calling on the government to "intern and remove . . . all persons
of Japanese descent irrespective of American citizenship," the *Scribe* did not
mention the order, the resolution, or Japanese Americans. It did, however,
publish on its editorial page the Wendell Wilkie call for tolerance quoted at
the start of this chapter. This plea echoed an earlier statement by New York
Mayor Fiorello LaGuardia, published by the *Scribe* in its January 2 issue. La-
Guardia's appeal "for fairness on behalf of 1,100,000 Italian, German, and
Japanese subjects by the United States," and urging Americans not to take
the law into their own hands, was the only mention of Japanese Americans
to appear in the paper during 1942. It was followed by an admonition from
the paper's editors: "Let us heed the warning, then, and do our best to avoid
the hysteria and confusion which will imperil liberty from within."[62] In doing so, they implied—as they did so often—that defending the rights of minorities was a central mission of the paper.

The failure to extend condemnations of prejudice and discrimination to
the policies directed against Japanese Americans was, in many ways, simply
a continuation of the pattern established earlier in the century. As demonstrated in chapter 1, western Jews had a history of divorcing their general-
ized concerns about civil rights from the particularly volatile local debate
about Asian exclusion. Their silence in the face of the alien land laws of the
1910s and 1920s was, in many ways, mirrored by their silence on the debate over Nikkei policy during the early days of World War II. Yet, as the
policy of mass removal of Japanese Americans emerged in the winter of
1942, the Jewish press's silence on the issue and the coverage surrounding
that silence suggest that editors were conflicted about the emerging alien
policy. Their sense of conflict is most visible in the stories that came closest
to addressing the plight of Japanese Americans: those on enemy aliens. Indeed, the coverage of this issue suggests that these publications may have
had an explicit policy of avoiding the Nikkei question.

From their earliest reports on the enemy alien issue, the Jewish papers
seemed to take special care to excise Japanese Americans from their coverage. To some degree, this was the natural result of the use of Jewish wire service stories, written in the East, where the Nikkei community was peripheral, if not invisible. Stories originating in the East, like those published in

Seattle's *Transcript* on December 12—one concerning the creation of an internment camp for enemy aliens and another on a proposed registration measure for foreign agents—reflected national Jewish interest in the issue and made no mention of Japanese Americans.[63]

Yet in the West, where enemy alien stories in the mainstream press focused almost exclusively on Japanese Americans and the "enemy alien" label was often used as a synonym for Japanese American, it required a deliberate effort to write—or read—about alien issues without referencing the Nikkei. Thus, when these publications reported on the arrests of enemy aliens immediately after Pearl Harbor, their coverage contrasted sharply with the mainstream dailies, which presented the arrests as primarily targeting the Japanese. *Emanu-El's* coverage was typical. On December 26, 1941, the paper published a news story headlined "FBI Steps In," reporting the arrest of German sympathizers and emphasizing that those rounded up were pro-Nazi anti-Semites. The FBI had also arrested a number of Japanese Americans during these December raids, and they were the main focus in the secular dailies, but this part of the story is left out of *Emanu-El's* coverage. By focusing on the arrest of Nazi sympathizers, the paper kept the story focused on a clear and useful theme: that fascists are both anti-Semitic and anti-American.

As restrictions on enemy aliens were issued, they were published in the Jewish press, as was advice to individuals for complying with the regulations.[64] While many of these stories were from the wire services, others focused on local concerns, such as the specific blackout instructions applying to these cities. The *Transcript* reported that efforts by the local Anti-Defamation League (ADL) representative had resulted in a positive ruling from the Department of Justice: the many Sephardic Jews from the island of Rhodes who made their home in Seattle would not be considered enemy aliens.[65]

Enemy alien stories had considerable salience in the Jewish press because German Jewish refugees were classified as enemy aliens. Locally and nationally, the possible impact of alien restrictions on German Jewish refugees was a central concern for groups like Los Angeles's Jewish Club of 1933 and Portland's Oregon Émigré Committee,[66] as well as for Jewish social service agencies. For example, in January 1942, the alien restriction issue was raised at a Jewish Service Association meeting in Portland. Members were warned, "There is the danger of political refugees in our midst losing their business licenses and their welfare is a serious problem for the Refugee Committee." In March, the possibility of evacuation of German aliens was raised, and the association was cautioned, "No partiality can be shown our people. There may be more evacuations and there may not be drastic action in cases where loyalty can be proven."[67]

When discussing the issue, all of these papers made the case that the "enemy alien" label was inappropriate for such refugees and that they should be exempt from restrictions. Again, this coverage reflected—and often was drawn from—eastern Jewish sources. When the papers published stories on various rulings and restrictions on aliens during the first few months of the war, they expressed concerns about the treatment of Italians and Germans but not Japanese. For example, on December 19, 1941, the *Transcript* published a wire service story headlined "Jews Included in F.B.I. Roundup" that mentioned the roundup of the Japanese briefly but focused on the Europeans, mentioning specifically the number of Italian and German aliens in America, and expressing particular concern about the "unknown number" of Jews among these detainees. Likewise, articles calling for a change in the "enemy alien" category questioned the appropriateness of this label for Europeans, but never for Japanese. Thus, a wire service story in the *Transcript* about the call by a medical society in New York for the government to "remove barriers for alien doctors" stressed the shortage of doctors in America and noted that some of the "refugee physicians" were graduates of "Europe's leading medical schools."[68]

It is important to emphasize that making such distinctions between European and Japanese aliens was unique to neither the western press nor the Jewish press but, instead, was part of the broader national distinction between European and Japanese aliens—a distinction that ultimately resulted in the mass removal and incarceration only of Japanese Americans. This coverage, then, was reflective of both the regional and the national context. To take just one example, in reporting on new registration requirements for enemy aliens residing in the Western Defense Zone, the *Messenger* relayed the text of the order, noting the numbers of Italians, Germans, and Japanese affected. It also paraphrased Attorney General Biddle's warning "not to dismiss 'loyal enemy aliens,'" because it "was stupid not to use the skilled technicians of German and Italian birth who have lived in this country for many years."[69] Failure to exploit the skills of Japanese immigrants was, apparently, not problematic.

Stories on the "enemy alien" issue often aimed to reassure refugee readers that they had no cause for concern. For example, on the same day as the FBI story, the *Transcript* published a separate story promising readers that "Loyal Aliens Need Not Fear," quoting a speech made by Eleanor Roosevelt at a Sephardic synagogue in New York.[70] An editorial appeared in Los Angeles's *Messenger* on the same day, emphasizing that "despite stringent regulations and powers affecting 'enemy aliens,' there need be no special fears for refugees, inasmuch as precautions are being taken by the Attorney General's office to prevent the unwarranted interference with activities of friendly aliens in America."[71] A month later, the *Messenger* published excerpts from a statement by Attorney General Francis Biddle, in which he emphasized the loyalty of "the great majority of our alien population."[72]

As concerns that restrictions on aliens would affect German Jews in-creased, the *Scribe* published a syndicated column by Phineas Biron assur-ing readers that such fears were exaggerated:

> Rumormongers are here-with invited to crawl back into the woodwork, and democratic-minded aliens are assured that they have nothing to fear from the American Government, which will continue to treat them exactly as it does its own citizens—notwithstanding the irresponsible gossipers who are trying to panic refugees from Central Europe by predicting that this country will put them in concentration camps.[73]

Biron went on to contrast the humane American policy toward German na-tionals with the internment policy of France, proclaiming, "Uncle Sam will not repeat the mistakes of the French Government, which interned well-known anti-Fascist fighters because Germany was their land of origin."[74] Several weeks later—just days before the Executive Order—the *Scribe* denied rumors that visas issued to enemy aliens would be canceled and empha-sized the loyalty of these so-called "enemy aliens."[75]

Concerns about the potential for Jews to be caught up in detentions of enemy aliens continued through the winter and, as restrictions on enemy aliens were enacted, this coverage grew more intense. The lead story in the March 20 edition of the *Scribe*, headlined "Urges Reclassification of Refugees in the 'Enemy Alien' Group," explained a government official's rec-ommendation that German political and religious refugees be exempted from the evacuation order.[76] Noting that "German refugees have by the very fact of their flight established themselves as enemies of Hitler," the article argued that individual cases should be investigated "with a view to clearing them of the stigma of enemy alien." Despite the tremendous attention in the secular press during this week to the Japanese removal getting underway in Oregon, the *Scribe* article failed to mention the Japanese. By urging ex-emptions only for Germans, the paper implied that individual investiga-tions were not needed for the Japanese. Yet rather than explicitly endorsing such a locally popular position, the *Scribe* remained silent on the Nikkei question.

Also in March, the *Scribe* published another of Biron's columns, urging readers and editors to investigate a bill passed by the House of Representa-tives "because it differentiates between foreign-born and native American citizens. . . . Its enactment might easily lead to abuses in the cancellation of the citizenship of foreign-born Americans."[77] Despite the editorial choice to feature this column just as the removal of Japanese American aliens and cit-izens alike got underway, *Scribe* editors again chose not to speak to the Nikkei question, neither endorsing nor condemning the removal policy.

In balancing their concerns about harsh restrictions on innocent German refugees against the potential presence of subversives, Portland's *Scribe* and

San Francisco's *Emanu-El* tended to emphasize the former, and Seattle's *Transcript* the latter. Within a week, all three papers published nearly identically headlined stories, *Emanu-El's* titled "Friendly Enemy Aliens" and both the *Scribe's* and the *Transcript's* titled "'Enemy Aliens' As America's Friends."[78] Yet, while the piece in San Francisco appeared as an editorial, the *Transcript's* and the *Scribe's* were presented as opinion pieces by Georg Bernhard, "distinguished German-Jewish editor." By introducing the column with a note explaining that it "gives the reaction of refugees in America to legislation affecting so called 'enemy aliens'" the *Transcript's* editors distanced themselves from the content. Their reasons are suggested by the appearance in the same issue of several other stories that balanced concern for German aliens with caution on the civil defense issue. An editorial called upon German émigrés to "be calm," expressing great sympathy for their situation, and assuring them that "Jewish leadership is not lying down on the job and what can be done will be done," but also reminding readers of the need for caution: "The United States of America **is at war with Germany** and its partners in international crime and all of us not only Germans but American citizens must bear with patience and forbearance whatever edicts the military authorities see fit to lay down"[79] [emphasis in original]. In the same issue, the paper's associate editor boasted, "If the Japs ever dare to make an attempt on this Coast they will find no Pearl Harbor or Singapore but a region well prepared to give them a warm reception. And better than that they will find no traitors within giving them signals from the hills. It is just too bad that some innocent people will have to suffer, but this is war and our own come first."[80]

Despite these variations in emphasis, the editorials on "friendly enemy aliens," published as the removal program was getting under way, were identical in their non-treatment of the Nikkei. All three specifically mentioned Germans among the friendly aliens, and *Emanu-El* included Italians, but they were uniformly silent on the Japanese. In each, visual markers distinguished discussion of European aliens from mainstream press coverage of the Nikkei: all implicitly questioned the term "enemy alien" by placing it in quotation marks. In this way, the German "enemy aliens" discussed in the western Jewish press were clearly distinguished from the "real" Japanese enemy aliens—without quotation marks—who appeared in the pages of the mainstream dailies.

This questioning of the "enemy alien" label as it applied to European refugees was not confined to the press. During the Tolan Committee hearings, a number of witnesses, including several representing Jewish groups, testified on behalf of German and/or Italian aliens. Most prominent among the German refugee witnesses was the intellectual Thomas Mann, who argued that many Italian and German nationals residing in the United States were enemies of fascism, so that "the idea and characteristic of 'enemy alien' has lost its logical justification in the case of the German and Italian émigrés."[81] Such objections did not, according to Mann, necessarily apply to the Nikkei aliens. Although Mann acknowledged them, he explicitly separated their situation from that of the Europeans: "All of us know that the burning problem on the west coast is the question of the Japanese. It would be a great misfortune if the regulations, perhaps necessary in their case—it is not my business to talk about the Japanese problem—would be applied to the German and Italian refugees, even with the intention of revising single cases later."[82]

Although Mann acknowledged the centrality of the Nikkei question, most of those who testified on behalf of European aliens did not mention Japanese Americans at all. Dr. Felix Guggenheim, for example, represented the Jewish Club of 1933 of Los Angeles and testified to the importance of avoiding repetition of "the experiences in France, when France made the terrible mistake of having detracted her attention from the fight against fifth columnists by fighting senselessly the loyal democratic anti-Nazi refugees in their midst."[83] The San Francisco Committee for Service to Émigrés—a group operating under the auspices of the Federation of Jewish Charities—presented a statement referring only to German and Italian refugees, concluding that

> It should be apparent that the German and Italian refugees, who have come to the United States since 1933, should not be classified as "enemy aliens" in any correct sense of the term. . . . They have every reason to abhor the German and Italian Governments which despoiled them and drove them out, and contrariwise, they have every reason to love and to serve the United States which offered them sanctuary and an opportunity to live again as freemen.[84]

Similarly, two representatives from the Washington Émigré Bureau spoke only to the Germans. Rabbi S. P. Wohlgelernter of Seattle presented a report on German-Jewish refugees.[85] None of them mentioned the Nikkei.

Even the one paper that stated opposition to the mass removal policy avoided direct mention of Japanese Americans. On March 13, 1942, the *Messenger* published an editorial titled "Mass Evacuation." In it, the editors endorsed a recent statement by the Council of Social Agencies "expressing confidence in the civil and military authorities to deal with the problems of disloyalty and sabotage" but "emphatically oppos[ing] the indiscriminate forcible mass evacuation of entire minority groups, citizens and aliens alike." The editorial noted the importance of "avoid[ing] action based on hysteria" and concluded, "we believe that the danger of real alien enemies, whether of foreign or native birth, whether yellow or white, can be handled without desecrating those fundamental principles for which we are fighting."[86] Although the references to "citizens and aliens alike" and to "yellow or white" aliens makes clear that the editors were speaking to the Nikkei issue, Japanese Americans are not mentioned—in contrast to the many occasions when the editors specifically mentioned Germans and Italians. This opinion, one of four short editorials to appear in this issue, was never again referenced or repeated in the paper.

While the failure of Jewish newspapers and Jewish groups concerned with enemy alien issues to mention the Japanese among the so-called "friendly aliens" implied that they fell into a different—presumably unfriendly—category, none directly suggested that this was the case. Indeed, although the tremendous outpouring of anti-Nikkei and pro-removal sentiment in the region may have discouraged the Jewish community from extending their concerns about enemy alien policies to the Japanese American community, it did not result in an embrace of that policy. Despite their vigorous support for other aspects of the war effort, neither the western Jewish press nor community organizations publicly endorsed removal and incarceration—with one exception.

That exception was Seattle's *Jewish Transcript*. For the most part, the *Transcript*'s coverage was strikingly similar to that of her sister papers. The paper reported extensively on the importance of support for the war effort, on anti-Semitism and other forms of discrimination, and on alien restrictions—generally, like other West Coast Jewish newspapers, without mentioning Japanese Americans. Yet on February 13, 1942, the *Transcript*'s editors endorsed the removal of "all Japanese aliens" in an editorial titled "Don't Compromise with Danger." The editors noted that the Bellingham American Legion post was forwarding to the National Board of the American Legion a resolution endorsing "the removal of all alien Japanese from the Pacific Coast Area" due to the alleged "activity and sabotage" of "subversive fifth columnist activity" and to the proximity of alien Japanese to vital defense industries. "Neglect and delay in this matter is a flirtation with definite danger," warned the editors. "War brings hardships on both the guilty and the innocent but the preeminent policy should be no compromise with danger."[87]

While the *Transcript* was the only western Jewish paper to publish such an endorsement, it is important to note that it expressed support only for mass removal of Japanese *aliens*. In the editorial, the *Transcript* specifically referred to the resolution passed by Bellingham's Albert J. Hamilton Post of the Legion—one of the more moderate legion resolutions, calling only for removal of Japanese aliens—rather than one of the broader resolutions, such as that passed by the Rizal Post in Seattle, which advocated "removing all Japanese aliens and American-born Japanese from the Pacific coast into concentration camps for the duration of the war."[88] In supporting any form of mass removal, the *Transcript* went farther than any of its sister papers. Yet its carefully worded editorial did not join the local press and prominent political leaders in calling for removal of the entire Nikkei community.

The *Transcript's* greater sympathy for restrictionist measures—both in its February endorsement of removal of Japanese aliens and in its March "patience and forbearance" warning to German aliens—may have been influenced by the presence of prominent community members in key civil defense positions. On December 26, 1941, the *Transcript* had reported that Lou Kessler, a well-known Jewish community leader, had been appointed by the American Legion to the position of "King County supervisor to the subversive investigations committee." The article explained that Kessler would "report to his chief on all persons suspected of enmity to the country or whose actions are of a suspicious nature." Kessler was not the only member of the Jewish community involved in such work—his supervisor would be Joe Marks, an executive of the Schwabacher Company, one of the most prominent Jewish firms in Seattle. The *Transcript* ran a picture with the caption "Louis Kessler—Digs up Enemies" with the article.[89] Later, it reported periodically on Kessler's activities in his new post, as when it praised his efforts to stop war rumors, enjoining readers, "All honor to Lou Kessler, the real American."[90] It is also notable that another prominent Seattle Jew, Abe Hurwitz, was named editor of the *Seattle Star*—a mainstream daily that was "the primary anti-Japanese voice in the Puget Sound area"—in January of 1942.[91] The *Star* published four "increasingly militant" editorials supporting internment in February and March. One responded to objections to the policy by arguing, "Isn't it preferable that they lose a few freedoms than for the traitors among them to blast war plants, air fields or guide invading forces?"[92]

Although the *Transcript* distinguished itself from its sister papers by endorsing a limited version of mass removal, it subsequently resumed its silence on the issue. Even as the Tolan Committee held hearings in Seattle in late February and early March, and as the evacuation began later that spring, the *Transcript* did not repeat its endorsement or join the chorus of groups calling for mass removal of the entire Nikkei community. Instead, it avoided further mention of Japanese Americans. In its March 13 article urging "patience and forbearance" for German Jewish refugees, appearing ten days after the *Seattle Times* had reported the coming "ouster of all Japs on the Coast,"[93] the *Transcript's* editors limited themselves to commenting on the situation of German aliens.[94]

With the exception of the *Transcript's* endorsement of a limited removal policy and the *Messenger's* one brief statement of opposition, the western Jewish newspapers, like the Jewish press nationally, maintained silence on the Nikkei question, as did local Jewish organizations. Yet examination of that silence and the words around it suggest that it was not merely a local example of a national phenomenon. While certainly born of the same conflict between commitments to supporting the war effort and upholding civil liberties, the regional silence suggests more tension over an issue that, in the local context, could not be ignored.

There is, for example, no evidence that the West Coast National Council of Jewish Women (NCJW) sections took any public stance on this issue, despite the fact that their national social legislation committee recommended a statement against the removal policy. Indeed, during 1942 and 1943, as the national NCJW debated the internment, drafted several resolutions, and participated in the Post War World Council meeting on "the Japanese situation," there was no mention of the issue whatsoever in the NCJW's Portland Section minutes.[95] Although Greenberg has demonstrated that President Blanche Goldman's position opposing a formal statement against the policy was informed by the San Francisco section's disapproval, the section did not make a public statement of its position.[96]

Tensions are clearly visible in the statement of the Los Angeles Committee for Church and Community Cooperation before the Tolan Committee. Three representatives of the Jewish community—Rabbis Morton Bauman and Edgar Magnin of Temple Israel and the Wilshire Boulevard Temple, respectively, and Mrs. Isaac Pelton of the Council of Jewish Women—were members of this group and signatories to its statement, one of the most tortured of those presented to the Tolan Committee. On the one hand, the group strongly opposed "mass evacuation" while, on the other, it explicitly acknowledged the potential for sabotage reported in a recently released report known as the "Yellow Paper" by the House Un-American Activities Committee.[97] Their written statement was reinforced with oral testimony by their spokesperson, George Gleason, who was regarded as an ally by the Pacific Coast Committee on National Security and Fair Play (henceforth, Fair Play Committee), a Berkeley-based group organized in late 1941 to defend Japanese Americans and oppose mass removal and incarceration.[98] Gleason's group avoided any specific recommendation regarding Japanese Americans, even when pushed by Tolan Committee members. Instead, they emphasized the need to defer to army and War Department decisions about who should be subject to removal orders. The testimony and written statement suggest a clear tension between the group's desire to avoid any policies based on race and their acceptance of the Yellow Paper's accusations that there were Japanese saboteurs residing on the West Coast. While the group emphatically opposed racially based actions and recommended a selective evacuation, Gleason conceded under questioning that Japanese represented a special danger:

Mr. Bender: Doctor, do you feel that Germans and Italians deserve different treatment than the Japanese aliens; or do you think that they are all of the same group and should be handled in the same way.

Dr. Gleason: I think they are all the same group, but I think there is a difference in the importance of dealing with the Japanese at this time, because we, on this coast, feel that our war is with Japan just now. You see, if the Japanese

Navy should come over to this coast, the Japanese who are loyal to Japan and disloyal to the United States would, and could, do something which the Germans and the Italians might not be so interested in doing. So I think on account of our nearness to Japan, the subversive elements among the Japanese are a little more dangerous to us immediately on this coast than the subversive elements among the Italians and the Germans.[99]

Examples of tension over the issue are also apparent in the pages of western Jewish newspapers. An excellent illustration came in a February 27 column by Rabbi Magnin.[100] The column, carried in the *Messenger* and in abbreviated form in the *Transcript,* was the text of Magnin's good will sermon for the National Conference of Christians and Jews' Good Will Sabbath. He had delivered the sermon from his pulpit at the Wishire Boulevard Temple, the most prominent congregation in Los Angeles, and on his weekly radio program. Titled "Labels that are Libels," the text focuses on tolerance, condemning prejudice in all its forms. With the Tolan hearings already under way in the West, it would have been difficult to read or hear Magnin's words without making a connection to the public discussion of Japanese removal. "We would never condemn a whole group of people by reason of the faults or sins of some of them," the rabbi declared. He cautioned that during wartime, prejudices flare and "history has demonstrated that in times of crisis minorities are always picked on by crooked politicians and unscrupulous statesmen to make the masses forget their real trouble and oppressors." Magnin reminded readers that each racial and religious group had made contributions to civilization—and pointed specifically to contributions of German and Italian artists and scientists. He called intolerance "patriotic blasphemy; patriotic prostitution" and argued that "no democracy can exist where there is hatred and suspicion between the citizens of that country." Although Magnin's sermon seems to pointedly critique a policy calling for mass removal based on race or ancestry, he did not specifically mention Japanese Americans.

An even more vivid example of tension surrounding the issue can be found in a March 27 opinion piece by Monroe Deutsch in *Emanu-El.* Informed readers would have immediately identified Deutsch as provost and vice president of the University of California, Berkeley. They would also have identified him for his prominent role as a founding board member of the Fair Play Committee.[101] Deutsch had been signatory to several Fair Play Committee statements presented to the Tolan Committee, urging that removals be carried out on the basis of individual examinations and arguing strongly against policies based on race. One read:

The proposed evacuation of the entire group of Nisei, but of no other group of citizens, apparently on the basis of race, is already embittering some of them and making them turn a ready ear to Communist and other subversive ideas.

It is also causing acute distress to many white citizens like ourselves who are concerned over every violation of the democratic principles for which we are fighting.

Since the Nisei are full-fledged American citizens by virtue of birth and up-bringing in this country, certainly they should be given not less consideration than German and Italian aliens, sympathetic as we are with those among them who are thoroughly loyal to democratic ideals.

Furthermore, the indiscriminate evacuation of Nisei citizens will, in our judg-ment, weaken rather than strengthen the civic morale which is an essential el-ement in national security during the war and of national unity after the war.[102]

Yet when *Emanu-El* published Deutsch's opinion piece "Rights of Enemy Aliens" on March 27, there was no reference at all to Japanese Americans. The full-page statement began with a bolded paragraph proclaiming, "The genius of democracy is its respect for the individual; and in consonance with this principle, this nation should engage in no witch-hunts against alien enemies and should give a favorable status to those among them who are friendly." While urging the necessity of cooperating with government authorities on necessary defense measures, Deutsch made a case for toler-ance and calm. With the evacuation already underway, Deutsch urged that it be followed immediately by investigations to determine individual loy-alty so that only those found disloyal would be detained in the long run. The specifics of this plea and Deutsch's public opposition to Japanese re-moval make it clear that he was, in fact, referring to that policy—the Nikkei were the only group for whom there was a policy of what Deutsch referred to as "mass resettlement." Likewise, Deutsch's argument that "people must be treated as persons—not 'lumped together' as this or that racial group," was clearly a reference to Japanese Americans, since no other group was subject to mass removal. Yet, despite these obvious references to the Nikkei, they were never named in this article. Rather, Deutsch's *Emanu-El* piece di-rectly mentions German and Italian refugees, noting that many were refugees from fascism and that they should be quickly "relieved from the stigma **enemy alien**," [emphasis in original].[103] That *Emanu-El* would run an opinion piece by a prominent community member known for his in-volvement in the Fair Play Committee and directly reflecting the commit-tee's stance on this issue implies sympathy for this position. Yet to run such a piece without specifically mentioning Japanese Americans suggests a de-liberate policy of keeping the Nikkei question at arm's length.

Such a policy is also suggested by *Emanu-El*'s failure to cover the Fair Play Committee activities of Deutsch and other prominent Bay Area Jews. Al-though *Emanu-El*, like the other West Coast Jewish papers, frequently covered the public activities of prominent local Jews, Fair Play Committee activities

were ignored, even though the region's most prominent rabbi, Temple
Emanu El's Irving Reichert, was an active member of its board of directors.
While the civil rights activities of Bay Area Jews were often reported in *Emanu-
El*, the Fair Play Committee's activities were never covered. Again, this contrast
in coverage suggests a deliberate policy of silence.

Evidence of this tension appears not only in the silence on the Japanese
American question but also in odd references to internment that crop up in
unexpected places, demonstrating a consciousness of the policy even as
these papers ignored it. For example, on February 20, 1942, the day after
Roosevelt issued Executive Order 9066, the *Scribe* published an editorial on
anti-Semitism including references to a "Colonel Sanctuary" who was distributing anti-Semitic tracts in New York. Under the headline "Disunity in
Our Midst," the editorial called for the unmasking and punishment of
Colonel Sanctuary even as it noted that "The United States is a democratic
government and does not like the idea of concentration camps even for
such men as Col. Sanctuary."[104] It is interesting that *Scribe* editors chose to
state their opposition to concentration camps for an individual whom they
clearly viewed as despicable while maintaining total silence on the steps being taken at that moment that would lead to the incarceration of their
Japanese American neighbors.

The consistent omission of Japanese Americans from stories in which
their plight was the obvious context strongly suggests that this silence was
not the result of disinterest or ignorance. The consistent appeals for tolerance even as the removal policy was carried out, and the condemnation of
blanket internment policies such as France's, suggest that these papers were
attempting to question the policy while avoiding any appearance of specific
support for Japanese Americans or criticism of a measure deemed "essential" to the war effort. Likewise, the failure of these papers to endorse the internment at a time when westerners overwhelmingly supported it, and
when they enthusiastically reported their communities' support for other
aspects of wartime policy, is suggestive. While silence often indicates indif-
ference, the words around this silence suggest conflict.

The page of the *Scribe* on which the Colonel Sanctuary piece appears effectively provides a framework for this tension (see Figure 2.1). It contains eight
brief stories, including several editorials, that literally surround the story with
news and opinion briefs laying out the concerns of the community. Concern
for European Jews was clearly expressed in one story reporting that a Presbyterian conference had called upon the United Nations to ensure "post war
equality for Europe's Jewish population as part of the peace settlement" and in
another relaying American Zionist support for the creation of a Jewish army in
Palestine to fight Nazi Germany. Anxiety about domestic prejudice was
demonstrated in three pieces: a rabbinical statement "deploring anti-Negro
discrimination"; a story noting the damage anti-Semitism does to a nation;

POST-WAR EQUALITY FOR JEWS URGED BY BRITISH CHURCH CONFERENCE

LONDON (W.N.S.) A resolution adopted by a special conference called to consider "Jewry's post-war position," held under the auspices of the Presbyterian churches of Great Britain and Ireland, called upon the United Nations to insure post-war equality for Europe's Jewish population as part of the peace settlement.

The churchmen urged "His Majesty's Government, in conjunction with other of the Allied and friendly nations, to provide some scheme for the emigration of Jews who cannot find a home in Europe."

AMERICAN RABBIS ISSUE STATEMENT DEPLORING ANTI-NEGRO DISCRIMINATION

CINCINNATI (W. N. S.) A statement deploring anti-Negro discrimination was adopted by the Commission of Justice and Peace of the Central Conference of American Rabbis in observance of Race Relations Week, Feb. 8-15. The statement was made public here by Dr. James G. Heller, president of the Central Conference.

"The plight of a large body of American citizens, children of the one God, members of the human family, brethren of us all, must challenge the conscience of every one who believes in the brotherhood of man," the statement read in part. "This situation is the harvest of sins of the spirit of which none of us is completely innocent. It results from the ignoring of God's word, that all men are created in His image. Race Relations Week should lead all to God's throne in prayer and repentence, seeking forgiveness for the sins of racial arrogance and injustice. We Jews, who ourselves have been victims of injustice, should be especially sensitive to this."

AMERICAN ZIONISTS ISSUE MANIFESTO

NEW YORK (Special) A stirring proclamation to all Zionists of America to throw themselves unreservedly into the effort to mobilize American public opinion for a Jewish fighting force in Palestine under British or United Nations command, has been issued by the American Emergency Committee for Zionist Affairs. A Jewish military forced based on Palestine, the call declares, is essential to strengthen the United Nations on one of the world's most vital fronts, and to vindicate the right of the Jewish People to national status in their national home.

ANTI-SEMITISM IS FAILING

"It is inconceivable that we can have anything even remotely resembling an America which is influenced by Christianity so long as anti-Semitism flourishes. All we know from good and substantial evidence, the Nazis have used hatred of the Jews as a means to induce Christians to deny Christ by inciting them to hate and to persecute their fellow men who are Jews. They have used anti-Semitism as the rallying point about which to build a following whose hatred of Jews has been transmuted into hatred and persecution of Christians.

"This method succeeded in Nazi Germany. It has been extended with every Nazi conquest, to other than German lands. It made its bid for support in America. But it is failing. It is failing because men like Mr. Ford, recognizing the dire effects of anti-Semitism upon a people, and evaluating its power aright, have had the courage to speak out, to renounce it, and to dissociate themselves from it."—*Rev. William C. Kernan.*

THE SCRIBE

DAVID E. COHEN—Publisher

Published Every Friday at Portland, Oregon—509-510 Davis Bldg. AT 7460.   Subscription per year, $3.00; Canada and Europe, $4.50

Entered as second-class matter Sept. 23, 1919, at the Post Office at Portland, Oregon, under the Act of March 3, 1879.

EDITORIAL BOARD

Rabbi Henry J. Berkowitz, L.L.D.   David Robinson
Rabbi J. B. Fain   Abe Eugene Rosenberg
Mrs. Arthur A. Goldsmith   Theodore M. Swett
Rabbi Philip Kleinman   Rabbi E. Chas. Sydney

Samuel B. Weinstein

EDITORIAL COMMENT

REFUGEE SKILLS

A SERIOUS shortage exists today in our medical reserves. There is a crying need for physicians, which is increasing as the armed forces drain the medical offices, universities and hospitals of the younger doctors.

That the situation is grave is evidenced by the fact that the N. Y. Times has commented in two editorials in as many weeks of this shortage and has advised the use of the skills of the refugee physicians now in the U. S.

It has been estimated that there are 5,000 refugee doctors who have emigrated to America since Hitler's assumption to power in Germany. Apparently none of the obstacles now standing in their way are insurpassable. English can be taught, hospital facilities opened to them and their presence in the U. S. is, in itself, a testament to their loyalty.

The Times suggested that a plan to place these doctors in rural communities might effect a solution. But whatever must be done, we should not waste the skills of those who are so eager to help at a time when the need is so great.

DISUNITY IN OUR MIDST

THE Non-Secretarian Anti-Nazi League, in a report this week, revealed that despite the national emergency, many of the dispensers of anti-Semitic wares are still carrying on their business as usual. In particular, the League draws attention to a certain Lieutenant-General Count Cherep-Spiridovich, who is president of what he calls a Mission in the Bronx from which he distributes anti-Semitic literature. Another who is very busy at the same work is a Col. Sanctuary, who sends forth such books as "The Holy Sea and the Jews," and "The Talmud Unmasked."

It is time to unmask Col. Sanctuary and see just how much holiness there is in this Sanctuary. These men carrying on their poisonous labors at this time when the nation faces the greatest peril in its history can be regarded only as the agents of the country's enemy. The United States is a democratic government and does not like the idea of concentration camps even for such men as Col. Sanctuary, but we remember that even the gentle Abraham Lincoln was forced during the war to send Vallandingham, who was breeding disunity in the north, into the ranks of the enemy.

The week intervening between the birthdays of the two greatest Americans, Lincoln and Washington, set aside as Brotherhood Week, is indeed a fitting time to take stock of these people to whom every week is Disunity Week.

HAMLET IN HEBREW—A BEST SELLER

The new Hebrew translation of "Hamlet," which has recently been published by the "Tarshish" Publishing Co. of Jerusalem, has turned out to be a best seller according to the Palestine Post of Jerusalem.

The translation, the first to be made into Hebrew in the last half a century, is by Dr. Harry S. Davidowitz of Tel Aviv, who formerly occupied a Rabbinical pulpit in the United States. He is now at work on a Hebrew version of Midsummer Night's Dream.

AMERICANS ALL

"This country's strength is the composite of persons of all descents—Irish, English, German, Italian and a myriad of other races, colors and creeds. No American has the right to impugn the patriotism or loyalty of any other American because of the accident of his birth or descent or religion. In times of war unthinkable persons sometimes forget the basic concepts of freedom for which America fights. Prejudices arise and persecutions are practiced.

"They must be protected in their rights and their liberty for they are of the very marrow of the bone of America."—*Wendell L. Willkie.*

Jewish Calendar
5702—1942

Purim	March 3
Passover	April 2-9
Shevuoth	May 22-23
Tisha B'ab	July 23
Rosh Hashanah	September 12

Holidays begin at sundown the day before the date designated.

Figure 2.1.   *The Scribe*'s editorial page on February 20, 1942, the day after Executive Order 9066, suggests the concerns of the Portland Jewish community. Oregon Historical Society.

[Handwritten annotations in margins: "Peace Dem. Copperhead", "Den US House Ohio", "formed 'New Departure' wing of Dems", "Clement Laird Vallandigham", "Lost to FDR 1940", "Episcopal Corp. Lawyer", "(Lib.) Rep. Party Nominee 1940"]

and the Wendell Wilkie statement against discrimination. All of these stories could easily have appeared in any Jewish newspaper in the country.

Yet perusal of the western mainstream dailies for the same week—the week of Executive Order 9066—provides a clearer sense of the local context in which editors selected and readers absorbed these stories. These dailies' extensive coverage of the Nikkei issue—their publication of alleged subversive activity, their tendency to use terms like "Jap" and "enemy alien" interchangeably as synonyms for Japanese Americans, their endorsements of mass removal of both Japanese aliens and American citizens of Japanese descent—made the issue, and the tension it created between national security concerns and civil liberties, inescapable. Although the regional silence on the Nikkei question echoes that of national Jewish organizations, it does not indicate that the issue "passed unnoticed."

Reading a silence presents many difficulties. While western Jewish newspaper editors and community leaders carefully placed the issues that they did discuss into the Jewish context that was their legitimate focus, they did not explain why they deemed other issues to be outside of their purview. Yet, the idea that there simply was no "Jewish connection" or that Japanese removal and incarceration "passed unnoticed" is implausible in the West Coast context. Unlikely, out-of-context references to internment, along with the careful avoidance of the issue even when the internment was the obvious context, demonstrate the kind of tension that existed over the issue. Similar discomfort is suggested by the failure to comment further on the isolated, individual editorials endorsing and condemning mass removal. Western Jewish communities faced the tasks of supporting both their anti-prejudice agenda and the war effort in a region where fear of invasion was real and majority opinion was overwhelmingly anti-Nikkei. The conflicting demands of this situation resulted, most often, in silence. Yet the words around this silence reveal that western Jewish newspapers and organizations did not just ignore these events but opted most often for a conscious, deliberate, and selective avoidance of the issue.

NOTES

1. *Scribe*, February 20, 1942, 4.

2. See discussion in the introduction to this volume. See also Cheryl Greenberg, "Black and Jewish Responses to Japanese Internment," *Journal of American Ethnic History* 14, no. 2 (Winter 1995); Judy Kutulas, "In Quest of Autonomy: The Northern California Affiliate of the American Civil Liberties Union and World War II," *Pacific Historical Review* 67, no. 2 (1998): 202; and Judy Kutulas, *The American Civil Liberties Union and the Making of Modern Liberalism, 1930–1960* (Chapel Hill: University of North Carolina Press, 2006).

3. Quoted in Greenberg, "Black and Jewish Responses," 13.

4. Greenberg, "Black and Jewish Responses," 12.

5. Lloyd Chiasson, "Japanese American Relocation during World War II: A Study of California Editorial Reaction," *Journalism Quarterly* 68, nos. 1 & 2 (1991): 265–68; Gary Okihiro, "The Press, Japanese Americans, and the Concentration Camps," *Phylon* 44, no. 1 (1983): 78–83.

6. Morton Grodzins, *Americans Betrayed* (Chicago: University of Chicago Press, 1949), 377–99. For further discussion of these findings see Okihiro, "The Press, Japanese Americans, and the Concentration Camps."

7. Chiasson, "Japanese American Relocation during World War II."

8. Floyd McKay, "Pacific Northwest Newspapers and Executive Order 9066," paper presented at The Nikkei Experience in the Northwest, Seattle, 2000. Looking more broadly at Washington state, the Tacoma *News Tribune*, like Tacoma's mayor, declined to endorse the policy. The weekly Bainbridge Island *Review* was openly sympathetic to the Nikkei, as was the Hood River (Oregon) *Hood River News*.

9. Linda Tamura, *Hood River Issei: An Oral History of Japanese Settlers in Oregon's Hood River Valley* (Urbana: University of Illinois Press, 1993), appendix A.

10. For example, the *Oregonian* included fifteen front page stories on the issue during February, 1942, eighteen in March, and fifteen in April.

11. *Oregonian*, December 8, 1941, 6.

12. *Oregonian*, December 19, 1941, 18.

13. *Oregonian*, February 12, 1942, 1.

14. *Oregonian*, February 26, 1942. See also Hearings before the Select Committee Investigating National Defense Migration (Tolan Committee), House of Representatives, 77th Congress, Second Session, parts 29, 30, 31: 11367.

15. *Oregonian*, April 26, 1942, 20.

16. *Oregonian*, May 2, 1942, 1.

17. *Oregonian*, March 31, 1942, 6.

18. *Oregonian*, April 19, 1942, 21.

19. For a discussion of the role of the press as shaper vs. reflector of public opinion and governmental policy, see Okihiro, "The Press, Japanese Americans, and the Concentration Camps," and Chiasson, "Japanese Relocation during World War II."

20. Roger Daniels, Sandra C. Taylor, and Harry H. L. Kitano, *Japanese Americans from Relocation to Redress* (Salt Lake City: University of Utah Press, 1986), xvi.

21. Chapter 3 examines some of those opposed to the removal program.

22. Tolan Committee Hearings, part 30: 11303, 11305.

23. Portland City Council, Resolution #22113, February 19, 1942. The text for the resolution can be found in the Tolan Committee Hearings, part 30: 11388.

24. Tolan Committee Hearings, part 30: 11366.

25. Tolan Committee Hearings, part 30: 11325.

26. Tolan Committee Hearings, part 30: 11389.

27. Tolan Committee Hearings, part 30: 11434–49. The language of the resolutions varied, with some legion posts endorsing evacuation and internment only for "alien Japanese," some for "all enemy aliens," and others for "both alien Japanese and American born Japanese residing in the United States."

28. Grodzins, *Americans Betrayed*, 113–14.

29. It should be noted that the mayors of Berkeley, California, and Tacoma, Washington, both spoke out against mass removal at the hearings.

30. Grodzins, *Americans Betrayed*, 100. By 1943, Bowron was arguing that descendants of Japanese immigrants should be barred from American citizenship.

31. Tolan Committee Hearings, part 30: 11404.

32. Tolan Committee Hearings, part 30: 11409.

33. Tolan Committee Hearings, part 29: 11009. Grodzins, *Americans Betrayed*, 97–98.

34. Tolan Committee Hearings, part 31: 11634. Olson had, shortly after Pearl Harbor, signed the statement by the Fair Play Committee, a group opposed to internment and based in the Bay Area. The Fair Play Committee is discussed in chapter 3.

35. Grodzins, *Americans Betrayed*, 128.

36. Grodzins, *Americans Betrayed*, 282.

37. *Emanu-El*, December 12, 1941.

38. It is notable that all of these papers had a Zionist orientation, even *Emanu-El*, despite the fact that San Francisco was notable for the strength of its anti-Zionist movement at the time.

39. *Seattle Jewish Transcript*, December 19, 1941.

40. *Seattle Jewish Transcript*, December 19, 1941, and December 26, 1941.

41. *Emanu-El*, December 12, 1941.

42. *Scribe*, December 19, 1941.

43. *Seattle Jewish Transcript*, February 27, 1942.

44. Marc Dollinger, *Quest for Inclusion: Jews and Liberalism in Modern America* (Princeton, N.J.: Princeton University Press, 2000), 84–86. The Japanese American Citizens League emphasized the importance of cooperating with restrictions and, later, volunteering for military service, as ways of demonstrating Japanese American loyalty and patriotism.

45. Fred Rosenbaum, *Free to Choose: The Making of a Jewish Community in the American West* (Berkeley: Judah L. Magnus Museum, 1976), 96–100.

46. Eric Goldstein, *The Price of Whiteness: Jews, Race and American Identity* (Princeton, N.J.: Princeton University Press, 2006), 191.

47. *Seattle Jewish Transcript*, February 6, 1942.

48. *B'nai B'rith Messenger*, February 13, 1942.

49. William Issel, "Jews and Catholics against Prejudice," in *California Jews*, ed. Ava F. Kahn and Marc Dollinger (Hanover, N.H.: Brandeis University Press/University Press of New England, 2003), 124.

50. Neighborhood House, Board minutes, November 10, 1942, Oregon Jewish Museum.

51. William Toll, *The Making of an Ethnic Middle Class* (Albany: SUNY Press, 1982), 190.

52. Steven Lowenstein, *The Jews of Oregon* (Portland: Jewish Historical Society of Oregon, 1987), 170.

53. The Los Angeles Jewish Community Committee is discussed in detail in chapter 4.

54. *Scribe*, January 30, 1942, 1.

55. *Seattle Jewish Transcript*, December 12, 1941.

56. See, for example, "Justice to the Negro," *Seattle Jewish Transcript*, December 19, 1941, 6.

57. *Scribe*, February 20, 1942, 4. See also March 6, 1942, 3.

58. *B'nai B'rith Messenger,* March 13, 1942. A year later, in 1943, a major race riot occurred in Detroit.

59. For example, see *Scribe,* January 2 and January 9, 1942.

60. In 1940, the African American population of Seattle numbered 3,789, while the Japanese population stood at 6,975. Calvin Schmid, *Social Trends in Seattle* (Seattle: University of Washington Press, 1944), 135–37. In Washington as a whole, there were 7,424 African Americans and 14,565 Japanese Americans; in Oregon, 2,565 African Americans and 4,701 Japanese Americans. In California, African Americans numbered 124,306 and Japanese Americans 97,717. All figures from the U.S. census.

61. *Emanu-El,* February 27, 1942.

62. *Scribe,* January 2, 1942.

63. *Seattle Jewish Transcript,* December 12, 1941.

64. For example, the *Seattle Jewish Transcript* published "Regulations for Enemy Aliens" and "Refugee Service Advises Aliens" on December 26, 1941.

65. *Seattle Jewish Transcript,* February 13, 1942.

66. See, for example, Oregon Émigré Committee, minutes, Oregon Jewish Museum.

67. Jewish Service Association minutes, January–March, 1942, Oregon Jewish Museum.

68. *Seattle Jewish Transcript,* December 19, 1941, and March 6, 1942.

69. *B'nai B'rith Messenger,* January 20, 1942.

70. *Seattle Jewish Transcript,* December 12 and 19, 1941.

71. *B'nai B'rith Messenger,* December 19, 1941.

72. *B'nai B'rith Messenger,* January 2, 1942.

73. Phineas Biron, "Strictly Confidential," *Scribe.* January 9, 1942, 8.

74. Biron, "Strictly Confidential," *Scribe,* January 9, 1942, 8.

75. *Scribe,* February 13, 1942.

76. *Scribe,* March 20, 1942.

77. Biron, "Strictly Confidential," *Scribe,* March 13, 1942, 8.

78. *Emanu-El,* March 13, 1942; *Seattle Jewish Transcript,* March 13, 1942; *Scribe,* March 20, 1942.

79. *Seattle Jewish Transcript,* March 13, 1942.

80. "In My Opinion," *Seattle Jewish Transcript,* March 13, 1942, 6.

81. Tolan Hearings, part 31: 11726.

82. Tolan Hearings, part 31: 11727.

83. Tolan Hearings, part 31: 11736.

84. Tolan Hearings, part 29: 11272.

85. Tolan Hearings, part 30: 11518 and part 29: 11270, 11278.

86. *B'nai B'rith Messenger,* March 13, 1942.

87. *Seattle Jewish Transcript,* February 13, 1942.

88. Tolan Hearings, part 30: 11434–37.

89. *Seattle Jewish Transcript,* December 26, 1941.

90. *Seattle Jewish Transcript,* January 30, 1942.

91. Hurwitz's appointment is reported in the *Seattle Jewish Transcript,* January 23, 1942. On the *Seattle Star,* see Doug Blair, "The 1920 Anti-Japanese Crusade and Congressional Hearings," Seattle Civil Rights and Labor History Project, http://depts.washington.edu/civilr/research_reports.htm; and Richard Berner, *Seattle*

Transformed: World War II to Cold War (Seattle: Charles Press, 1999), 27–30. Also of note is the fact that one of the chief architects of the removal and incarceration policy was Karl Bendetsen, first in the office of the California Attorney General and later at the Western Defense Command under General DeWitt. Bendetsen had grown up as a Jew in Washington. However, he had begun "passing" as a non-Jew while in college, and by the time of the war had no connection to the Jewish community. The *Transcript* did not report on his involvement in the policy. For more on Bedetsen, see Klancy Clark de Nevers, *The Colonel and the Pacifist: Karl Bendetsen—Perry Saito and the Incarceration of Japanese Americans during World War II* (Salt Lake City: University of Utah Press, 2004).

92. Quoted in McKay, "Pacific Northwest Newspapers and Executive Order 9066," 11.

93. Berner, *Seattle Transformed*, 35.

94. "German Emigres Must be Calm," *The Jewish Transcript*, March 13, 1942.

95. Portland Section, National Council of Jewish Women, minutes, Neighborhood House, Oregon Jewish Museum. On the 1946 resolutions, see minutes from May 1, 1946.

96. Greenberg, "Black and Jewish Responses," 14.

97. The committee was also called the Dies Committee, after its chair, Representative Martin Dies. Its report, known as the Dies Yellow Paper, is discussed in more detail in chapter 4.

98. Fair Play Committee correspondence with Gleason, June–August, 1942. Pacific Coast Committee for National Security and Fair Play, The Bancroft Library, University of California, Berkeley (BANC MSS C-A 171), box 1.

99. Tolan Hearings, part 31: 11623–29.

100. *B'nai B'rith Messenger* and *Seattle Jewish Transcript*, February 27, 1942.

101. The Fair Play Committee and Deutsch's role in it are discussed in more detail in chapter 3.

102. Tolan Hearings part 29: 11266.

103. *Emanu-El*, March 27, 1942.

104. *Scribe*, February 20, 1942, 4.

3

To Be the First to Cry Down Injustice? Western Jews and Opposition to Nikkei Policy

In February 1942, CIO official Louis Goldblatt testified before the Tolan Committee at its San Francisco hearings. Goldblatt argued that using racial or ethnic characteristics to determine loyalty compromised American values and accused the "yellow press" of acting as a "fifth column" by whipping up hatred against Japanese Americans. He charged that "local and State authorities, instead of becoming bastions of defense of democracy and justice, joined the wolf pack when the cry came out, 'Let's get the yellow menace.'" "Where is this to end, Mr. Tolan?" he asked,

> Italians will be the next to be evacuated, then the Germans. Why stop with the Germans? According to the present Federal order Hitler could stay in San Francisco in a prohibited area and one of German nationality would have to leave because Hitler is an Austrian. So it will extend to the Austrians. It will go to the Hungarians, to Bulgarians, to Finns, to Danes. These are countries, many of them which have declared war on us. Where is the mark to be drawn?

> And, Mr. Tolan, if we follow such a procedure we can land in only one place. We will do a perfect job for those who want to sabotage the war effort. We will have the American people at each other's throats.[1]

Although Goldblatt was Jewish, there is nothing in the record to suggest that he thought of himself as a representative of the Jewish community. Goldblatt's words in support of the Nikkei community are generally framed as driven by his progressive views. Likewise, when Al Wirin of the Southern California ACLU took an active role in opposing the internment, both by testifying before the Tolan Committee and taking on Japanese American cases, there is no indication that either he or any Jewish organization saw

71

his activities as driven by his Jewish identity. The same can be said for Fair Play Committee supporters like UC-Berkeley professor Max Radin. Although many progressive organizations failed to take a stand against the removal and incarceration policies, individuals who came from such organizations were prominent among the activists who did speak out. While one might make the case that, for those who were Jewish, that upbringing and sensibility informed their activities, their principled stand was similar to that of other non-Jewish progressives and activists. It would be difficult to make the case that their opposition was specifically Jewish.

In contrast, when Rabbi Irving Reichert joined the Fair Play Committee, he acted in his official capacity as a Jewish leader. When his name appeared on committee letterhead, he was listed as a rabbi. He recruited support for the committee among his coreligionists. When he urged others to speak out in defense of Japanese Americans—as he did in his December 12, 1941, sermon—he rooted his opposition in his Jewish identity, explaining, "we Jews, who have for 19 centuries suffered persecution because of the alleged conduct of some of our forbears in Judea 1900 years ago, ought to be among the first to cry down the unjust persecution of the foreign-born in our midst whose patriotism is equal to ours."[2] Similarly, when prominent lawyer and Jewish community leader Joseph P. Loeb was approached by the Fair Play Committee, he conveyed that "he, *as a Jew*, was especially concerned at the hypocrisy the West Coast is showing in the 'handling' of the Japanese minority" [emphasis added].[3]

Although silence was the most common response of the organized western Jewish community to the removal and incarceration policy, there were voices that pierced that silence. Individual Jews, including several who were prominent community leaders, questioned the need for mass removal. Some demonstrated their discomfort through acts of kindness and support for Japanese American friends and neighbors. Others played a vocal role in the public debate about the policy, arguing that Japanese Americans, like German and Italian Americans, should be incarcerated only selectively, based on individual actions. This chapter explores the extent of Jewish opposition in the four largest Pacific Coast cities, Los Angeles, San Francisco, Portland, and Seattle. "Jewish opposition" is defined as that which can be said to flow out of the Jewish community, whether because the individuals involved attributed their actions to their Jewish identity, drew on Jewish community connections, or presented themselves and were perceived by others as representatives of a Jewish organization or community.

In exploring this opposition, it is important to keep several caveats in mind. First, although individual acts of kindness and support offered to friends and neighbors were, undoubtedly, far more common than public protests, they are far more difficult to document. Determining the motives behind such actions, and whether they were in some way specifically Jewish, is often impossible. Second, it is important to emphasize that the "Jewish opposition" explored in this chapter consists of deeds performed by individuals, on their own, or through secular groups. There is no evidence of an organized western Jewish opposition to the mass removal and incarceration of Japanese Americans.[4]

Several factors influenced Jewish opposition. Chief among them was the local context. Although both Jewish and Japanese Americans were concentrated in the major West Coast cities, the spatial relationship of their communities varied. Jewish and Japanese American residents of Portland, for example, were far less likely to share neighborhoods, schools, and commercial relationships than those in Seattle or Los Angeles. Since the development of personal relationships was a key factor influencing active opposition to these wartime policies, the residential pattern in each city influenced the extent of opposition, particularly in the form of individual acts of kindness and support for Japanese American neighbors. Jewish responses to Nikkei policy were also shaped by the degree of local opposition, and the four cities provided quite different contexts for active opposition to the policy. San Francisco emerged quickly as the center for the secular opposition movement; Seattle developed a religiously based opposition; Los Angeles was home to some activists affiliated with the opposition based in San Francisco but did not generate its own organization and leadership; and Portland failed to produce any organized opposition movement at all. The presence or absence of an organized opposition group and the dynamics of that opposition were critical to shaping Jewish responses within each city. Finally, Jewish opposition was influenced by political ideologies within the Jewish community. Specifically, anti-Zionism, an ideological movement that rejected the idea of Jewish nationhood and raised concerns that Zionism would lead to accusations of Jewish dual loyalty, appears to have informed several of the most prominent Jewish opponents to Japanese American removal and relocation.

When a correspondent suggested to Dr. Galen Fisher, secretary of the Fair Play Committee that his personal ties with Japanese Americans motivated him, Fisher took exception. "What most moves me," he contended, "is the denial of the due process of law which the Constitution guarantees . . . and the appearance of race discrimination in that all persons of Japanese stock were removed and no others."[5] Although opponents of the mass incarceration like Fisher saw their stance in principled, moral terms, it is clear that personal contact with Japanese Americans *was* a critical factor informing their dissent. Organizers of the Kansha Project database of those who stood with the Nikkei community in the face of wartime policy have concluded that one commonality among many supporters was that they often had "preexisting relationships with Japanese Americans as teachers, neighbors, or friends."[6] Testimony before the Tolan Committee confirms this conclusion. Again and again, witnesses arguing in favor of selective rather than mass removal cited familiarity as the basis for their conclusion that the Nikkei were overwhelmingly loyal.

Evidence of the influence of personal ties runs throughout the hearings. For example, Dan McDonald, a farmer from Washington's Yakima Valley, had worked with Japanese agriculturalists for three decades. He testified to their work ethic, skill, and loyalty, based on these personal connections. "My contact with the Japanese has proved to me that they are good citizens of the United States. . . . I know a good many young Japanese born here, and I know that they feel this is their country; they have no other; and they wish to do what they can to defend it."[7] Likewise, Esther Boyd, a businesswoman active in women's clubs and former president of a Yakima Valley PTA group, testified that she had "come to know the Japanese there very well. I have visited them in their homes. Some of them have been in my home as welcome guests." Based on these personal and business ties, she argued that the Nikkei were reliable, productive, and loyal.[8]

For many who spoke out, connections with Japanese Americans had been forged in religious settings.[9] Thus, a number of Christian missionaries who had worked in Japan and with Nikkei churches in America testified against mass removal. In San Francisco, Reverend Frank Herron Smith, the head of Methodist Japanese missions in the West, was typical when he explained, "it is my belief from this close association over many years with these Japanese that fully 90 percent of the first generation Christian aliens are loyal to America." Herron testified that Nisei Christians, "boys whom I have known 15 years, boys whom I married to their wives, are as truly American as your son, Congressman Tolan, or my son with whom these boys went to school and where they received the same education."[10] Many of these missionaries spoke more broadly about the Nikkei community, as did Reverend Gordon Chapman, who was responsible for Presbyterian work with the Nikkei community. Chapman explained in his written statement to the Tolan Committee, "Long and wide experience with American citizens of Japanese race has convinced the writer that they have become more thoroughly Americanized than is the case with the children of certain other racial groups. And it is true that these young people of Japanese parentage have again and again demonstrated their loyal Americanism."[11] Floyd Schmoe of the American Friends Service Committee in Seattle characterized the Nisei as "American citizens by birth and training" and explained, "Those of us who have known them well have confidence in them. We have come to value them as neighbors, as friends, and as business associates."[12] In Los Angeles, five representatives of Christian churches and a Buddhist priest spoke out against mass removal[13]; in Seattle, several "church related people" testified in defense of the Nikkei.[14]

Although clergy voiced opposition to mass incarceration most frequently, those who had taught or studied with the Nisei were also vocal. At the University of Washington, for example, where 458 Nisei students were enrolled,[15] a number of their classmates and professors defended them. Senior Curtis Aller was one of several students to testify, and he claimed to do so on behalf of an "informal group of students." Like many of the clergymen, Aller based his defense of the Nisei on his own connections with individual Nisei, explaining,

> I know many of these students personally, am pleased to count some of them as my intimate friends, have gone to school with them, studied with them, participated in student activities with them, gone to the same parties, and visited their homes and so I feel at least partially qualified to speak in their behalf.

> What are the Nisei students like? I am convinced that the majority of university students will agree with me when I say that the answer can be given in just one word—American. Aside from superficial differences of skin color, you would be unable to tell them from the average American college student. They dress the same, talk the same, and most importantly they think and believe the same. . . . They are loyal and intend to remain loyal and also intend to do everything in their power to prevent subversive activity in the Japanese community.[16]

In addition to supporting their classmates, more than one thousand UW students signed petitions protesting a decision by the Seattle public school system to fire its Nisei employees.

UW students were joined in their defense of the Nisei by faculty and administrators, including Jesse Steiner, chair of the Sociology Department, who argued in favor of a selective removal plan for the Nisei.[17] Robert O'Brien, assistant to the Arts and Sciences dean, testified that during his three years at the University of Washington he had "come in contact with second generation Nisei" and had found them well integrated into university affairs and willing to serve their country. He also presented the committee with a list of "Japanese students, club members and alumni who have either volunteered or have joined the army under selective service."[18]

A similar response came from the Bay Area. Many faculty from the University of California at Berkeley, the only school with a population of Nisei students greater than UW's, were active in the Fair Play Committee.[19] Berkeley provost and vice president and Fair Play Committee board member Monroe Deutsch framed his opposition in terms of personal ties:

> As one who has lived almost all his life in California and has seen a great deal of the Japanese population, I feel able to express a considered judgment on them. I have never had occasion to doubt the loyalty of any of those with whom I have been in contact; I have found them hard working, devoted, and law-abiding. On the Berkeley campus of the University of California, we have

had some four hundred American-Japanese; they have acquitted themselves well not only in their studies but in their conduct also. It has been a joy to me to see how in the days preceding the war these students were accepted more and more as part of the student life on the campus.[20]

Likewise, Galen Fisher, professor of religion at the Pacific School of Religion and research associate at UC-Berkeley, testified, "Like many other Americans who have long known hundreds of Japanese, I would testify that among their most marked traits are loyalty and gratitude. I strongly believe that the Nisei citizens will, with few exceptions, be as loyal to the United States as any other group of citizens."[21] Berkeley law professor Max Radin also likely had familiarity with the Nikkei community through his brother, Paul Radin, an anthropologist who had conducted a study of San Francisco's Japanese community in 1935.[22]

In Los Angeles, where no single campus had a Nisei population exceeding Berkeley's, UCLA and Los Angeles City College had a combined total of more than five hundred Japanese American students.[23] George Knox Roth, testifying before the Tolan Committee, indicated that his Public Affairs Committee of Los Angeles—a group of leading citizens opposing mass removal—was made up chiefly of "a group of young university professors."[24] There was a strong overlap between the religious and university-based opposition, exemplified by Roth, who was a Quaker, as were many of the leading activists at the University of Washington.[25]

Along with those motivated by religious or university ties, opposition leaders also emerged from the civil liberties community and leftist political organizations. Historian Robert Shaffer has argued that "this opposition reflected the growing rejection of racism among left-liberals in the 1930s and 1940s." Among the few national organizations to oppose the policy were the Socialist Party and the Fellowship of Reconciliation,[26] although it is important to remember that many prominent "left-liberals"—both within the administration and outside it—supported the policy, as did many organizations of the same stripe.[27] Westerners who were members of such organizations often drew on personal ties as well as ideological commitments in their support for Japanese Americans. For example, in his testimony before the Tolan Committee, CIO leader Louis Goldblatt pointed out that the Nisei, some of whom "are members of our unions," were "the only people who have shown a semblance of decency and honesty and forthrightness in this whole situation."[28]

While the national ACLU voted not to oppose the mass removal policy as it unfolded in the winter of 1942, a position shared by many members of the West Coast branches of that organization,[29] some local ACLU leaders in California dissented from this policy and actively pursued cases. Northern California ACLU (NC-ACLU) leader Ernest Besig defied the decision of the national office by taking on the Korematsu case.[30] ACLU historian Judy Kutulas explains, "Besig's membership . . . [in contrast to the national ACLU] saw those policies from the ground up. They visited the camps, dealt with the defendants in wartime cases and clashed with local officials who seemed racist and dictatorial."[31]

Since much of the opposition to Nikkei policy was based in universities, the political left, and the civil liberties communities, it is to be expected that individual Jews would become involved in that opposition. Although there was a strong history of Jewish Republicanism among western Jews, and Jewish involvement in the labor movement—with the exception of Los Angeles—was not as strong as in the East, Jewish westerners were well represented in these circles. Jews were among the founding members and leaders of the ACLU, for example, in Portland, San Francisco, and Los Angeles. The Communist Party in Los Angeles was overwhelmingly Jewish.[32] Not surprisingly then, some of the Jews in these organizations, like their comrades from other backgrounds, became involved in the opposition. Notable among them were A. L. Wirin, director of the Southern California ACLU (SC-ACLU), who also frequently represented the Communist Party in his private practice. Wirin testified pointedly at the Tolan Hearings and doggedly defended Japanese Americans, although, unlike Besig, he felt obligated to stay within national ACLU policy.[33] Likewise, among the faculty at Berkeley who were involved in the Fair Play Committee, there were several Jews, including Max Radin, a professor of law. Radin, Goldblatt, and Wirin serve as examples of Jewish individuals who spoke out. Yet none of them identified himself as the representative of a Jewish organization or community. Nor did they articulate their opposition in Jewish terms. Likewise, despite the fact that Jews tended to be overrepresented in the left-leaning political groups that were an important source of opposition, Jews were not particularly numerous or prominent among the activists.[34]

In understanding the extent and limitations of Jewish opposition, it is important to keep in mind that, as this testimony vividly demonstrates, familiarity and personal ties with the Nikkei community were important factors informing the positions of many of their defenders. This is not, of course, to say that such familiarity led inevitably to empathy or compassion. Certainly, many individuals who wholeheartedly embraced an anti-Nikkei position also claimed to know the community well.[35] While familiarity with the Japanese American community did not *necessarily* lead to sympathy, it was one important factor. Therefore, understanding the extent of contact between Jewish and Japanese American communities in the major West Coast cities can explain some of the regional variations in Jewish responses to the events of 1942.

In Oregon, the relatively small size of the Japanese American community limited opportunities for interaction. Portland's Nikkei population, which numbered 1,680 in 1940, was the smallest of the major West Coast communities. The majority of Oregon's 4,071 Nikkei lived in more rural areas like the Hood River Valley, an agricultural area that was notorious for its anti-Japanese agitation both before and during the war.[36]

Although Portland's Jewish community was the state's largest, it was far smaller than the major communities in Washington or California. A 1937 Jewish population survey showed that of Oregon's 11,649 Jews, 10,700 lived in Portland, making that community smaller than Seattle's at 14,500 and tiny compared to San Francisco's 40,900 or Los Angeles's 82,000.[37] Concentration of the Oregon Jewish community in Portland limited contact with the rural Japanese American community. The Hood River Valley, for example, was home to few if any Jews and no organized Jewish communities.

In Portland, the Japanese American community, concentrated north of Burnside Street, did not overlap with the major Jewish neighborhood in South Portland.[38] Both communities contained thriving business districts catering to their separate neighborhoods, as well as an array of cultural institutions. Children attended different public schools, and many spent their afternoons in Hebrew or Japanese schools in their respective neighborhoods. Even at the university level, Jewish students, who began to attend college in large numbers in the 1920s and 1930s, did not encounter a significant number of Nisei peers at Oregon's colleges and universities. The University of Oregon, in Eugene, for example, had only twenty-seven Nisei students in 1941–42, and Oregon State College in Corvallis, with more Japanese American students than any other Oregon institution of higher learning, had but forty-one.[39] In Portland, there was as yet no state university, and the smaller colleges had only a handful of Nisei students each.

The demographics of the Nikkei community in Oregon not only minimized the chances of contact between the state's Jews and Japanese Americans but also was a critical factor limiting opposition more generally. In California and Washington, academics, civil libertarians, and clergymen who had significant contact with Nikkei populations were among those most likely to protest mass removal. But in Oregon, the potential opponents of the policy were far less likely than their counterparts in the other coastal states to have had meaningful contact with Japanese Americans. While academics at UC-Berkeley and the University of Washington were able to testify based on their personal contact with scores or even hundreds of Nisei students, faculty at the University of Oregon in Eugene were unlikely to encounter Japanese Americans at work or in their daily life: the 1940 census listed only sixty-two individuals who were neither "white" nor "negro" in all of Lane County, home to the university.[40]

If opposition was most often grounded in personal connections with the Nikkei community, then it should be no surprise that nowhere on the West

Coast did anti-Nikkei sentiment meet as little opposition as in Oregon. During the Portland Tolan Committee hearings only one lone voice, that of a former Methodist missionary to Japan, Azalia Emma Peet, directly questioned the rationale behind mass relocation. "These are law abiding, upright people of our community," she argued. "What is it that makes it necessary for them to evacuate? Have they done anything?" In contrast to the clergymen who testified in other cities, Peet spoke as an individual, without any organizational support. Although groups like the Seattle Council of Churches expressed sharp opposition to mass removal, the Portland Council of Churches failed to question the policy and instead only advised the government about process and logistics.[41]

The lack of any organized opposition to the emerging policy combined with distance from the Nikkei community to mute protest by potential critics in the Jewish community. Thus, Gus Solomon, a prominent Jewish civil libertarian (and later federal judge), was active in working to bring about the return of Japanese Americans to Oregon later in the war, but he did not speak out in 1942. He explained later, "I am sorry to say that I was not involved in the beginning, when the Japanese-Americans were moved into concentration camps. I knew about it; I didn't like it; but I didn't protest."[42] In an interview, Solomon "guiltily recalled his own near-paralysis" and attributed his inaction at the time to the fact that he personally knew few Japanese Americans and was aware of no active opposition to the policy in Portland. He noted that the Portland ACLU was "virtually extinct" at the time and that his efforts to urge the national ACLU to participate in the Minoru Yasui case were rejected.[43] He also remembered urging the local American Jewish Congress to speak out against the incarceration of Japanese American citizens, arguing that "they have got to speak up against the treatment of the Japanese because today it's the Japanese and tomorrow it's the Jews." He found, however, that he "was the only Jew in Portland willing to stand up."[44] Although he served as one of several court-appointed advisors to the judge in the case and shared with the court his opinion that the curfew order that Yasui had violated was unconstitutional, Solomon did not speak out publicly against alien restrictions or the removal policy.[45] His failure to do so, which, according to his biographer, "lay forever on Solomon's conscience,"[46] demonstrates vividly the way in which unfamiliarity with the Japanese American community and the absence of a cohesive opposition group could stifle supportive impulses among potential activists.

In Oregon, the historic strength of anti-Asian sentiment,[47] the relatively small size of the Nikkei community, particularly in Portland and Eugene, and the consequent limited opportunity for interaction with academics and civil libertarians worked against the formation of an opposition movement. While Portland Jews had a history of defending minority rights, as evidenced by their opposition to the Klan and to the mandatory public school bill of the early 1920s, there was, as we have seen, no history of applying such concerns to Asian Americans. With neither a history of personal contacts nor an organizational framework for opposition, it is not surprising that no opposition to mass removal emerged among Jewish Oregonians.

Although the evidence for close interaction between Jews and Japanese Americans in San Francisco is almost as scant as for Portland, had Solomon lived in the Bay Area he would have had little difficulty finding an outlet for his dissent. Civil libertarians and academics in the Bay Area were successful in organizing an extensive and active opposition to Nikkei policy, a movement in which several prominent Jews played key roles. Their involvement, however, appears to have grown not out of neighborhood ties but through connections within the civil libertarian community and an ethos informed by the anti-Zionist movement.

Like Portland, San Francisco had a history of strong anti-Asian sentiment. Indeed, while Portland's reputation as a city hostile to Nikkei emerged most forcefully in the immediate prewar years, San Francisco's went back to the nineteenth century. The city had been the center of the anti-Asian movement since the late nineteenth century, led by local labor unions. The crisis that precipitated the Gentlemans' Agreement grew out of San Francisco, and the city remained a center for exclusionist activity for decades afterward.[48]

Although both Jews and Japanese Americans moved into the Fillmore District in the years after the 1906 earthquake and established strong ethnic neighborhoods in the 1920s and 1930s, sources suggest relatively little interaction. Jerry Flamm's book-length reminiscence of life in San Francisco in this period profiles the Fillmore as a "lively Jewish section" where Jews "bought Kosher meats and chickens at the butcher and poultry counters. On Saturday night stores opened after sundown when the twenty-four hour Jewish Sabbath ended and stayed open until eleven o'clock."[49] Despite the fact that the Fillmore was a diverse area that also included African American, Mexican, Italian, Russian, and Japanese American communities,[50] among others, accounts of the Jewish Fillmore scarcely mention their presence. For example, Flamm's book mentions Japanese Americans only to note that the "Japanese colony was concentrated in a few blocks on Post and Sutter Streets, east of Fillmore."[51]

Likewise, descriptions of the *Nihonmachi* (Japantown) in the Fillmore tend to minimize the presence of Jews and other non-Nikkei residents and fail to distinguish among "Caucasian" ethnic communities:

> There were non-Japanese establishments in the area, but very few. Ace Restaurant was run by a Japanese but catered to African Americans and some whites. A Chinese laundry existed next to a Japanese drugstore. At the end of Webster Street was a chimney-cleaning shop, a "Negro" church, a restaurant, a Japanese gymnasium, and a grocery store. A Filipino barbershop was next to a "shady" hotel, Nishikawa Rooming, "with its unmistakable red sign reading 'Rooms.'"

Further down was a restaurant specializing in fresh eel from Japan. A fish store was run by Kiichiro Murai and legally owned by his son Hajime; it did a thriving business. Down the street was a dry goods store, Nichi Bei Bussan, owned by Shojiro Tatsuno. Nakagawa's Shohin Kan was across the street; Tatsuno and Nakagawa once had been partners but had become competitors after a misunderstanding. A small vegetable store was tended by Mrs. Nakata while her husband delivered his wares all over the city. A landmark of the area then and now, fifty years later, was Soko Hardware, owned by Masayasu Ashizawa. Both Nichi Bei Bussan and Soko Hardware survived the evacuation because sympathetic property owners helped the Japanese proprietors reestablish their businesses.[52]

Flamm's map of the Jewish Fillmore in the 1920s and anthropologist Paul Radin's of "Japantown" in 1935 show largely the same area, but do not identify any of the same businesses. Flamm does not mention Japanese Americans or their businesses at all. Although Radin mentions an African American presence, his only reference to Jews comes when he noted that a Buddhist temple had been created in a building that had earlier served as a synagogue.[53]

Personal relationships did develop in this mixed area and resulted in support from neighbors and business associates in the face of anti-Nikkei policies. For example, two different Jewish couples were recalled by Pat (Yamakawa) Yamamoto, a San Francisco native and child at the time of the war, as "the only non-Japanese persons my parents ever talked about having helped them during that time." One couple, the Clurmans, were the Yamakawa's landlords, renting out the upstairs apartment in their O'Farrell Street home to the family. When the Yamakawas were forced into confinement, the Clurmans safeguarded their belongings and sent care packages to them in camp. The families remained so close that when Mrs. Clurman was unable to attend Pat's wedding after the war due to poor health, Pat "went to see her, still in my wedding gown so she could be part of my special day." The second couple, Barney and Mary Barnard, were business associates of Pat's father, David. In addition to offering the Yamakawas financial assistance, the Barnards and Yamakawas corresponded during the latter's incarceration at Heart Mountain, and the Barnards sent the family supplies including a hot plate and a large stuffed panda. As David Yamakawa recounted in a letter to the Barnards from Heart Mountain, "the children raised one 'whoopee' after another and could not be coaxed to eat their dinner nor could we get them to bed in the evening after I opened the package you sent to them."[54]

Although the proximity of the Japanese American and Jewish neighborhoods in San Francisco's Fillmore make it likely that many such acts of kindness and support from individuals occurred, they are difficult to document. What is clear, however, is that the most extensive organized opposition to Nikkei policy emerged in San Francisco and attracted several prominent Jewish community leaders. Presumably, these individuals, like others in their community, felt the strain between their commitments to support the war and to fight prejudice. Yet for them, the commitment to civil liberties weighed more heavily than their compulsion to support *all* defense measures and led them to break the silence.

The Fair Play Committee, based in Berkeley, was the most prominent organized opposition group, forming early in the crisis and ultimately working to coordinate Nikkei defense activities along the West Coast. From the outset, its stance against removal and incarceration based on race or ancestry was clearly articulated. As its secretary, Galin Fisher, explained in his testimony before the Tolan Committee,

> I fully accept as our paramount aim: Win the war—maintain national security. Therefore, I approve any measures for control of either aliens or citizens that may be required to achieve these ends. . . . But I am fully convinced that the sweeping evacuation of Japanese residents, whether aliens or citizens, would hinder, not help, the attainment of these ends. Removal of persons of any race or nationality should be confined to such as special investigation shows to be dangerous or decidedly suspicious.[55]

Throughout the war, the Fair Play Committee kept up its defense of the Nikkei, arguing first for selective rather than mass removal and, once Japanese Americans had been incarcerated, arguing for individual investigations aimed at clearing and releasing the overwhelming majority whom they believed were loyal. They worked to pave the way for the return of the Nikkei to their home communities on the West Coast and were also involved in the effort to place Nisei college students in universities outside of the Western Defense Zone.[56]

From the outset, Temple Emanu-El Rabbi Irving Reichert and UC Berkeley Vice President and Provost Monroe Deutsch, two of the Bay Area's most prominent Jews, served on the board of the Fair Play Committee. Reichert became the earliest and most prominent Jewish leader to speak out on the issue with his December 13, 1941, sermon, "The Price of Freedom." As we have seen, Reichert referred specifically to "American citizens of Japanese parentage," claiming their loyalty was as "assured as that of President Roosevelt himself" and reminding Jews of their own persecution based on prejudice.[57]

Rabbi Reichert had a long history of involvement with progressive causes. He was an active member of the Northern California branch of the ACLU and had taken public stances in support of striking California farm workers and against lynching.[58] He saw such causes as central to his role as rabbi. As historian Fred Rosenbaum demonstrates, Reichert frequently preached a message of social justice to his congregation and to his larger radio audience, and he saw his role as "identifying society's ills and motivating his flock to cure them." For example, in a sermon titled "The Duty of Hating," he asked, "How much liberty do we want? Do we want it only for white men and not for others? How much justice do we want? Do we want it only for people of wealth and power, or for the humble and friendless too?"[59] His commitment to social justice and tolerance went back several decades. As a college student in Cincinnati, he had won an oratory contest with a speech defining acceptance as the "Mission of America": "To be true to our noblest impulses, we must break down forever the forbidding walls of bigotry and prejudice and with welcome hand hail the stranger who knocks at our gates, for we, too, have been strangers in the land."[60] Reichert's long commitment to the fight against prejudice and his framing of it as part of his mission as a rabbi made him a particularly articulate advocate of Jewish involvement in liberal causes, including the fight against mass removal.

Likewise, Monroe Deutsch has been described as a "champion of civil rights" who "put himself in the place of the disinherited, the exiled, the downtrodden."[61] He is remembered at Berkeley as a staunch supporter of academic freedom and particularly for his stance against loyalty oaths in the postwar period. In addition to his Fair Play Committee activities, he was heavily involved in the effort to place Nisei students in colleges and universities outside of the defense zone and letters from these students suggest that they viewed him as a trusted mentor.[62]

While Reichert and Deutsch's long involvement in civil liberties causes and in the fight against prejudice and discrimination clearly informed their stance against mass removal and incarceration, they had another commitment that set them apart from many of the Jews who were involved, locally and nationally, in liberal causes and gave them a special sensitivity to the dual loyalty issue. Reichert was one of the key national leaders of a faction of Reform rabbis who joined together to oppose the Reform Movement's swing toward Zionism in 1941–42 by forming the American Council for Judaism (ACJ). Reichert became national vice president, and his San Francisco congregation, with Deutsch serving as ACJ section president, became an organizational stronghold.

Anti-Zionists embraced the Classical Reform ideology, which defined Judaism solely as a religion and rejected both Jewish nationalism and the connection to Palestine as homeland, arguing that American Jews needed no other homeland than America. Reichert and his like-minded colleagues believed that Jewish nationalism would lead to charges of dual loyalty and would threaten the status of Jewish citizens in America and other liberal nations. As Reichert had warned in a 1936 sermon that was widely reprinted in American Jewish newspapers, "There is too dangerous a parallel between the insistence of Zionist spokesmen upon nationalism and race and blood and sinister pronouncements by Fascist leaders in European dictatorships. . . . We may live to regret it."[63]

Although an anti-Zionist position had been embraced by the Reform mainstream in the late nineteenth and early twentieth century, it was increasingly out of step with the majority of American Jewry by the 1920s and 1930s. Both the increasing influence of pro-Zionist East European Jews and the growing threat to European Jewry led to a swing toward Zionism, even among Reform Jews, in the 1930s. During that decade, the Reform Central Conference of American Rabbis (CCAR) moved from anti-Zionism to non-Zionism and official neutrality and, finally, to sympathy with Zionism. Within months of the American entry into the war, the CCAR voted to endorse the formation of a Jewish army in Palestine, a central demand of Zionists.[64]

Anti-Zionists like Reichert and Deutsch had become a beleaguered minority within the Reform Movement by early 1942 and moved to create the ACJ as an organization dedicated to fighting the movement's embrace of Zionism. The coincidence of the timing of their work as founding members of both the ACJ and the Fair Play Committee is suggestive, as concerns about the dangers of a real or imagined dual loyalty figured prominently in both organizations. One of the central goals of the Fair Play Committee was to present Japanese Americans as loyal U.S. citizens and residents without any allegiance to Japan. The ACJ's major concern about Zionism was that it would lead to accusations that American Jews had "dual loyalties" and to a questioning of their patriotism. The mass internment of Japanese Americans on the basis of dual loyalty accusations seemed to prove exactly what the ACJ had preached: that ethnic groups with perceived ties to other nations were vulnerable to charges of disloyalty.

The overlap in themes and timing is demonstrated vividly through examination of Reichert's anti-Zionist and anti-internment statements, both issued during the final weeks of February 1942. On anti-Zionism, Reichert published in the temple newsletter a statement explaining his refusal to support the formation of a Jewish army in Palestine. Reichert argued that the Jewish army would create the perception of the Jew "as a ubiquitous nationality within every nation where they dwell, unified in a higher allegiance to the soil of Palestine and its nationalistic claims than to the countries whose protection and freedom they enjoy on terms of equality with their fellow citizens." Reichert composed this statement less than a week after the Fair Play Committee submitted its statement to the Tolan Committee, trying to convince the panel that Japanese Americans were loyal only to the United States. Reichert, as a Fair Play Committee board member, was a signatory to that statement.

Reichert, Deutsch, and other Fair Play Committee board members were kept informed about continuing attacks on "dual loyalty" in the California state legislature. For example, during the 55th legislative session in 1943, House Bill 1881 proposed "disciplinary proceedings against employees . . . who claim citizenship in a foreign country; hold dual citizenship; pledge allegiance to an enemy country; act disloyally and disrespectfully to the United States or its flag; or do anything to impede the war effort." Likewise,

Senate Joint Resolution 3 memorialized Congress to revoke the citizenship of individuals with dual citizenship.[65] The Fair Play Committee carefully documented these measures as part of its effort to monitor anti-Nikkei activity. For anti-Zionists like Reichert and Deutsch, such measures seemed to confirm their concerns about the dangers of real or perceived dual loyalty.

Given these connections, it is not surprising that anti-Zionism was a common thread among several prominent Jewish community leaders who spoke out against the policy. In addition to Deutsch and Reichert, Seattle's Rabbi Samuel Koch, who was also an ardent anti-Zionist, spoke out early in defense of Japanese Americans—although his final illness prevented him from taking a prominent role in the spring of 1942. The following year, the Fair Play Committee group in Seattle brought in Alfred Shemanski, a Jewish community leader, UW regent, and ACJ activist. When a Fair Play Committee contact approached Joseph P. Loeb, a prominent lawyer and ACJ activist in Los Angeles, he reported that "Mr. Loeb told [him] that he, as a Jew, was especially concerned at the hypocrisy the West Coast is showing in the 'handling' of the Japanese minority," and concluded, "he should be a good man for your Los Angeles committee."[66] In San Francisco, Deutsch recruited Daniel Koshland, another ACJ activist, to write a letter in support of the Fair Play Committee later in the war.[67]

Certainly, Reichert and Deutsch also used networks beyond the ACJ to build support for the committee. Reichert was instrumental in recruiting Los Angeles rabbi Edgar Magnin for the board in 1943. Magnin, in turn, brought Los Angeles-based Judge Benjamin Scheinman on board.[68] Yet the prominence of ACJ activists among the Jewish names in the Fair Play Committee records is striking. For the majority of Jews in America by 1942, the solution to the problem of European Jewry was to defeat Nazism and settle refugee Jews in Palestine. While western Jewish newspapers, like most Jewish newspapers and congregations across the country, preached an increasingly Zionist message during the war, ardent anti-Zionists like Reichert and Deutsch believed that Zionism would fan the flames of anti-Semitism. They believed the Zionist program had the potential to lead American Jews down the path of Germany—to the perception of American Jews not as Americans but as a foreign element. For these anti-Zionists, a heightened sensitivity to the dual loyalty issue was an important factor that helped to resolve the dilemma that Nikkei policy posed. They broke the silence and spoke out.

Although the involvement of Rabbi Koch and Alfred Shemanski in Seattle suggests that anti-Zionist sensibilities contributed to Jewish opposition there, Jewish responses in Seattle seem to be more influenced by personal connections. The same is true for Los Angeles. Many Jews in both of these cities interacted extensively with Japanese Americans. If close contact were the key factor influencing support for Japanese Americans, one would expect

the strongest Jewish support to come from those two cities, where their ethnic neighborhoods overlapped. Yet, while there is evidence of close relationships and individual actions by Jews in support of Japanese Americans in
both cities, a Jewish-based opposition did not arise in either.

Since the turn of the century, the Yesler Way area had been the heart of
Seattle's Jewish and the Japanese communities.[69] In 1940, on the eve of
World War II, the neighborhood was still home to approximately 85 percent of Seattle's Jews.[70] All of the Jewish community's institutions were lo-
cated in this area, including all of the major congregations. Nikkei, who
were Seattle's largest nonwhite group, comprised approximately 40 percent
of the district's population in 1940,[71] and, like the Jewish population, were
concentrated in the trade sector. Children from both groups attended the
same schools, particularly Broadway, Franklin, and Garfield High Schools,
and mixed in classes and in extracurricular activities.[72]

Similarly, in Los Angeles Jews and Japanese Americans both resided in the
diverse Boyle Heights neighborhood, although the area was far more heavily Jewish than was Seattle's Central district. In 1940, there were about thirty-
five thousand Jews in the area and five thousand Japanese Americans, along
with significant African American, Mexican, Italian, Armenian, and Russian
communities.[73] Although Jewish and Japanese American children interacted,
especially in school, contact between adults in the different ethnic communities was limited, with most socializing within their own groups.[74] In Los
Angeles, however, where there was a strong working-class, leftist political
movement, there was some contact among Jewish and Japanese American
activists. The Los Angeles Communist Party, for example, was largely Jewish,
but tried during the 1930s "to be more inclusive and to reach out to other
minorities," and did have Japanese American members and leaders.[75] Elaine
Black, the daughter of immigrant Russian Jews, met her future husband Karl
Yoneda at a demonstration in Los Angeles. Both were Communist Party
leaders in the Los Angeles area. In 1942, Elaine Black Yoneda opted to join
her husband and young son during their incarceration at Manzanar.[76]

As in Seattle, however, the most frequent interactions came in the Boyle
Heights area schools. Although Jewish and Japanese American children attended different primary schools, they encountered one another in both
junior and senior high schools, especially Roosevelt High School, where, in
1936, 35 percent of the student body was Jewish and 6 percent Japanese
(Mexicans made up 24 percent of the school population).[77] Oral histories
from Jews and Nisei who were students at the time recall positive interactions at school and references to the school as a "melting pot" are common.[78] Despite this perception, former students reported only limited contact outside of school. George Yoshida, who moved from Seattle's Central
District to Boyle Heights as a child in 1936, recalled several Jewish friends
at Roosevelt High School, but noted that "although we were very close in

school—we had lunch together, had same classes together—outside of class, there was no contact at all with these people except the first few young guys that I met." His Boy Scout troop, for example, was made up of "exclusively Japanese American kids."[79] Still, Yoshida noted that both Jews and Japanese Americans were involved in school-based extracurricular activities and members of both groups frequently held leadership positions. One informant who attended Roosevelt in the 1930s reported that "during the three years (six semesters) that I attended the school, the student body presidents were Nisei, Black, Mexican-American and Jewish."[80] Wendy Elliot-Scheinberg's analysis of Roosevelt yearbooks in the 1930s demonstrates that students of varied ethnic backgrounds mixed in clubs and sports, as well as in the classroom, and that many friendships developed across ethnic lines.[81] It is notable that both the Seattle and the Los Angeles schools in these diverse neighborhoods embraced an "internationalist" curriculum that encouraged appreciation of diverse cultures.[82]

As was the case in the universities, it seems clear that interaction in school increased student empathy for Nisei students. In Seattle, the editors of the Garfield school newspaper, for example, openly expressed feelings of loss when more than two hundred of their classmates were forced to leave school for relocation camps in the spring of 1942. Although the editors did not express opposition, their good-bye message's affirmation of the Nisei students' American identity is notable:

> Garfield has always drawn her strength from a cosmopolitan student body. Her great football teams, her famed track squads, her aggressiveness—these are the results of a dynamic school spirit which in its pursuit of a greater Garfield, has overlooked racial prejudices and recognized us all only as Garfieldites—not as black, or white, or brown, or yellow men, but as classmates and comrades.

> Today the war has made it necessary for all people of Japanese descent to be removed from Seattle. This action will affect not only the evacuees themselves, but also the communities which they must leave. Garfield will suffer. No school can lose 225 loyal, capable students and not be the worse for it. Even as these students are reluctant to abandon their homes and friendships, so does it sadden Garfield to see so many who have represented her so well, go.

> But we all know the necessity of such action. We all realize that the principles at stake far outweigh the happiness of the individual even as we know that the ultimate happiness and success of each one of us is dependent upon the survival of those principles.

> Best of luck, then, to those fellow Garfieldites and Americans, who, in the service of their country, must leave home and school behind![83]

In the same issue, the regular sports columnist discussed the impact of the "evacuation" on the school's sports program and detailed the many contributions of Nisei athletes to the school's various teams. Although the Nisei students were forced into relocation camps before graduation that spring, the *Garfield Messenger* listed their names along with the other seniors in its graduation issue.[84] The continuing attachment to the Nisei students is suggested in a news article in early June, reporting that Makiko Takahashi, a former Garfield senior and copy editor for the *Messenger*, would be working on a newly organized camp paper, serving the Nikkei incarcerated at the Puyallup relocation center.[85]

Similarly, Roosevelt High School in Boyle Heights lost a substantial number of students when its Nisei were forced into camps in April 1942. The Roosevelt *Rough Rider* covered the story, publishing "A Tribute to Japanese American Students" and reporting on a "farewell exercise" held for the students prior to their departure.[86] Jewish columnist Harry Rosenberg opined, "This action will affect all of us here at Roosevelt. Many of our school officers and friends are of Japanese lineage. There is nothing that can be done to remedy the situation. I'm sure that our Japanese students realize the necessity of the action. That we shall miss them, should they leave, can go without saying. They have done many fine things here at Roosevelt."[87]

Likewise, oral histories with Jewish students from the diverse Boyle Heights area schools indicate sympathy among Jewish classmates for their Nisei peers. For example, Claire (Orlosoroff) Stein recalled,

> I remember when the war was declared and President Roosevelt announced that we were going to war with Japan, it was very scary for them. In fact, the president of the school [Hollenbeck Junior High] was Kei Ozawa, and he was really kind of torn. I remember that the national anthem was being played, and he didn't know what to do. He stood up, but he just didn't know what to do. It was very heart-breaking, because we were good friends, all of us, and they were sent away. . . . We had to say goodbye to a lot of our friends. It was awful.[88]

Leo Frumkin, also in junior high school at the time, remembered a sense of "bewilderment" when "all of a sudden, the Japanese friends we had just disappeared." He wondered, "What happened to Frankie Yamamoto? What happened to him. And then people would say they went off to the concentration camps. It was sort of a shock." When the Nisei students returned during his senior year of high school, Frumkin ran unsuccessfully for school president "on the program that a great injustice had been done to our fellow students, and we had to go out of our way to try to welcome them back and help integrate them in."[89]

Overlapping neighborhoods and business districts, and Nisei integration in classes, sports, and other extracurricular activities at the schools attended by Jewish Seattleites and Angelinos all indicate that there was a far higher level of interaction between the two ethnic communities than in Portland. Yet this interaction did not always lead to strong affinity. Perhaps not atypical of ethnic communities that occupy similar residential space and economic niches, these similarities could breed competition and friction as well as affection. Although it may not accurately reflect prewar relations, it is interesting that a 1948 study of social relations among students at several Seattle high schools found particularly strained relations between Jewish and Japanese American students. At Garfield, where nearly 16 percent of the students were Jewish and nearly 10 percent Japanese American (down significantly from before the War), Jewish and Nikkei students rated one another less desirable as potential friends, dates, coworkers, and leaders than members of their own group, non-Jewish whites, and, in some cases, other minorities. The study noted a "marked antipathy which Japanese and Jews showed each other on all questions," and speculated that, "perhaps the fact that both groups value scholastic success and also that they are the two largest minority groups in school make for competition."[90]

Jewish and Japanese American adults met as parents at the schools and in their daily lives in their overlapping neighborhoods and business districts— although accounts from both groups suggest fairly segregated shopping patterns, with Jews and Japanese tending to patronize their "own" stores. Not surprisingly, their close proximity and familiarity led to a range of responses. For example, there is evidence that individual Jews and Jewish organizations—like others in the region—took advantage of the opportunity to purchase Nikkei property, which was available at very low prices due to the sudden, forced departure. The most notable example is the purchase by orthodox Seattle Congregation Bikur Cholim of an adjacent property. The congregation's board minutes show that on April 26, 1942, two days before the city's first Japanese Americans were incarcerated at the Pullyup assembly center, a special meeting was called to consider an opportunity "to purchase a house at 1706 Washington St., adjacent to the Synagogue." After continuing the meeting on April 30, the board authorized the purchase, without ever mentioning why the opportunity appeared so suddenly or who the seller was. City directories reveal that the previous owner was Roy Nakagawa.[91]

In Boyle Heights, Leo Frumkin recalled the outrage of his parents when they learned that a friend had purchased a Japanese-owned store, taking advantage of fire sale prices:

> I remember one of my parents' friends bought a drugstore on First and Soto, which was owned by Japanese people. And I remember my parents angrily telling them how could they have done this to these people; I'm assuming they bought it for a song because people just had to leave. And I remember that my parents were just furious that they would take advantage of a situation like that. You know, 'Why didn't you rent it from them?' I remember that was the discussion, why didn't you rent it, or something like that. . . .[92]

There is also evidence of more gallant responses. According to a history of Educational Center, the Council of Jewish Women's settlement house in the

Central District, there was considerable concern for the plight of local Nikkei. Rose Levin, who served as president of the board of the center, recalled that "Many Jews were openly in sympathy with the Japanese. Jewish people could understand the situation." Mrs. Levin and her brother visited the Puyallup Assembly Center to personally express their concern. She recalled years later in an oral history,

> My brother had rented a store from a Japanese family who owed the building . . . on Sixth or Seventh Avenue and Jackson. And he felt very badly about the fact that these wonderful, wonderful Japanese people who were marvelous landlords—he felt they had nothing to do with the war—that they were elegant, very fine, up-right citizens—and here the whole family was uprooted from this entire building where they had a store of their own. And they had to board up the place. And so my brothers, who were in business on the corner of that particular building, really oversaw that building, that whole area, while these Japanese were sent away to the relocation center.[93]

In Los Angeles, there are similar accounts of Jewish neighbors looking after the property of incarcerated Japanese American neighbors. Other kindnesses by individuals included visits at the assembly centers. According to historian Mark Wild, who has written about the diverse neighborhoods of Los Angeles in the early twentieth century, "Observers noted that a steady stream of African American, Jewish, Chinese, Mexican and Anglo visitors traveled to the Santa Anita and Pomona assembly centers in Southern California."[94] Touru Yenari recalled that his Jewish neighbor and junior high school classmate, Joe Portnoy, "bicycled ten miles from Boyle Heights to visit him and deliver a load of fresh laundry [at the Santa Anita Assembly Center]."[95] Milton Goldberg, a Boyle Heights native who served as a Boy Scout official, worked to keep Japanese American troops functioning not only at the Santa Anita Assembly Center but also at Manzanar. He visited them there and arranged for them to participate in backpacking trips in the Sierra Mountains near the camp.[96] Fred Okrand, a young Jewish lawyer beginning his first job at A.L. Wirin's law firm, was able to draw on personal ties when a Japanese American plaintiff was needed to challenge local wartime restrictions. Okrand, who grew up in Boyle Heights and attended Roosevelt High and UCLA, recalled, "I'd gone to Santa Anita to try to find a plaintiff. . . . You needed a plaintiff. I couldn't file a lawsuit. I couldn't get inside, barbed wire. Then right across the way was a fellow I went to UCLA with, Johnny Yamasaki. . . ."[97]

Despite these and other examples of actions taken by individual Jewish Seattleites and Angelinos to support their Japanese American friends and neighbors, there is no evidence that such actions translated into any organized Jewish opposition to the mass removal policy. In Seattle, where there was a strong opposition movement, its pacifist and Christian identity likely muted Jewish involvement. In Los Angeles, the heavy investment of the most powerful community organizations and leaders in efforts to fight local anti-Semitism pushed the Jewish civil rights community in a quite different direction, as I explore in chapter 4.

As we have seen, Seattle's Rabbi Samuel Koch had delivered a plea for tolerance, in which he specifically addressed the plight of Japanese Americans, immediately after Pearl Harbor.[98] His sermon was not out of step with the attitude in the mainstream press at that time. Yet Koch was a likely candidate for continued activity as an opponent of mass removal. He had a long record as an advocate for social justice, and he was deeply involved in a wide variety of local philanthropic and interfaith initiatives, as well as serving on the national Reform rabbis' social justice group.[99] He was also, like Rabbi Reichert in San Francisco, an ardent anti-Zionist who worried about the potential for Jews to be accused of dual loyalty. At the time, however, he was suffering from what would be his final illness and had already announced his intention to resign his pulpit. As hostility toward Japanese Americans mounted in early 1942, Koch did not repeat his supportive statements in the temple newsletter, although he retained control of the publication through the winter. His successor, Rabbi Raphael Levine, whose last position had been at a London congregation, did not assume his new position until after the Nikkei had been removed from the Seattle area. At any rate, as a newcomer to the West and a survivor of the Blitz, Rabbi Levine was focused on the threat of Nazi Germany and the fate of European Jewry, not the plight of the Nikkei, with whom he had no personal experience.

Organizational and congregational minutes from Seattle—even from progressive groups like the Council of Jewish Women—show no engagement with the issue. Neither the minutes of Congregation Bikur Cholim nor those of any other congregation in the Central District, which are only available in fragmented form, provide any evidence that they took a stand on—or even acknowledged—the removal policy. Even in the minutes of the Seattle Section of the Council of Jewish Women—recorded by Secretary Rose Levin who, as we have seen, felt great personal affinity for her Japanese American neighbors—there is no mention of Japanese Americans in this time period.[100] The only reference to the alien issue came when Miss Morgenstern reported to the Board of Directors of the Education Center on a February 15 mass meeting in the neighborhood on civil defense, which included a speech by Seattle Mayor Earl Millikin titled "The Status of Enemy Aliens." While the minutes do not reflect the content of Millikin's speech, it seems reasonable to assume that, as when he testified before the Tolan Committee two weeks later, he expressed concerns about the potential for sabotage by Japanese American fifth columnists and endorsed mass evacuation.[101] Whatever Mrs. Levin's and others' private thoughts about these speeches or about the *Transcript's* endorsement of selective internment earlier in the week, there is no evidence that concern about the policy was raised at the meeting.

The lack of engagement with the issue in the Jewish community contrasted sharply with the strong opposition that emerged among some Christian communities and within academic circles in Seattle. Yet the particular constellation of that movement would have been problematic for many Jews. Although the University of Washington played a central role, the key activists—including many of the academics—were Quakers, pacifists, and Christian missionaries. Sociology Department Chairman Jesse Steiner, who testified at the Tolan Hearings, for example, had longstanding contacts as a researcher within the Nikkei community and had also taught in Japan at a Christian mission school.[102] Likewise, Robert O'Brien, a college dean and sociologist who played a key role in organizing student protest in response to the attempted ouster of Nisei public school secretaries and who later took a leave of absence in order to work with Nisei students, rooted his protest in his pacifist, socialist upbringing and was an active Quaker. Another Quaker activist, Professor of Biology Floyd Schmoe, resigned to work full time on American Friends Service Committee activities on behalf of Japanese Americans. Schmoe and his wife had five Nisei students living with them at the time, and his daughter would later marry UW student Gordon Hirabayashi, a Quaker who violated curfew laws in order to challenge alien restrictions. Both Hirabayashi and Schmoe had been involved in a conscientious objectors group at the University of Washington.[103] Former Washington State Senator Mary Farquharson, who was a key member of this defense group, was also a Quaker and a socialist. She worked with Arthur Barnett of the Seattle Council of Churches to organize Hirabayashi's defense. The group established an office at the University Friends Meeting, which also housed a hostel where a number of female Nisei students lived.[104]

The Seattle Council of Churches was, along with the American Friends Service Committee, central to this effort. Within days after Pearl Harbor, the group organized an Emergency Committee on Aliens. Initially, the committee offered assistance to Issei detained in the December FBI arrests. As the mass removal policy took place, the group argued that racism was the motivating factor behind the policy and its representative, Harold Jenson, told the Tolan Committee that the group was "disturbed by the manner in which the question of Japanese evacuation was separate from any consideration of evacuation of people of German or Italian descent."[105] Some individual churches also took a stand in support of the Nikkei. The First Baptist Church of Seattle ran frequent articles in its newsletter "encouraging the congregation to support its Japanese brothers and sisters."[106]

Although these overlapping groups criticized the emerging policy for its "race prejudice,"[107] their networks were Christian and pacifist. Given the

Jewish community's tremendous focus on supporting the war effort in order to save European Jewry, as well as its long history of concern about Christian missionary activity, this particular coalition of activists would have been unattractive to many Jews. This issue would later be recognized as a problem by the Fair Play Committee as it tried to coordinate opposition activities under its umbrella. In a 1943 letter from Ruth Kingman of the Fair Play Committee in California to Mary Farquharson regarding the hiring of a part-time secretary for the region, Kingman asked Farquharson for suggestions, reminding her, "As you may remember from our conversations, she should be free from any strong religious or other pacifist groups, and should have good contacts in the community and experience in meeting with such persons as might be effective in our organization."[108]

Implicitly acknowledging Kingman's concerns, Fraquharson responded several months later that her own name would be left off of the local executive committee, "because I am afraid some persons whom we want on the advisory board might be afraid of it," presumably because she was a known pacifist and socialist.[109] Ultimately, a Mrs. E. E. Siegley, the wife of a "well established businessman" with "good contacts in [the] business community," was recruited as executive secretary. Farquharson explained that they were "very conservative Republicans on most issues, but both Bob O'Brien and I were impressed with the fact that Mrs. Siegley evidently feels strongly on the issues around which the Fair Play Committee is organized." The first target in their recruiting drive once Siegley was on board was Alfred Shemanski, a member of the Board of Regents of the University of Washington, a trustee of Temple de Hirsch, and an active anti-Zionist.[110] Until that point, well over a year after the removal of Seattle's Japanese Americans, there is no evidence of Jewish involvement in the coalition of groups opposing government policies.

In Los Angeles, as in San Francisco and Seattle there was a university-based effort to organize Nikkei defense, as indicated by George Knox Roth in his testimony.[111] Yet, as was the case in Seattle—and in contrast to the situation in San Francisco—there is no evidence of Jewish involvement in that movement as the crisis unfolded in early 1942. Rather, the most prominent Jewish Angelinos took a more moderate course. While Rabbi Edgar Magnin did eventually affiliate himself with the Fair Play Committee, he took a circuitous route and communicated conflicting signals during the first year of the war.

If any Jewish community leader had the standing and background to play an active role in the opposition movement, it was Rabbi Magnin. A native-born Californian, Magnin, like Reichert and Koch, was the leading Reform rabbi of his city, with a regional and national reputation among Jews and non-Jews and with a special prominence due to his reputation as "rabbi to the stars" and his leadership in the fight against racist depictions in film.[112]

His sermons, lectures, and articles, frequently broadcast and published lo-cally and regionally, emphasized universal values and social justice.[113] Un-like Reichert and Koch, Magnin was "favorable to Zionism."[114]

Magnin walked a fine line during the winter of 1942. In his "Labels that are Libels" sermon, delivered to his Wilshire Boulevard congregation, pub-lished in several Jewish newspapers, and broadcast on his weekly radio pro-gram, he spoke out strongly against prejudice and intolerance, and he specif-ically cautioned against blaming an entire group for the acts of some. Yet he refrained from specific mention of Japanese Americans. And despite this plea for tolerance, Magnin, as one of three Jewish signatories to the statement by the Los Angeles Committee for Church and Community Cooperation, en-dorsed a statement to the Tolan Committee that emphasized the danger of subversion on the West Coast, expressed confidence in the army's handling of the matter, and affirmed that "any evacuation proposed is not prompted by race hatred, prejudice or selfish business interests, but is contemplated only for military protection." Although the statement stressed the need for "a selective evacuation," it did so in the context of a discussion of enemy aliens from all three Axis nations, and it failed to specifically endorse selec-tive evacuation for the Issei or for their children. While this statement did not specifically recommend mass removal and incarceration of the Nikkei, by accepting false accusations of sabotage, arguing that "in case of a Japa-nese attack, most Americans believe that some enemy aliens, and even some claiming citizenship, would attempt to aid the invasion," and urging obedi-ence, the statement suggested no opposition to such a policy.[115]

Although Rabbi Magnin neither specifically endorsed nor opposed mass removal and incarceration, his affiliations suggest conflicting impulses. On the one hand, Magnin was listed through early 1943 as a board member of the Americanism Educational League. The AEL was founded in the late 1920s as a civic group working against prejudice, but after some initial hes-itation in the early months of the War, it emerged in the spring of 1942 as an organization that was vigorously anti-Nikkei and pro–mass incarcera-tion.[116] By the fall, it was working closely with the American Legion and campaigning to prevent Japanese Americans from returning for the dura-tion of the war. Rabbi Magnin had joined the league's board before the war, when it was working to expose intolerance and anti-Semitism as anti-Amer-ican. Although he dissociated himself from the group, explaining, "my ex-istence on the Board has been of much embarrassment to me on the Japan-ese question," he did not take this step until the summer of 1943.[117]

At the same time, Rabbi Magnin was apparently considered to be sympa-thetic to the Nikkei. When a group representing organizations known to be supportive including several church groups, the YMCA, the YWCA, the Council of Social Agencies, the Fellowship of Reconciliation, and the Bud-dhist Brotherhood—formed in April of 1942 to provide services to the

Nikkei housed at the temporary relocation camp at Santa Anita, Rabbi Magnin was contacted. Although he was unable to attend the meeting, it was noted that "Rabbi Magnin will be happy to speak at some religious service at Santa Anita, if asked to do so."[118] By April 1943, Rabbi Magnin had joined the Fair Play Committee Board, and he was used as a contact for recruiting other Jewish board members in the Los Angeles area, including judges Benjamin Scheinman and Harry Hollzer.[119] His name also appeared in June 1943 on a Fair Play Committee pamphlet endorsing segregation of disloyal Nikkei from the loyal, opportunities for the loyal to serve in the military, and "fair play" and resettlement for loyal Japanese Americans.[120]

Rabbi Magnin's actions during this period suggest an internal conflict. The words of his sermon indicate a clear understanding of the fundamental wrong of mass removal and incarceration based on race or ancestry. Yet his endorsement of the Committee for Church and Community Cooperation statement and his continued association with the AEL into 1943 suggest that allegations of subversive acts by Japanese Americans led him to stifle his objections to the policy during 1942 and early 1943. The Committee for Church and Community Cooperation statement placed great stock in the allegations of subversion and potential fifth-column activity that had been publicized by the Dies Committee in its February 1942 Yellow Paper. As chapter 4 demonstrates, Magnin felt he had good reason to trust the Dies report, as much of its content was developed by the News Research Service, a Los Angeles–based group with which he was closely affiliated and had deemed "thoroughly reliable."[121]

For western Jews, local context was an important factor. Those living in cities where they encountered Japanese Americans as classmates and neighbors were more likely to recognize the racism of the policy than those who did not. For those who did recognize that racism, local context also greatly influenced the potential for action. While there was a forum for Jewish opposition in San Francisco, local dynamics hindered Jewish involvement in Seattle and Portland.

Internal politics also influenced Jewish opposition. As the American Jewish community moved toward a strong embrace of Zionism, staunch anti-Zionists found themselves to be increasingly outside the mainstream and concerned about the perils of dual loyalty. Such concerns appear to have sensitized this minority to the plight of the Nikkei. At the same time, in Los Angeles, where organized anti-Semitic groups had found a stronghold, an influential but secretive Jewish community group had forged close ties with government entities and patriotic groups focused on exposing fascists and anti-Semites as anti-American. These ties, which are explored in chapter 4, not only distanced prominent Jewish Angelinos from opposition groups but actually led them to contribute to the case for mass removal and internment.

NOTES

1. Tolan Committee Hearings, part 29: 11179, 11183.

2. Rabbi Irving Rechert, sermon, December 12, 1941, reprinted in *Temple Emanu El Chronicle*, December 19, 1941.

3. William Carr to Ruth Kingman, June 13, 1943. Pacific Coast Committee for National Security and Fair Play, Bancroft Library, Berkeley, box 6.

4. The Fair Play Committee became a sort of clearinghouse for opposition groups, and its files contain correspondence with many sympathetic groups, including a number that were religiously based. These files present no evidence of any Jewish opposition group. Pacific Coast Committee for National Security and Fair Play records, Bancroft Library, University of California, Berkeley.

5. Galen Fisher to George Gleason, August 17, 1942. Pacific Coast Committee for National Security and Fair Play, Bancroft Library, Berkeley, Box 1, correspondence.

6. Shizue Seigel, *In Good Conscience: Supporting Japanese Americans during the Internment* (San Mateo: AACP, 2006), 263. See also Robert Shaffer, "Opposition to Internment: Defending Japanese American Rights during World War II," *The Historian* 61, no. 3 (Spring 1999): 598.

7. Tolan Committee Hearings, part 30: 11582–83.

8. Tolan Committee Hearings, part 30: 11583–84.

9. The Kansha Project found that "religious people, mainly foreign and domestic missionaries and members of the peace churches, particularly Quakers," were prominent among defenders of the Nikkei. See Seigel, *In Good Conscience*, 263.

10. Tolan Committee Hearings, part 29: 11208.

11. Tolan Committee Hearings, part 29: 11206.

12. Tolan Committee Hearings, part 30: 11527.

13. Tolan Committee Hearings, part 31.

14. Floyd Schmoe, "Seattle's Peace Churches and Relocation," in *Japanese Americans: From Relocation to Redress*, ed. Roger Daniels, Sandra C. Taylor, and Harry H. L. Kitano (Salt Lake City: University of Utah Press, 1986), 115.

15. Allan W. Austin, *From Concentration Camp to Campus: Japanese American Students and World War II* (Urbana: University of Illinois Press, 2004), table 1.

16. Tolan Committee Hearings, part 30: 11590.

17. Tolan Committee Hearings, part 30: 11558.

18. Tolan Committee Hearings, part 30: 11598–99.

19. Austin, *From Campus to Concentration Camp*, table 1. There were 485 Nisei students at Berkeley. Other than the University of Washington and Berkeley, there was no other university with a population of Nisei exceeding 300.

20. Monroe Deutsch, September 12, 1942. Pacific Coast Committee for National Security and Fair Play records, Bancroft Library, University of California, Berkeley, box 63.

21. Tolan Committee Hearings, part 29: 11199. Fisher had served as a missionary in Japan and spoke Japanese fluently. See Ruth Kingman, "The Fair Play Committee and Citizen Participation," an oral history conducted in 1974 by Rosemary Levenson in *Japanese-American Relocation Reviewed, Volume II: The Internment*, Regional Oral History Office, The Bancroft Library, University of California, Berkeley, 1976.

22. Paul Radin was a student of Franz Boaz and spent much of his career studying Native Americans. He conducted the survey of what later became known as "Japantown" but was at the time referred to as "Japanese town" in 1935. By 1941, he was no longer residing in California, but his brother, Max, was a longtime member of the law faculty at Berkeley. On the survey, see Sandra Taylor, *Jewel of the Desert: Japanese American Internment at Topaz* (Berkeley: University of California Press, 1993), 34.

23. Austin, *From Campus to Concentration Camp*, table 1.

24. Tolan Committee Hearings, part 31: 11799.

25. On Roth, see Seigel, *In Good Conscience*, 29–31. The Kansha Project's listing of supporters of Japanese Americans demonstrates clearly the critical role of Quakers, including many who were academics.

26. Robert Shaffer, "Cracks in the Consensus: Defending the Rights of Japanese Americans During WWII," *Radical History Review* 72 (1998): 85.

27. For a discussion of leftist and liberal involvement in the opposition, see Shaffer, "Cracks in the Consensus," 95–96.

28. Tolan Committee Hearings, part 29: 11180. In addition to Louis Goldblatt, San Francisco's CIO president also protested the mass removal. See Shaffer, "Cracks in the Consensus," 90.

29. Even within the Northern California ACLU branch, there was considerable disagreement over Nikkei policy. A March 1942 survey of the group leadership and members "showed majority support among both groups for Executive Order 9066 and General DeWitt's evacuation program." The branch's executive committee membership "rejected an ACLU test of the orders, although substantial majorities favored the establishment of hearing boards for Japanese American citizens," by votes of 9–8 and 103–96, respectively. See Peter Irons, *Justice at War: The Story of the Japanese Internment Cases* (Oxford: Oxford University Press, 1983), 112.

30. Rather than leave the Bay Area, Fred Korematsu, a Nisei, had plastic surgery to alter his appearance and went into hiding, but he was soon found and arrested. He lost his challenge to the evacuation order and was convicted of violating that order in federal court. That ruling was upheld by the Supreme Court in 1944. However, this decision—and those in the parallel Yasui and Hirabayashi cases—were found in the early 1980s to be fundamentally flawed and were vacated in an unusual procedure called *coram nobis*. On the *coram nubis* cases, see Peter Irons, *Justice Delayed: The Record of the Japanese American Internment Cases* (Middleton, Conn.: Wesleyan University Press, 1989).

31. Judy Kutulas, "In Quest of Autonomy: The Northern California Affiliate of the American Civil Liberties Union and World War II," *Pacific Historical Review* 67, no. 2 (1988): 202. See also Kutulas, *The American Civil Liberties Union and the Making of Modern Liberalism, 1930–1960* (Chapel Hill: University of North Carolina Press, 2006).

32. Shana Bernstein, *Building Bridges at Home in a Time of Global Conflict: Interracial Cooperation and the Fight for Civil Rights in Los Angeles, 1933–1954*, Ph.D. Diss., Stanford University, 2003, 72–73.

33. Irons, *Justice at War*, 111. For Besig's testimony, see Tolan Committee Hearings, part 31, 11797–98.

34. An extensive database of individuals supporting Japanese Americans during the war has been compiled by the Kansha Project. Among the several hundred individuals listed, only a few are identified as Jewish. Siegel, *In Good Conscience.*

35. To take just one example, State Senator Ronald E. Jones of Brooks, Oregon, testified that he knew the local Nikkei community well. He claimed, "I know some of those families, especially the heads of the families, that there is no question about their affiliation with the Japanese people; their sympathies are entirely with them." Tolan Committee Hearings, part 30: 11314.

36. Japanese American population figures for Oregon are from "The 'Japanese Question' Confronts the State" in *Oregon Responds to World War II,* a web exhibit by the Oregon State Archives, http://arcweb.sos.state.or.us/exhibits/ww2/threat/question.htm.

37. Population figures from *American Jewish Year Book,* American Jewish Committee, 1942–1943; tables 1 and 6, pages 422, 425–26. A note indicated that an updated 1942 estimate put the Los Angeles Jewish population at 125,000.

38. For a map of Nihonmachi (Japantown) see http://www.discovernikkei.org/nikkeialbum. See also "A Glimpse of Portland's Japantown, 1940" (Oregon Nikkei Legacy Center, undated) and *Nihonmachi: Portland's Japantown Remembered,* Doug Katagiri, editor (Oregon Nikkei Legacy Center, 2002). For a map of the Jewish neighborhood in South Portland, see Steven Lowenstein, *The Jews of Oregon* (Portland: Jewish Historical Society of Oregon, 1987), 102.

39. Austin, *From Campus to Concentration Camp,* table 1.

40. Historical Census Browser, 1940, http://fisher.lib.virginia.edu/collections/stats/histcensus. This issue is discussed further in Ellen Eisenberg, "As Truly American as Your Son: Voicing Opposition to Internment in Three West Coast Cities." *Oregon Historical Quarterly* 104, no. 4 (2004): 542–65.

41. Tolan Committee Hearings, part 30: 11386, 11620.

42. Gus Solomon, interview transcript, Portland Jewish Oral History Project, Oregon Jewish Museum.

43. Peter Irons credits Solomon with bringing the Yasui case to the attention of the national ACLU, but they chose not to get involved. Irons, *Justice at War,* 114.

44. Harry Stein, *Gus Solomon: Liberal Politics, Jews, and the Federal Courts* (Portland: Oregon Historical Society Press, 2006), 76.

45. Solomon interview. See also Stein, *Gus Solomon,* 76–82.

46. Stein, *Gus Solomon,* 76.

47. It is notable that hostility toward Japanese Americans in Oregon, while particularly strong by 1942, was relatively late in coming. As late as 1920, the Oregon legislature defeated an alien land law similar to those passed earlier in Washington and California, and, at least in Portland, anti-Nikkei sentiment was muted until the 1920s. Oregon's Alien Land Law was passed in 1923 by the Klan dominated legislature elected in 1922. See William Toll, "Permanent Settlement: Japanese Families in Portland in 1920," *Western Historical Quarterly* 28, no. 1 (Spring 1997): 24.

48. Roger Daniels, *The Politics of Prejudice* (Berkeley: University of California Press, 1962).

49. Jerry Flamm, *Good Life in Hard Times: San Francisco in the 1920s and 1930s* (San Francisco: Chronicle Books, 1999), 72.

50. Alison Varzally characterizes the Fillmore in this period as a multiethnic neighborhood, similar to Seattle's Central District and Los Angeles's Boyle Heights.

Varzally, "Romantic Crossings: Making Love, Family and Non-Whiteness in California, 1925–1950," *Journal of American Ethnic History* 23, no. 1 (Fall 2003): 10.

51. Flamm, *Good Life in Hard Times*, 72.

52. Taylor, *Jewel of the Desert*, 35.

53. "A Walk Through Japantown—1935," *Hokubei Mainichi*, Sunday, January 1, 1989, Supplement. This supplement is a reprint of a survey by anthropologist Paul Radin. See Taylor, *Jewel of the Desert*, 34.

54. David Yamakawa to Mr. and Mrs. Barney Barnard, April 3, 1943. Account of the Yamakawa family's experiences was shared through correspondence from Mrs. Pat (Yamakawa) Yamamoto with the author, July 12, 2007.

55. Tolan Committee Hearings, part 29: 11199.

56. See Pacific Coast Committee for National Security and Fair Play records, The Bancroft Library, University of California, Berkeley. On activities to support Nisei college students, see Austin, *From Concentration Camp to Campus*.

57. Reichert's sermon is quoted on page 1 of the introduction.

58. Fred Rosenbaum, *Architects of Reform: Congregational and Community Leadership Emanu-El of San Francisco, 1849–1980* (Berkeley: Judah L. Magnus Museum, 1980), 127–29; and Rosenbaum, *Visions of Reform: Congregation Emanu-El and the Jews of San Francisco, 1849–1999* (Berkeley: Judah L. Magnes Museum, 2000), 183–213.

59. Rosenbaum, *Visions of Reform*, 186.

60. "Mission of America," (1917), Irving Reichert Papers, Western Jewish History Center, Berkeley.

61. Benjamin Lehman, "Homage to Monroe Deutsch: Three Addresses Delivered at a Gathering in His Memory" (Berkeley: University of California, 1955), 25, 19.

62. Austin, *From Concentration Camp to Campus*, 12; Seigel, *In Good Conscience*, 287; Roger Daniels *Asian America: Chinese and Japanese in the United States since 1850* (Seattle: University of Washington Press, 1988), 243–44, 262.

63. Rosenbaum, *Architects of Reform*, 135.

64. Thomas Kolsky, *Jews against Zionism: The American Council for Judaism, 1942–1948* (Philadelphia, Temple University Press, 1990), chap. 1; Howard Greenstein, *Turning Point: Zionism and Reform Judaism* (Chico, Calif.: Scholars Press, 1981), chaps. 1 and 2.

65. Pacific Coast Committee for National Security and Fair Play, Bancroft Library, University of California, Berkeley, carton 1, folder 60.

66. William Carr to Ruth Kingman, June 13, 1943, Pacific Coast Committee for National Security and Fair Play, Bancroft Library, University of California, Berkeley, box 6.

67. Shemanski, Loeb, and Koshland are identified as "key members" of ACJ in Kolsky, *Jews against Zionism*, appendix D, 502–9.

68. Ruth Kingman to Rabbi Irving Reichert, April 26, 1943, Pacific Coast Committee for National Security and Fair Play, Bancroft Library, University of California, Berkeley, box 1.

69. Calvin Schmid, *Social Trends in Seattle* (Seattle: University of Washington Press, 1944), 121, 133.

70. Craig Degginger, "Washington's Jewish Heritage," Jewish Genealogical Society of Washington State, www.members.tripod.com/~JGSWS/history.htm.

71. Jean Porter Devine, *From Settlement House to Neighborhood House* (Seattle: Neighborhood House, 1976), 18.

72. Franklin, Garfield, and Broadway yearbooks and newspapers, 1941–42, Seattle Public Library and Seattle Public Schools Archives. The yearbooks from all three schools provide evidence of Jewish and Japanese participation in a wide range of school activities, ranging from athletics to yearbook and newspaper.

73. George Sanchez, "What's Good for Boyle Heights Is Good for the Jews: Creating Multiracialism on the Eastside during the 1950s," *American Quarterly* 56, no. 3 (September 2004): 635. "Neighborhood Profile," *The Boyle Heights Oral History Project*, Japanese American National Museum: 41. For an excellent account of the development of Boyle Heights, see Wendy Elliot-Scheinberg, *Boyle Heights: Jewish Ambiance in a Multicultural Neighborhood*, Ph.D. diss., Claremont Graduate University, 2001.

74. Leo Frumkin oral history transcript, December 19, 2001, "The Boyle Heights Oral History Project" Japanese American National Museum. Allison Varzally contrasts the tendency of youth in these areas to cross ethnic boundaries with their parents' preference for socializing within their ethnic group. Varzally, *Ethnic Crossings: The Making of a Non-White America in the Second Quarter of the Twentieth Century California*, Ph.D. diss., University of California, Los Angeles, 87.

75. Bernstein, *Building Bridges at Home*, 72–73.

76. Mark Wild, *Street Meeting: Multiethnic Neighborhoods in Early Twentieth Century Los Angeles* (Berkeley: University of California Press, 2005), 1–2.

77. Elliot-Scheinberg, *Boyle Heights*, 289.

78. See, for example, Hershey Eisenberg oral history transcript, December 18, 2000, "The Boyle Heights Oral History Project," Japanese American National Museum; see also Wendy Elliott, "The Jews of Boyle Heights, 1900–1950," *Southern California Quarterly* 78, no. 1 (1996): 7, and Elliot-Schienberg, *Boyle Heights*, chap. 6.

79. George Yoshida oral history transcript, July 23, 2001, "The Boyle Heights Oral History Project," Japanese American National Museum. There were three Japanese American Boy Scout troops in Los Angeles's Little Tokyo, sponsored by the Buddhist, Catholic, and Methodist churches, respectively. See Seigel, *In Good Conscience*, 288.

80. Elliot-Scheinberg, *Boyle Heights*, 306.

81. Elliot-Scheinberg, *Boyle Heights*, 303–12.

82. On Los Angeles, see Wild, *Street Meetings*, 112–13; on Seattle, see Yoon K. Pak, *Wherever I Go, I Will Always Be a Loyal American: Schooling Seattle's Japanese Americans during World War II* (New York: Routledge Falmer, 2002), chap. 4.

83. *Garfield Messenger*, May 1, 1942. Seattle Public School Archives.

84. *Garfield Messenger*, May 19, 1942.

85. *Garfield Messenger*, May 29, 1942.

86. Japanese American National Museum, *Los Angeles's Boyle Heights*, Images of America Series (Charleston, S.C.: Arcadia Publishing, 2005): 77.

87. *Rough Rider*, March 19, 1942, cited in Varzally, *Ethnic Crossings*, 177–78.

88. Claire Orlosoroff Stein, oral history transcript, November 11, 2000, "The Boyle Heights Oral History Project," Japanese American National Museum.

89. Leo Frumkin oral history transcript, "The Boyle Heights Oral History Project" Japanese American National Museum.

90. Lenore Dickson, "Social Distance in Two Seattle High Schools," M.A. thesis, University of Washington, 1951, 26–27.

91. Congregation Bikur Cholim papers, Washington State Jewish Historical Society, archives, University of Washington.

92. Leo Frumkin oral history transcript, Boyle Heights Oral History Project, Japanese American National Museum.

93. Devine, *From Settlement House to Neighborhood House*, 19.

94. Wild, *Street Meeting*, 2.

95. Seigel, *In Good Conscience*, 262.

96. Seigel, *In Good Conscience*, 288–89.

97. Yamasaki did not become the plaintiff himself but helped to make connections for Okrand. Fred Okrand, Boyle Heights Oral History Project, Japanese American National Museum, 23.

98. *Temple Tidings*, December 12, 1941, Temple de Hirsch, Seattle. Koch's sermon is quoted on page 1.

99. Samuel Koch papers, University of Washington Archives. See also David Buerge and Junius Rochester, *Roots and Branches: The Religious Heritage of Washington State* (Seattle: Church Council of Greater Seattle, 1988), 162–63.

100. Council of Jewish Women, Seattle Section papers, Washington State Jewish Historical Society Archives, University of Washington.

101. Tolan Committee Hearings, part 30: 11404–5.

102. Shaffer, "Opposition to Internment," 610. Steiner's research on Japanese Americans is discussed in chapter 1.

103. Schmoe, "Seattle's Peace Churches," 115. See also Berner, *Seattle Transformed*, 39.

104. Richard Berner, *Seattle Transformed: World War II to Cold War* (Seattle: Charles Press, 1999), 40.

105. Douglas M. Dye, *The Soul of the City: The Work of the Seattle Council of Churches during World War II*, Ph.D. diss., Washington State University, 112.

106. Dye, *Soul of the City*, 102.

107. Tolan Committee Hearings, Seattle, part 30: 11565.

108. Ruth Kingman to Mary Farquharson, July 26, 1943, Mary Farquharson papers, University of Washington Archives.

109. Farquharson to Kingman, September 3, 1943, Mary Farquharson papers.

110. Farquharson to Kingman, September 9, 1943, Mary Farquharson papers. Shemanski's name appears on a list of anti-Zionist activists in Kolsky, *Jews against Zionism*, app. D, 502–9.

111. Tolan Committee Hearings, part 31: 11799.

112. Felicia Herman, "Jewish Leaders and the Motion Picture Industry," in *California Jews*, ed. Ava Kahn and Marc Dollinger (Hanover, N.H.: Brandeis University Press/University Press of New England, 2003), 98. Magnin's activities in this area are discussed briefly in chapter 1.

113. Max Vorspan and Lloyd Gartner, *History of the Jews of Los Angeles* (Philadelphia: Jewish Publication Society, 1970), 158.

114. Max Vorspan and Lloyd Gartner, *History of the Jews of Los Angeles* (Philadelphia: Jewish Publication Society, 1970), 192; see also William Kramer and Reva

Clar, "Rabbi Edgar F. Magnin and the Modernization of Los Angeles Jewry," part I, *Western States Jewish History* 19, no. 3 (1987): 240–41.

115. Tolan Committee Hearings, part 31: 11623–25. Along with Rabbi Magnin, Rabbi Morton Bauman of Temple Israel in Hollywood and Mrs. Isaac Pelton of the National Council of Jewish Women were members of this group.

116. The AEL is discussed in more detail in chapter 4.

117. Rabbi Edgar Magnin to Ruth Kingman, August 25, 1943, Pacific Coast Committee for National Security and Fair Play, Bancroft Library, University of California, Berkeley, box 6.

118. Committee to Coordinate Religious and Social Service Activities at Santa Anita Racetrack and the Pomona Fair Grounds, April 7, 1942, Pacific Coast Committee for National Security and Fair Play, Bancroft Library, University of California, Berkeley, carton 2, folder 5.

119. On Magnin joining the board, see Rabbi Irving Reichert to Fair Play Committee, April 22, 1943, Pacific Coast Committee for National Security and Fair Play, Bancroft Library, University of California, Berkeley, carton 2, folder 27. On Magnin's cooperation in attempting to recruit others, see Ruth Kingman to Rabbi Reichert, March 17, 1943, box 1.

120. Fair Play Committee pamphlet, June 1943, Pacific Coast Committee for National Security and Fair Play, Bancroft Library, University of California, Berkeley, box 2, folder 4.

121. Magnin to Minneapolis ADL office, telegram, October 7, 1940, box 164, Jewish Federation Council of Greater Los Angeles' Community Relations Committee Collection series 2 (CRC2), Urban Archives Center, Oviatt Library, California State University, Northridge.

4

Fighting Fascism: The LAJCC and the Case for Removal

Long before the Japanese attack on Pearl Harbor or the Tolan Committee hearings on the West Coast, a variety of agents working for federal, state, and private groups had begun to assemble allegations of Japanese American disloyalty that would ultimately be used to justify their mass removal and incarceration. In his testimony before the Tolan Committee in February 1942, then California Attorney General Earl Warren presented a list of "dozens of allegedly subversive Japanese American organizations" and provided reports of their pro-Japanese sentiments and activities. According to historian Peter Irons, "What Warren did not reveal to the Committee was that the bulk of this material, and the conclusions he drew from it of a subversive conspiracy bent on espionage and sabotage, came directly from the files of the notorious House Committee on Un-American Activities [the Dies Committee], which in turn relied heavily on the amateur sleuthing of right-wing and anti-Oriental groups."[1] In fact, the Dies Committee's scathing and alarmist "Yellow Paper" of February 1942 was drawn from a variety of previously published anti-Japanese materials.[2] Among these were reports published in the summer of 1941 by a group that Irons characterizes as "an obscure Los Angeles organization known as the News Research Service." These reports would inform not only Warren's testimony but also General DeWitt's 1943 *Final Report* on the removal program and even the Supreme Court's opinions on challenges to alien restrictions, such as the *Hirabayashi* case.[3]

In his attempt to challenge the Dies Committee report on the House floor in late March 1942, Congressman Vito Marcantonio (American Labor Party-NY) "traced these charges, point-by-point and word-for-word, from the Dies Committee report to their origins in publications of the News Research Service [NRS]." A member of the Dies Committee revealed only that "the material that has been quoted from the report and from the [NRS] *News Letter* is material that was obtained from the same source and authorized by the same person who gathered it but did not want to be quoted."[4] Yet Marcantonio—like historians examining the report in the years since— was unable to determine who was behind the News Research Service. Historian Irons speculates, "Since the ONI [Office of Naval Intelligence] and FBI break-in at the Japanese consulate in Los Angeles took place shortly before the first espionage charges published by the News Research Service, the source of this material might well have been one or both of these intelligence agencies."[5]

It was reasonable for both contemporaries and, later, historians to assume that these explosive and ultimately influential allegations came from "right-wing and anti-Oriental" groups. Any number of conservative and vigorously anti-Japanese groups had long been operating in California and participated actively in spreading the propaganda that would generate public and official support for the emerging mass exclusion policy. Neither contemporaries nor historians would guess that the News Research Service and its *News Letter* were actually run by the Los Angeles Jewish Community Committee (hereafter, LAJCC; later known as the Community Relations Council of the Jewish Federation Council of Los Angeles, or CRC),[6] an organization whose primary goal was to fight both prejudice and fascism.

The LAJCC's role in the development of the case for mass removal is a unique episode in the story of relations between organized western Jewish communities and Japanese Americans. In contrast to both the studious silence of the western Jewish press and community organizations in the face of the mass removal and the outspoken advocacy for Japanese Americans by a few individual Jewish leaders, this appears to be the only case in which the resources of the organized Jewish community were used to actively contribute to anti-Nikkei measures. This participation, which seems antithetical not only to the general American Jewish commitment to fighting prejudice but also to the LAJCC's own dedication to rooting out discrimination and ethnic hatred, can only be explained through a careful examination of the local context in which it took place. This study demonstrates that the group's investment in fighting forms of fascism that it believed were linked directly to local and international anti-Semitism led it to investigate the Nikkei community. Although prevailing racial ideas about Japanese Americans clearly informed the group's perception of the Nikkei as foreign nationals rather than as a beleaguered American minority group, the LAJCC was motivated primarily by its commitment to fighting fascism and anti-Semitism. In contrast to the many pro-exclusion groups that had a long history of anti-Asian sentiment, the LAJCC acted *in spite of* rather than *in accordance with* its general attitudes about the place of ethnic and racial minorities in America.

The pattern of growth in Los Angeles during the first half of the twentieth century was an important factor distinguishing it from its sister cities on the coast and, ultimately, shaped the context within which Jewish Angelinos would respond to the events of 1942. From the end of the nineteenth century through the 1930s, Los Angeles grew explosively, due in large part to a dramatic migration of white, American-born Protestants from the Midwest, "drawn to the promise of an exotic landscape and determined to transform it into a white refuge."[7] The newcomers' desire for a "homogeneous utopia" transformed a city that had been diverse and relatively inclusive into one that became known for increasing discrimination and exclusionary practices. Jewish Angelinos, who had earlier touted their city's tolerance, found themselves, like their counterparts in other parts of the country but unlike others in the Pacific West, facing exclusion from "corporate directorships, law firms, philanthropies and clubs that in many cases they had helped to establish."[8] Civic groups like the Chamber of Commerce began an "unspoken but recognized policy" of excluding Jews, despite the fact that several Jews were among the founders of that organization. Similarly, elite social and business clubs that had long accepted Jews reversed that practice.[9] In the 1910s and 1920s, Congressman Julius Kahn, Congresswoman Florence Prag Kahn, and California Immigration and Housing Commissioner Simon Lubin were examples of the many California Jews who held appointed or elected office. Yet in Los Angeles during the same years, politics became the province of "white Protestantdom," and Jewish Angelinos came to see bids for elected office as "unrealistic."[10]

Anti-Semitism in the area was not confined to elite efforts to exclude Jews from clubs, civic organizations, and law firms. While Jewish concerns about public expressions of anti-Semitism by national figures like Henry Ford, Father Coughlin, and Charles Lindbergh increased during the 1920s and 1930s, most West Coast Jewish communities prided themselves on the relative absence of overt anti-Semitic activities in their backyards. Yet while its sister communities on the West Coast experienced only muted versions of the wave of anti-Semitism sweeping the country, in southern California, Jews were alarmed by the growth of local, overtly anti-Semitic groups. Among these were the Silver Shirts, whose Pacific Coast Division, based in San Diego, claimed the strongest concentration of members in the country. By 1935 the group had generated sufficient attention to become the subject of investigation by the Special Committee of the House Un-American Activities Committee.[11] In late September of the same year, "thousands of virulently anti-Semites leaflets were distributed throughout Los Angeles." The incident so alarmed journalist and Progressive activist Carey McWilliams that he responded by writing a pamphlet titled *It CAN Happen Here: Active Anti-Semitism in Los Angeles*, in which he linked anti-Semitism and racial prejudice in general to fascism, arguing that "fascism was a means of channeling economic discontent into a hatred of racial minorities."[12] McWilliams warned, "I have come to believe that California is that state of the union which has advanced furthest toward an integrated fascist set-up. For these reasons, the anti-Semitic plotting described in the pamphlet has considerable symptomatic significance."[13]

While white, Protestant Midwesterners dominated the migration to Los Angeles during this period, the surge in Jewish population was, proportionately, even greater.[14] As the other major western Jewish communities stabilized during the interwar years, Los Angeles experienced incredible growth, even during the Depression. The Jewish community had increased from just 2,500 at the turn of the century to 30,000 in 1920. By 1930 its population reached 70,000, and on the eve of the war it stood at 130,000, on its way to passing Chicago as the nation's second largest Jewish community by 1950.[15] This meant that, at a time when other Jewish communities in the region were consolidating and creating institutions like Jewish Community Centers that served and helped to unify the entire community, the Los Angeles community became increasingly complex and lacked a focused center. While working-class and lower-middle-class newcomers concentrated in diverse neighborhoods and created an array of institutions reflecting their East European heritage, the native-born, well-connected Reform community was joined by Hollywood moguls in posh residential areas and elite clubs.

The increase in anti-Semitism in Los Angeles more directly affected the elites than the working class or small business owners. The latter lived in areas like Boyle Heights, among neighbors from diverse ethnic, racial, and religious backgrounds. Boyle Heights residents tended to regard their community as accepting and tolerant, and that atmosphere informed their reactions to wartime developments.[16] Since they had not resided in Los Angeles during its earlier, more tolerant days, and since they were generally not candidates for elite clubs or for positions in top firms or city offices, they were less conscious of the shifting attitudes. Elites, on the other hand, felt the sting of being excluded where they were formerly included.

While groups and individuals from both segments of the population participated in efforts to fight domestic and international anti-Semitism and fascism, the differences in background and experience shaped their responses. In Boyle Heights, the rich organizational structure created by East European Jews included a number of left-wing entities such as labor unions and socialist and communist political groups. Although these organizations shared with elites a desire to fight anti-Semitism, they were unlikely to choose to do so through cooperation with governmental investigative groups like the Dies Committee or the FBI, which heavily targeted leftist groups as "un-American." On the other hand, wealthier, Reform, and native-born Jews tended to share the mainstream American view that communism was a threat to the United States and, therefore, had fewer qualms about cooperating with such investigations.

Issues surrounding the movie industry also shaped the politics of the Los Angeles Jewish community. As concerns about anti-Semitism in America increased after World War I, Jewish organizations hoped to combat this trend by shaping the image of Jews in motion pictures. The Los Angeles Jewish community, and its most visible leader, Rabbi Magnin, played a key role in such efforts. After an outcry in 1927 over *The King of Kings*, which was replete with anti-Semitic images despite Magnin's efforts, the Motion Picture Producers and Distributors Association (MPPDA) invited an "official Jewish representative" to help "improve cinematic representations of Jews." Leon Lewis, who as ADL national secretary in the 1910s had spearheaded its efforts to convince filmmakers to "avoid spreading negative stereotypes of Jews," became the coordinator of the MPPDA-ADL committee.[17]

This group, which was loosely organized in its early years, was spurred to action in 1933, as concerns that had been growing for decades about increasing exclusions in elite circles combined with alarm about the rise of anti-Semitic and fascist groups internationally and locally.[18] In addition to its original concern about negative images of Jews in film, the group was also sensitive to the ways in which anti-Semites might use the historic and continuing strong presence of Jews in the industry to their advantage. For example, the group was concerned about the "morality" issue—the charge that immorality in films was the result of Jewish influence—and it, therefore, worked to convince industry moguls to produce moral films. They also "acted on the seemingly paradoxical notion that films that were explicitly anti-Nazi or pro-Jewish were also dangerous" because they "strengthened the notion that 'the Jews controlled Hollywood.'"[19]

When these efforts were stymied by organizational rivalries, Lewis coordinated their consolidation under one body. Forty representatives of a variety of Los Angeles Jewish organizations including the Anti-Defamation League (ADL) and the American Jewish Committee (AJC) came together to formulate a plan. Among them were some of Los Angeles's most prominent Jewish leaders, including Rabbi Magnin, Marco Newmark, Mendel Silberberg, Judge Isaac Pacht, Judge Harry Hollzer, Judge Lester Roth, and Judge Ben Scheinman.[20] The result was the 1934 formation of the Los Angeles Jewish Community Committee (LAJCC) dedicated to "combating 'un-Americanism' by infiltrating and exposing pro-Nazi and anti-Semitic organizations" and turning over to federal authorities the information uncovered. Many Jewish communities embraced such strategies in the mid to late 1930s across the country.[21] Lewis served as executive secretary to the group from its founding until 1946,[22] and, perhaps due in part to Lewis's ties to the ADL, there were close relations between the two groups. As historian Felicia Herman observes, "philosophically and methodologically, the

LAJCC closely resembled the ADL: it was a group of self appointed notables, largely of central European descent, who preferred a quiet, behind-the-scenes approach to anti-defamation work."[23] Beginning in 1940, the LAJCC and the Southern California ADL shared a suite of offices in Los Angeles.[24]

Lewis brought to the group not only his experience with the ADL but also his close ties to veterans' groups. A disabled World War I veteran, Lewis moved to Los Angeles from Chicago on the advice of his doctors and quickly became active in both the Disabled American Veterans of the World War and the American Legion. His connections with these groups were important for two reasons. First, as Lewis explained in a long memorandum summarizing the work of the LAJCC's publication arm, the News Research Service (NRS), he "was fortunate in having in his possession a great mass of direct information on Nazi activities in the United States and in foreign countries, accumulated during his terms of office as Americanism Chairman for the Department of California of the Disabled American Veterans (DAV) of the World War, and as a member of various Americanism committees of the American Legion." The information, originally intended for a book to be titled *Nazi Fifth Column Activity in America*, was instead used extensively in the group's publication, the *News Letter*.[25] Second, Lewis, believing that it was helpful to have non-Jewish groups take public positions against anti-Semitism, encouraged these veterans' groups to pass resolutions "which would repudiate fascist discrimination policies, recognize fascism's threat to American democracy, and emphasize 'American' values of brotherhood, tolerance and religious equality."[26] Similarly, the LAJCC sometimes used the veterans' groups as conduits for bringing information into the public light. For example, Roy P. Monahan, chairman of the DAV's National Americanism Committee, offered to "publicize any additional material you may have dug up but not printed" about potentially subversive groups when he testified before the Dies Committee.[27] It is notable that the LAJCC's long-serving chair, Mendel Silberberg, was also an active Legionnaire (as well as a "major figure" in the state Republican Party).[28]

Like the ADL and the Survey Committee in San Francisco with which it also cooperated closely, the LAJCC embraced the belief that the fight against anti-Semitism was part of the larger fight against discrimination and prejudice in America. Indeed, by the mid- to late 1930s, all of the major West Coast Jewish communities had publicly embraced the idea of interfaith cooperation in the fight against discrimination in all of its forms. As we have seen, the Jewish press on the West Coast frequently ran stories and opinion pieces expressing support for African Americans and other minorities. LAJCC leaders kept abreast of national and local civil rights and civil liberties issues, subscribing to publications like the Julius Rosenwald Fund's *Trends in Race Relations* and the NAACP's *Negroes* and maintaining files on topics like intercultural education.[29] They cooperated with civil liberties groups like the ACLU, as when they shared with that organization their files on the Ku Klux Klan.[30] A study of civil rights groups in Los Angeles in the 1930s lists the LAJCC along with the local chapters of the NAACP, the JACL, and the Mexican American Community Service Organization (CSO) as "among the most interracially-minded, politically moderate activist organizations in Los Angeles."[31]

While supporting a broad civil rights agenda, the LAJCC leadership tended to be quite cautious about taking public positions on these issues. Despite the fact that the Los Angeles *B'nai B'rith Messenger*, on whose editorial board a number of LAJCC founders and leaders, including Lewis and Silberberg, served, often took editorial positions in support of ethnic and racial minority groups, this elite group privately expressed caution.[32] This caution was shared by counterparts in San Francisco, as evidenced in a February 1941 report from the director of the Southern California ADL, David Coleman, recounting a meeting in San Francisco with Jesse Steinhart and other Bay Area leaders. The aim of the meeting was to discuss whether Jewish leaders in California should take a position on state level legislation and to coordinate any response. The group discussed a series of "civil liberties" bills, mostly introduced "by the Negro Assemblyman, [Augustus] Hawkins," focusing on the question, "Are the bills of sufficient importance for us to draw ourselves into action as Jews?"[33]

The notes on this discussion shed considerable light on the palpable insecurity felt among a small group of well-heeled, well-educated, and well-connected Jewish leaders. In discussing bills such as one that would prohibit questions about race in state employment, participants expressed concern that, if Jews took a public position in favor of the bill, it would have the negative effect of implying that they considered themselves a racial group. Jesse Steinhart urged "that definitely we should not get behind so-called racial bills as Jews and classify ourselves with the colored group." These concerns echo those of late-nineteenth-century southern Jews who, when facing increasing uncertainty about their own status, feared that conflating discrimination against them with discrimination against African Americans might "lend credence to the comparison."[34] While the group seemed to agree that Jews must avoid action that might create the appearance that they were a racial group, they disagreed on strategy. Thus, one participant expressed opposition to a state senate bill aimed at setting up a "committee on race relations" "because he does not want the situation to arise where the Jews will be classified as a race." Steinhart disagreed with this tactic, arguing, "Jews would not come under the provisions of this bill and that opposition on our part might indicate our belief that we were so included." Later, in discussion of anti-discrimination bills passed in New York, Steinhart urged the group to take a position against such legislation, arguing that "it cannot be enforced, and we cannot force Jews down the throats of employers who do not desire to have them."[35]

The anxiety over anti-Semitism apparent in the discussion of the racial and employment bills is not present in the discussion of several bills designed to crack down on subversion. One "creating committees to protect civil liberties and guard against subversive activities" was received positively by the group. Another, requiring registration of secret societies, was characterized as "favorable legislation." Memos such as these reveal that while national and regional Jewish community organizations and newspapers were publicly embracing the fight against discrimination in all of its forms, these elite leaders were anxious that support for civil rights might undermine Jewish status and acceptance. In contrast, embracing the fight against subversion and "un-American" activity presented no such dilemma: Jews could participate actively without endangering their identity as white Americans.

Their anxieties were rooted in concerns about local anti-Semitism. Indeed, as the LAJCC took shape, Lewis soon found that the group was "more interested in their local problems with antisemitism [sic] than with the national anti-defamation agenda."[36] Like its eastern counterparts in the American Jewish Committee and the ADL,[37] the LAJCC developed a network of informants and undercover agents and successfully infiltrated local chapters of groups including the Silver Shirts, the German American Bund, and American First. In 1939, the LAJCC established the News Research Service (NRS) to disseminate the intelligence gathered through its weekly *News Letter*, edited by Lewis's law partner, Joseph Roos, who had come to work for the LAJCC in 1938. Initially, the NRS operated under the LAJCC's Motion Picture Division, but it soon moved, along with Roos, to a new Fact Finding and Community Relations Division. There, Roos spearheaded an expansion of the organization's intelligence efforts. In addition, Roos edited both the *News Letter* and reports written for the Dies Committee.[38]

Roos was well-suited to the task. Born in Austria in 1908, he had been raised in Germany and moved to Chicago in 1927. There, he began work as a translator for a German-language newspaper. By 1929, he was employed as a foreign correspondent, first for Chicago's *Daily News* and then for *The Chicago American*, part of the Hearst chain. Sent to Berlin in 1929, he became aware of the power of Nazism, and on his return to Chicago he "began paying attention to what the Nazis in Chicago were doing." Working with other opponents of Nazism, he created a publication, *The National Free Press*, "to awaken America to the danger over there." Roos's reports caught the attention of *The Chicago American*'s publisher, Roy D. Keehn, a commander in the Illinois National Guard, who placed Roos in contact with Colonel George C. Marshall (future general and secretary of state). Marshall appointed Roos to the Illinois National Guard, where he served as an investigator, with a team of four or five undercover agents, monitoring pro-Nazi activities. This was, according to Roos, "the very first governmental investigation of Nazi activities" in the United States.[39]

Roos first became aware of Leon Lewis when he learned through his investigative work on Nazis in the Midwest that Lewis, who had worked as executive secretary of B'nai B'rith in the Midwest, was identified by local Nazis as an "enemy." After arriving in Los Angeles but prior to coming to work for the LAJCC, Roos performed undercover work for Lewis in the local German community. He recalled in his oral history,

> I became a volunteer, going down with my wife to German House, doing the "Heil Hitler" business, watching them operate, watching even some of the fistfights that took place down there. And I kept reporting to Leon Lewis. He had other operators, most of them coming out of the Disabled American Veterans, who saw in this Nazi business what then was called "un-American."[40]

By the time he began work at the LAJCC, Roos, therefore, had extensive experience both as a journalist and as an investigator.

Printing stories without attribution, the *News Letter* masthead revealed only that it was produced by the NRS at a Los Angeles address, without any indication of a connection to the LAJCC or the Jewish community or attribution to Roos, Lewis, or any other contributor.[41] The *News Letter* was distributed to a variety of allied groups and individuals, including government bodies such as the FBI and the Dies Committee and sympathetic journalists, like the popular radio and print personality Walter Winchell.[42] In addition to sharing information through the *News Letter*, the LAJCC used its contacts to disseminate its stories through a wide variety of media outlets. Journalists who had used information from the *News Letter* for a story frequently contacted the NRS for follow-up stories. For example, George Britt of the *New York World Telegram* wrote to ask for additional information on the Bund, and to thank "my useful, unseen friend, Leon L. Lewis, for the fine, helpful material he has sent me," reporting, "I am guarding it as if it were crown jewels."[43] In 1942, the group was the source of a story on the controversial economist Lawrence Dennis in the leftist New York biweekly, *PM*.[44]

An internal NRS memorandum, compiled in April 1940, and an addendum produced ten months later offered considerable detail on the organization's efforts to distribute its intelligence findings. The sixty-eight-page memorandum traced the history of the *News Letter* and proudly touted its growing influence, noting that "various government offices . . . have come to accept NRS as a reliable source of information," as had "authors, newspapermen, columnists, radio commentators, public speakers, educators, and a number of publications."[45] These documents are filled with testimonials from members of these groups, praising the publication's thorough and informative reports and requesting more information. For example, a letter from Walter Winchell read, "You might like to know that I am using your tips a lot to help fight the lice. If you have anything I can use for my new radio feature 'Some Americans Most Americans Can Do Without,' please send it on."[46]

The reach of the *News Letter* is suggested by these testimonials, submitted by educators and church leaders, journalists and government officials. Although the weekly distribution was limited to one thousand copies, care was taken to circulate it "only among those most actively engaged in creating a sound public opinion."[47] According to Lewis, an incomplete tally indicated that NRS stories had been picked up by eleven columnists and fifty-three news publications or news services, including the Associated Press, United Press, International News Service, *The New York Times*, *The New York Post*, *The New Republic*, *Life*, *Look*, a variety of Los Angeles newspapers, Jewish press outlets, and foreign newspapers in Paris, London, Johannesburg, and Basel.[48] Eleanor Roosevelt's daily column revealed that "she reads the NRS very attentively," and Lewis received a letter from her secretary, expressing the First Lady's appreciation for the publication. When the editor of *Look* wanted to do a story on the German-American Bund, he instructed his Los Angeles representative by telegram, "PLEASE GET IN TOUCH TODAY WITH LEON LEWIS WHOSE OFFICE IS IN YOUR BUILDING AND SEE WHAT HE CAN SUPPLY IN WAY OF BUND DOPE AND PICTURES."[49]

In addition to disseminating information through the press, the LAJCC also acted to ensure that the government was well informed about pro-fascist, anti-Semitic, and un-American activities. By supporting the efforts of the Dies Committee, the FBI, and state-level investigations of subversive groups such as those of the California legislature's Tenney Committee (nicknamed the "Little Dies Committee"), the LAJCC could help to ensure that the government's definition of subversive groups included those whose philosophies were anti-Semitic. The 1940 NRS memorandum and 1941 update provide considerable detail on the extent of the group's government contacts. A chapter titled "NRS Accepted by U.S. Government Officials" in the 1941 document opens with the statement that "investigators of the Federal Bureau of Investigation are going through each NRS issue with a fine tooth comb, breaking down the material presented and starting case reports on each individual and organization mentioned."[50] Among the testimonials were one from FBI Director J. Edgar Hoover and another from Secretary of the Interior Harold Ickes. According to the report, the latter "used a great deal of material from NRS in his many public utterances."[51] The report identified, usually by name, contacts throughout the federal government, including the FBI, the army, naval intelligence, the Senate, and the Departments of Interior and Justice. In September 1941, in response to a request from M. A. McKavitt, director of libraries at the Department of Justice, Roos sent a complete set of *News Letters* for the department's collection and offered additional information from the NRS files.[52]

The closest collaboration was with the Dies Committee. It was natural for the LAJCC to see the committee, which had grown out of the House Special Committee on Un-American Activities, as an ally. The Special Committee was founded in 1934 through the efforts of Congressman Samuel Dickstein of New York, an East European immigrant Jew and the chair of the House Committee on Naturalization and Immigration, to investigate pro-Nazi activities.[53] During the next year, the Special Committee, with Congressman John McCormack as chair and Dickstein as vice-chair, held a series of hearings focusing on Nazi activities in the United States.[54] Dickstein was an important force behind the establishment of HUAC in 1938 under the chairmanship of Martin Dies. Although Dies's primary concern had long been communists, he had "added fascists to his agenda" by 1935, and his committee concentrated its hearings through the late 1930s and into the war years on "the twin threats of communism and Nazism."[55] NRS involvement with the committee began early, when the NRS intervened in an attempt by anti-Semitic groups to use the Dies Committee's investigations of leftist groups to further their anti-Semitic goals. Instead, it reported, the "NRS conducted a well planned campaign, exposing Dies's would-be friends and showing them up for what they really were," resulting in the exposure of various anti-Semitic groups and individuals as Nazi agents and sympathizers.[56] Such outcomes were extremely helpful, as they reinforced the message that groups that were anti-Jewish were also anti-American. In the following years, HUAC investigators proved receptive to—and actively encouraged—NRS contributions to its investigations. Thus, in August 1938, Martin Dies sent a telegram to Leon Lewis asking that he share the "considerable information on Nazism" that the group had gathered and inviting him to appear in person before the committee or to file a brief "to be published in the record."[57] By 1940, according to the NRS memorandum, "A book could be written describing the practical value derived from NRS in the dealings of this office with the Dies Committee and its investigators who were assigned to Los Angeles."[58]

The effort to link the rise of fascism abroad and the activities of groups like the Silver Shirts at home to more genteel forms of anti-Semitism was an important priority for the LAJCC, as it was for other local and national groups fighting anti-Semitism.[59] The Jewish press, in the West as elsewhere in the country, highlighted this link, emphasizing that since fascism was clearly undemocratic and un-American, and since fascist movements explicitly espoused anti-Semitism, anti-Semitism, too, could be labeled undemocratic and un-American. For example, on September 24, 1937, the Los Angeles *B'nai B'rith Messenger* reported that radio preacher Martin Luther Thomas had been forced to resign from a local committee organizing the celebration of the U.S. Constitution. Labeling him "a Fascist and anti-Semite," the paper reminded its readers, "As Jews, we must take note of his rantings not only because of his indirect attack against democratic institutions but because of his vicious propaganda against Jewry generally. . . . The importance of Jewish alignment with liberal forces becomes more and more apparent in the light of contemporary events."[60] The *Messenger* further explained, "What we should bear in mind is not so much the importance of refuting his propaganda, as the necessity of making clear to what few converts he may win . . . *the light in which Thomas is regarded by authorities* and the facts about his record"[61] [emphasis added]. Helping both the press and the government to publicly identify subversion among anti-Semitic groups and individuals not only had the tangible effect of curtailing their activities but also elevated Jewish efforts to expose these groups from self-interested defense efforts into patriotic acts.

The files of the LAJCC are testimony to its vigorous efforts to infiltrate suspect groups and to their close collaboration with the government in investigating and exposing those groups. They contain scores of boxes filled with intelligence on a wide array of organizations and individuals, including reports filed by informants and agents identified only by code names. Office contact files document frequent and cooperative relationships with a wide variety of government agents.

The overwhelming majority of these files focus on local pro-fascist groups, including European immigrant groups (such as the German American Bund or local Italian American pro-fascist organizations) and home-grown nativist and anti-Semitic groups like the KKK. The information on these groups was supplied by a small group of "undercover investigators" supervised by Roos, who himself also sometimes posed as a German sympathizer and attended the meetings of pro-Nazi groups.[62] The sheer volume of this material conveys quite clearly that organizations that were explicitly anti-Semitic were, by far, the greatest concern of the group. Yet the coupling of anti-Semitism with fascism and, more generally, un-Americanism, led them to investigate some local groups that were not anti-Semitic but whose actions made them vulnerable to the charge of being "un-American." For example, after the American entry into the war, the group began keeping files on pacifists, including the Absolutist War Objector Society and the American Friends Service Committee.[63] These files consist of clippings and leaflets, without any commentary or indication that infiltrators or informants were used against them by the LAJCC. Such meager files, in contrast to virtual mountains of material on the KKK or the German American Bund, suggest that the LAJCC was only mildly interested in the activities of pacifist groups. Still, the fact that pacifists would be subjects of investigation at all is indicative of a familiar pattern of the expansion of the definition of "subversive" in times of crisis.

The LAJCC saw the NRS monitoring of these groups as tightly linked to its more conventional civil rights work. Once the United States entered the war, these activities were, in turn, blended with civil defense efforts as the group "began working with patriotic organizations, veterans' groups, interfaith religious organizations and local schools and colleges to combat rising bigotry and discrimination."[64] The need for unity in the face of foreign threats led the Roosevelt administration to tie the campaign against bigotry to the fight against fascism. Faced with a threatened march on Washington by African Americans in 1941, Roosevelt issued an executive order establishing the Fair Employment Practices Committee, which protected African Americans, Jews, and other minorities from discrimination in the war-related industries. Like African Americans who called for a "Double V" campaign to fight both the fascists abroad and discrimination at home, Jewish groups like the LAJCC believed that the fight against anti-Semitism at home was inextricably tied to the international war against fascism and Nazism.

As the relationship between the LAJCC and government investigative bodies grew closer, it sometime put a strain on the organization's ties with former allies. Liberal groups and individuals shared LAJCC concerns about anti-Semitism and prejudice and could join together in exposing and condemning the KKK or the Silver Shirts. However, individuals like well-known California Progressive Carey McWilliams and organizations like the ACLU did not share the LAJCC's comfort in working with the Dies Committee, which targeted leftists for their political beliefs and had accused the ACLU of being controlled by Communists.[65] Although, according to ACLU historian Judy Kutulas, it appears that there was, by 1939, "an informal or tacit deal between Dies and ACLU representatives promising the Union a public 'cleansing' if the group got rid of its Communists,"[66] by early 1941, the ACLU was publicly urging the discontinuation of the Dies Committee, arguing that it was violating the rights of individuals to free speech and assembly. Interestingly, as Kutulas demonstrates, there were sharply divided opinions within the ACLU on this question, as the increasing contingent of liberals within the union "opposed censorship but were troubled when fascists asked for the same rights as Communists or Catholics or Democrats."[67] Despite their disagreements, the LAJCC maintained a cooperative relationship with the ACLU on other matters during the war years. For example, after announcing that it would not represent individuals who were actually disloyal, the ACLU used the NRS to conduct background checks on potential defendants. In February 1943, Joseph Roos of the NRS received a letter from the ACLU national secretary thanking him for his assistance: "I am most appreciative of all the help you have given me in all these cases. I believe I informed you in the beginning it is my task to discover whether the defendant who appeals to us for legal assistance has been cooperating with or working on behalf of the enemy."[68]

Just as some in the ACLU objected to working with the Dies Committee, there were those within the LAJCC who had qualms about cooperating with the American Legion, even though several leaders, including Lewis and Silberberg, were active Legionnaires. As Roos recalled, "The fact is that many Jews just didn't feel comfortable in the American Legion. It just didn't fit into their way of thinking." Roos himself saw the Legion as "authoritarian" and even "leaning towards fascism" but not anti-Semitic. The Legion's work in opposition to Nazism, justified for Roos (and apparently for others in the LAJCC leadership) continued engagement with them. As he later explained, "The local Americanism Committee of the American Legion was intelligent enough to understand that Nazism . . . national socialism . . . is as much a menace to the United States as the enemy whom they had identified long ago . . . 'communism.' And because they were intelligent enough to understand that, it was possible to do this sort of work with them."[69]

Similarly, the LAJCC, whose efforts to expose the Silver Shirts had benefited tremendously from the Dies Committee's public hearings, disagreed strongly with the ACLU's call for the committee's dissolution and continued to cooperate closely with the committee throughout 1941 and into the war years. In April of that year, an internal report noted that James Steedman, an investigator for the Dies Committee, had requested that the LAJCC summarize all of its information about "Nazi and other subversive propaganda activities in Southern California." When the LAJCC indicated a need to question witnesses in order to fully follow their leads, Steedman assured them that he had "full authority" to subpoena. In addition, Steedman assured the group that their report would "be printed as a *Dies Committee* document as presented to him by the Committee [LAJCC]" [emphasis in original]. That summer, the committee asked the LAJCC to check 1,200 names of individuals under investigation against their "card file index." The names were checked and the LAJCC provided short reports on individuals of interest.[70]

The strong relationship with the Dies Committee was extremely beneficial for the LAJCC. The Dies Committee's heavy reliance on the group's reports and tips significantly advanced the LAJCC campaign to expose the fascist and anti-Semitic groups that it considered dangerous. As early as February 1941, the NRS was able to claim that "if one were to watch the various steps undertaken by the Dies Committee, it would become apparent soon that many of its moves were inspired by News Research Service, which is read regularly by members and investigators of the Committee."[71] In several instances, as suggested by Steedman's 1941 promise to publish their report on Nazi propaganda "as presented," the LAJCC's own materials were published as the work of the Dies Committee, giving them the weight of a congressional investigation while allowing the organization to remain out of the public eye. Certainly, these benefits played an important role in the group's decision to continue to work with the Dies Committee despite the ACLU's public condemnation of it and their own discomfort with the excesses of the committee, and its chair, Martin Dies.

As early as 1940, Leon Lewis had voiced concerns about Dies in correspondence with California Congressman Jerry Voorhis, a member of the committee, writing, "I was somewhat appalled at some of the statements in the first instalment [sic] of Congressman Dies's articles in Liberty Maga- zine." Lewis expressed specific concerns about Dies's very sweeping defini- tion of Marxists, including "not merely Communists and fellow travelers, but all Socialists and even liberals—or those at least whom the Congress- man thinks are not 'well-intentioned.'" Voorhis agreed with Lewis, writing, "Frankly, I have some of the same misgivings as you about the methods sometimes employed."

Lewis's continued cooperation with Dies indicates that, like Voorhis, who voted to continue the committee's work because "many of its findings have been of unquestioned importance," he believed that the benefits of expos- ing fascists, subversives, and anti-Semites outweighed concerns about meth- ods.[72] In a January 30, 1942, memo that he asked be kept "strictly con- trolled," Lewis explained his view, writing critically of the ACLU condemnation of HUAC, and arguing that the problem of subversion

> is not one that can be solved by academic discussions of the limits of liberty. This is the stock-in-trade of the American Civil Liberties Union, which has been in the forefront in defending the license displayed by the subversive agi- tators. Noble may be a crackpot but so was Hitler. He may be psychopathic but dangerous psychopaths cannot invoke the Bill of Rights to secure release from an institution.
>
> As I see it, the fundamental fallacy in the entire situation derives from the un- realistic and impractical viewpoint of those who consider that the slightest in- fringement of the constitutional guarantee of freedom of speech and assembly would lead inevitably to dictatorship. The fallacy in this reasoning, as I see it, is that it does not recognize the established principle of police power to curb license and, second, that unity of purpose in the community, particularly in war time, is equally as important as unbridled freedom of speech to prevent dictatorship; for where there is no such unity the essential need for dictator- ship becomes obvious and the route to it much shorter. Civil libertarians will quarrel with this viewpoint, and would permit matters to become progressively worse until we might become entangled in a spiral of repressions that could end only in tyranny.[73]

While he did not quote or cite it, Lewis's argument closely paralleled the views of liberal theologian Reinhold Niebuhr that appeared in an article in *The Nation* on January 24, 1942, and that was filed together with Lewis's cor- respondence on this issue. Niebuhr argued that the debate over civil liberties during wartime divided "absolutists," who "refuse to countenance any re- striction of liberty of expression and who are inclined to hold to their posi- tion without regard to the political consequences which may flow from it," and "relativists," who argue that "freedom of speech should be withheld from those political groups which intend to destroy liberty." Niebuhr explained his "broad agreement with the relativists," making the case for "a flexibility in tactics which does justice to momentary contingencies while maintaining an inflexibility in strategy which does justice to the basic principles of human society."[74] Niebuhr's article is an important reminder that the position that Lewis outlined on the question of civil liberties during wartime was one that was broadly accepted, not only within the government but also by many liberals, including a strong faction within the ACLU. Niebuhr himself had a history as a pacifist and socialist, although he had become, by the early 1940s, a critic of pacifism and a strong supporter of the "just war" against fascism and Nazism. It is in the context of this position on national security and civil liberties that the LAJCC's cooperation with government agencies to investigate alleged subversion, and particularly its role in building the case against Japanese Americans, must be understood. Given Lewis's acute awareness of the dire peril that the Nazi regime posed for European Jews, it is not surprising that he embraced Niebuhr's relativist position.

For the first several years of its existence, the LAJCC's efforts were focused on explicitly anti-Semitic groups, and there is no evidence that the organization took any interest in Japan or the Japanese American community. The first sign of concern came in 1939, when the NRS *News Letter* reported on contacts between local Japanese and German American Bund agents.[75] After Japan entered into the Tripartite Pact with Germany and Italy in September 1940, the *News Letter* published several issues focusing prominently on the alliance between Japan and Nazi Germany and painting pro-Japanese propaganda as largely the product of Nazi agents and sympathizers.[76] As war with Japan began to be seen as a real possibility by the summer of 1941, the group began publishing reports on local Japanese American groups as part of their more general coverage of fascists, subversives, and un-American activities.

During the summer of 1941, the NRS published two editions of its *News Letter* focusing specifically on subversive activity within the Japanese American community. The July 9, 1941, edition centered on claims that while Japanese language schools in California publicly claimed to "stress Americanism" the NRS investigation "revealed the exact opposite to be the case." The five-page report asserted that the schools used two sets of textbooks: "One set, usually shown to curious Occidentals, contains no objectionable text whatsoever. . . . However, practically every page of the other set preaches loyalty to Japan and treason against the American government." The report went on to detail NRS efforts to obtain the second set and presented lengthy quotations from it, demonstrating its inculcation of Japanese unity and superiority and loyalty to the Emperor. After students' graduation from language school, the *News Letter* claimed that they continued to be inundated with "an unending flow of pro-Japanese and anti-American literature" through books and lectures from Japanese officials. One such book, quoted in the report, highlighted the importance of the Nisei in pro-Japanese propaganda efforts in response to the situation in China and linked that role to the success of the language schools: "Nisei always take the leadership. In the world where English language newspapers and magazines are most influential, the Nisei are in an excellent position to do their share. We have seen to it that they shall be well prepared for their task." The *News Letter* also alleged that the Los Angeles Japanese American newspaper, the *Rafu Shimpo*, had a dual policy that paralleled that in the language schools: while the English section "reeks of patriotic sweetness," the Japanese portions of the paper encouraged loyalty to Japan, going so far as to advocate creation of a "Nisei oversea division," aimed at helping to "accomplish the aim of the Fatherland, the establishment of a Greater Asia." In summarizing the issue, the *News Letter* claimed, the "NRS has shown how American citizens of Japanese ancestry are taught to be loyal to the Land of the Rising Sun."[77]

The following edition, on July 16, 1941, continued the *News Letter*'s examination of alleged Japanese American disloyalty, turning to the examination of a "spy manual for Japanese-American Quislings." Here it was reported that a book titled *The Triple Alliance and the Japanese-American War*, published in Tokyo the previous year, laid out a strategy for war with the United States and the role that Japanese Americans were to play in that war. According to this report, Japanese military officials had toured Japanese American communities on the Pacific Coast, holding secret meetings and circulating the book. The aim of this activity, according to the *News Letter*, was "to inspire courage among sabotage and espionage agents, and to recruit new men for the Japanese-American Trojan Horse Brigade."[78] Despite the secrecy involved, the *News Letter* reported that it had successfully obtained a copy of the book that was "a well-camouflaged textbook for Japanese espionage." The *News Letter* then presented the table of contents and a number of excerpts from the book, revealing details about Japan's plan for an attack on the United States, occupation of Hawaii, and establishment of control over the Panama Canal. The result of a war between the United States and the Triple Alliance would be that "only the flag of the sun, which symbolizes our nation, would fly over the Pacific. On the Atlantic, the swastika, which also symbolizes the sun and life, will be active with might. In addition, the meaningful flag of Italy would flash."[79]

The same edition of the newsletter linked the messages of *The Triple Alliance and the Japanese-American War* to similar messages allegedly appearing in the Japanese language version of *Rafu Shimpo* and in other books distributed by Japanese authorities among Japanese Americans. These books and articles encouraged "Nipponese faith in the might of the Mikado's Empire" and presented the Japanese view of contemporary world conflicts. Finally, readers were reminded that, to fulfill her imperialistic goals, "Japan relies not only on her military arms and her Axis allies, but also upon Japanese-American Quislings who will gladly volunteer."[80]

Correspondence provides a rare and revealing glimpse into the attitudes toward Japanese Americans that informed these issues of the *News Letter*. On July 10, 1941, a "very rough first draft for next week's News Research Service story" was sent to Dies Committee investigator James Steedman along with a letter, likely written by Lewis.[81] After warning that the report was still in need of editing, the writer urged Steedman to send it on to the Dies Committee's Washington office, explaining,

> Hope the office in Washington sees the significance in this and goes to town on it. . . . I think it should be pointed out to the people in Washington that Shintoism calls for a kind of loyalty to the family which is unknown to the Occidental. The family comes before everything else. . . .
>
> The Japanese government takes advantage of this fact in the following manner: If a Japanese-American is not ready to tow the mark, pressure is brought to bear upon his relatives in Japan. In most cases this pressure is in financial form. Then the Japanese is told that the pressure will stop if he gets in touch with his relative in America and begs him to do as he is told by the Japs. Family loyalty being more than any of our Ten Commandments, the Japanese-American usually falls in line and that is the way the Japs have succeeded in building up a tremendous force which they can use at a moment's notice.

The writer concluded by suggesting that Steedman call in Kilsoa [sic] Haan[82] and "spend many hours with him and make him talk."

Examination of this letter—a very rare case in which an LAJCC leader elaborated on the *News Letter*'s coverage of Japanese Americans—helps to reveal how anti-Nikkei accusations were reconciled with the group's vision of themselves and their organization as antiracist. The repeated use of the term "Japs" suggests that this racial epithet was commonly used within the organization, as it was in general in California. However, the letter writer's attempt to explain why Japanese Americans might engage in subversive activity does not employ biological or racial arguments. Rather, he argues that Japanese Americans are vulnerable to blackmail by the Japanese government. On the one hand, Japanese are stigmatized as completely foreign (possessing "a kind of loyalty to the family which is unknown to the Occidental") but, on the other, potential subversives are described not as people who respond to biologically based loyalties to the Emperor but as individuals coerced through pressure.

While the letter writer's hope that the Dies Committee "goes to town on this" conveys his enthusiasm about NRS efforts to expose Japanese American subversion, it is not clear where these allegations originated. Much of the material for the exposes of pro-Nazi groups came from the NRS's own covert agents who infiltrated meetings. It seems unlikely that similar methods were used here, both because of the difficulty of passing unnoticed at a

Nikkei gathering and because the reports published in the *News Letter* focus on printed materials rather than on accounts of meetings. In addition, there are no files focusing on Japanese American language schools, the JACL, the *Rafu Shimpo*, or other Nikkei organizations among the LAJCC files on "investigated groups."[83] This suggests that, unlike editions of the *News Letter* focusing on anti-Semitic or pro-Nazi groups, these issues were not based on information gathered by the LAJCC's network of informants and agents, although there is some evidence to suggest that the group employed translators to study the local Japanese press.[84] The use of materials translated from Japanese suggests cooperation with groups like the Office of Naval Intelligence, with which the LAJCC worked closely and whose Los Angeles staff included officers with Japanese language skills.[85]

In addition, there is evidence that at least some of the information on Japanese nationals was obtained from foreign (Allied) governments. For example, Joseph Roos revealed in an oral history that, "the day after Pearl Harbor I turned over to the intelligence agencies a complete list of all the Japanese agents in the country." He explained that he did not develop the list. Rather, it was given to him by a British intelligence officer who had been forced to leave the country several months before. Because foreign agents were not legally allowed to operate in the United States, "he [the British agent] couldn't turn it over to his allies . . . [because officially] he isn't here. That's where the list came from."[86] There is also correspondence in the file that indicates that Roos made an unsuccessful effort to gather materials for the July 1941 editions from the Chinese Information Service in Washington, D.C.[87] Several months later, he wrote to both the Chinese Embassy and the China Emergency Relief Committee in New York, requesting information on Japanese propaganda.[88] While these particular efforts did not yield information, it is possible that intelligence was gathered from other, similar groups.

Furthermore, the specific allegations about the language schools, as well as the more general accusations of Japanese American disloyalty, had a long history in California. Exclusionists, frustrated that alien land laws were circumvented by Issei who passed land ownership to their American-born children, had been painting the Nisei population as disloyal as part of their campaign to revoke Nisei citizenship. Since the 1920s, exclusionists had "manufactured" a "Japanese language school 'problem'" to support their argument "that Nisei educated as Japanese subjects were unworthy of American citizenship, and thus they should be ineligible to own their own piece of California land."[89] Such allegations led to the passage of a 1921 law that placed the language schools under state control, requiring testing and licensing of teachers and administrators, imposing a limit on hours of operation, and giving California's superintendent of public education "full control over the course of study, textbooks, and the right to issue and revoke teaching permits."[90] Thus, popular pro-exclusion groups, including the American Legion, the Native Sons of the Golden West, and the Native Daughters of the Golden West, had been circulating accusations similar to those appearing in the NRS *News Letters* for decades. Given Lewis's strong connection to the American Legion and the similarities to materials in the *News Letter*, it seems likely that it was the source of at least some of the *News Letter* allegations.

While the *News Letter* did not focus on the Japanese issue again between the July issues and Pearl Harbor, it did offer support when Senator Guy Gillette of Iowa, in a speech focusing primarily on the dangers of Japanese subversion, called for a special Senate investigation of activity by Axis powers to organize aliens and dual citizens. Within days of Gillette's speech, titled "Japanese Activities in the U.S.," Lewis wrote to the senator, offering "to place at your disposition our files and records, which cover the results of several years investigation of foreign propaganda techniques and foreign propaganda agents."[91]

After the attack on Pearl Harbor, the NRS quickly put together a special edition of the *News Letter* based on their previously published reports. Correspondence in the files makes clear that a decision was made not to distribute this issue, dated December 10, 1941. However, it was shared with a few individuals during the early months of 1942.[92] Because it aimed to consolidate the previous NRS investigations of Japanese Americans, it provides a useful summary of these activities. While this issue of the *News Letter* focused some attention on pro-Nazi and other groups, the bulk of it was devoted to reminding readers of the NRS's pioneering work in exposing Japanese American disloyalty and examining the German-Japanese alliance. "Since its inception," the *News Letter* claimed, "NRS has collected information on pro-Japanese activities in this area." Readers' attention was called to a May 10, 1939, NRS report on meetings between Fritz Kuhn, a leader of the German American Bund, and his "Japanese allies" in the Los Angeles area. Presumably drawn from informant reports, the story detailed visits between "Kuhn and Y. Hajaschi, Japanese undercover agent, whose address is 831 No. Townsend Ave., Los Angeles," claiming frequent visits back and forth between German-American Bund leaders and Hajaschi. The *News Letter* followed the reprint of the 1939 article with a commentary on the "parallels existing between Nazi and Japanese activities here," referring to fundraising efforts and other activities in support of the German and Japanese governments. In detailing contacts among pro-German groups, isolationists (specifically America First), and pro-Japanese groups, another article characterized some "Japanese-American citizens" as having "loyalty to the God-Emperor [that] is greater than their love for America." Several articles examined Japanese and German war goals and discussed the implications of their alliance.

The *News Letter* did moderate its accusations against Japanese Americans by noting that "the majority of the Japanese element is loyal to the United

States" and informing readers that loyal Nisei had established a new, loyal, English-language newspaper and a coalition called the "Anti-Axis Committee of the Southern District Council of the Japanese American Citizens League," which had pledged its loyalty and dedication to an American victory. Despite these statements, which appeared in one paragraph on page 7 of an eight-page edition, the thrust of the *News Letter* was clearly in the opposite direction. Pages 4 and 5 consisted of a spread displaying the front pages of six previous editions of the *News Letter*, all focusing on alleged actual or potential Japanese disloyalty. In addition to the July 9 and July 16 editions, the spread included front pages headlined "Japa-Nazis Over Hawaii" (October 1940), "Aiding and [Abet]ting the Japanese!" (December 1940), and "Historical Distortions Betray Pro-Japan Propagandists" (August 1941), and one with the lead story "Axis Aided by Japa-Nazi Auxiliaries in the United States" (date not visible). In addition to reminding its readers of this previously published material, the editor added, "Findings by NRS with regard to Japanese propaganda activities were published from time to time. . . . However, information which was of greater value to the authorities was withheld from publication. NRS will continue practicing self-imposed censorship."[93] (See Figure 4.1)

The extent of the impact of the newsletter's allegations within the Jewish community is difficult to determine. There is no direct evidence that the *News Letter*, which was distributed to leading Jewish organizations like the Anti-Defamation League, influenced their position nationally. Locally in Los Angeles, where the ADL and the LAJCC had very close relations and even shared a suite of offices, there is some evidence of a direct influence. George Knox Roth, a Quaker and civil rights activist who was active in defending the Nikkei during the war, told historian Bill Hosokawa in an interview that

> he and his anti-Axis Committee friends were astonished to find the Anti-Defamation League among those hostile to Japanese Americans. When Roth investigated he found the ADL, heavily financed by Jews in the movie industry, had made extensive records of anti-Semitic and pro-Nazi activity in California. As part of the project ADL had employed translators to study the Japanese press in Los Angeles and San Francisco over a period of several years. They discovered the Japanese sections supported Japan's aggression in Asia whereas the English sections took a strong pro-American stand. This apparent schizophrenia was interpreted by ADL as evidence of the unreliability of the entire Japanese American population, and this judgment led to the decision to support their removal from the West Coast.[94]

Although Roth was clearly conflating the ADL with the LAJCC/CRC, as well as overstating the Los Angeles ADL's support for removal (they did not publicly endorse the policy), his account is suggestive.

Figure 4.1. The center spread of the *News Letter* on December 10, 1941 featured the News Research Service's coverage of the Japanese issue. CRC/2 205,2, Urban Archives Center, Delmar T. Oviatt Library, California State University Northridge.

While direct evidence of the influence of the *News Letter* on Jewish communal attitudes toward Japanese Americans is scanty, its broader influence is unmistakable. The *News Letter's* claim of close cooperation with authorities is strongly supported by archival evidence. Nowhere is this clearer than in the group's work with the Dies Committee in support of its "Report on Japanese Activities," released on February 28, 1942. The NRS played a pivotal role in shaping the report, which was initially referred to as a "White Paper" but ultimately came to be known as the "Dies Yellow Paper." On January 4, 1942, Roos sent a five-page letter to Dies Committee investigator Steedman. Roos began, "In the following, I am giving you a few pointers for the Japanese White Paper. . . ." Roos then went on to frame the broad outline that the report should take, explaining which parts should be concise and which should be "painstakingly detailed in order to overwhelm the reader with the mass of 'evidence'." For example, he explained the importance of dividing the report into "as many chapters as possible," with "many forceful and far-reaching subtitles, so that certain parts of the Table of Contents will immediately appeal to those newspapermen and magazine writers through whom the desired publicity can be achieved." He suggested that "photostatic copies and photographs" ought to be used in sections that might otherwise be "too dry," and he emphasized that "wherever possible—parallels should be drawn between the German and Japanese technique." He then went on to provide twenty-four specific points to include in the document, often noting NRS stories and those in other newspapers that might be used for reference. Roos assured Steedman that "all the Japanese material published in the NRS Bulletins can be used and is authentic" and suggested that the *News Letter* stories would provide examples of "dramatic presentation of dry material."[95] Finally, Roos made clear that he would be happy to provide further assistance on the project and reminded Steedman that "everything will be kept strictly confidential."

Steedman clearly welcomed Roos's offer and, in the weeks leading up to the release of the report, he repeatedly visited the LAJCC/CRC offices. The record of executive office contacts indicates that on January 15, 1942, "Steedman (Dies Committee) wants further details on 'Japan's Progress,' quotations which were turned over to him for use in the Dies Yellow Paper re: Japanese Fifth column activities."[96] The next day, the record noted that an item in the committee's report "is based on the old NRS expose of the Japanese Language Schools." Similarly, on January 21, a notation was made that "Steedman (Dies Com) wants dope on Shuji Fujii (editor of 'Do Ho' [sic], Japanese language newspaper). Also wanted information on P.D. Perkins. Information on both individuals given."

The completed Dies Committee report reflected this close cooperation. The October 1940 *News Letters* were "reprinted, word for word, in Martin Dies Yellow Book as the product of Dies own investigation," according to an investigator working on the Japanese American Evacuation and Resettlement Study in 1943.[97] Several sections, including those titled "Japanese Language Schools" and "Pro-Axis Propaganda in Japanese Publications" included strings of paragraphs reproduced verbatim from the July 1941 issues of the *News Letter*.[98] While, as we have seen, the committee refused to reveal its sources, the key role of the LAJCC/CRC and its NRS was acknowledged privately, as shown in a February notation: "Lunch with Steedman (Dies Com). Says in writing Yellow Paper for Dies Committee he followed our outline. Returned material loaned to him. Very grateful for our help."[99]

The Dies Yellow Paper brought the NRS reports on the Japanese and Japanese American community to a far broader audience than the original *News Letter* editions had reached and generated widespread press coverage.[100] Released during the Tolan Committee Hearings, the Yellow Paper clearly had an impact on the testimony. For example, Dr. George Gleason, executive secretary for the county-appointed Los Angeles Committee for Church and Community Cooperation, quoted the Dies report to support his statement on the potential for a fifth-column attack in California. Gleason testified that all of the members of his group, which included Jewish leaders Rabbi Edgar Magnin of the Wilshire Boulevard Temple, Rabbi Morton Bauman of Temple Israel of Hollywood, and Mrs. Isaac Pelton of the National Council of Jewish Women, had studied the Dies report.[101] Magnin, who had close connections to the LAJCC and had been among its founders, was likely already familiar with much of the material in the Dies report from the *News Letter*—a publication that Magnin considered "thoroughly reliable."[102] That Gleason and his organization, considered allies by the Fair Play Committee,[103] presented a statement to the Tolan Committee that was so influenced by the Yellow Paper is a testament to its power. The report also, as we have seen, found its way into the testimony of California Attorney General Earl Warren and General DeWitt's 1943 *Final Report*.

Because of the Yellow Paper's broad influence, the LAJCC's contacts with the Dies Committee have particular significance. Yet the group's cooperation with authorities in the months after Pearl Harbor extended well beyond the Dies Committee. During the period from January to April 1942, for which a listing of "office contacts" is available, the LAJCC/CRC was visited, in many cases repeatedly, not only by members of the Dies Committee but also by FBI agents, naval intelligence officers,[104] members of California's Tenney Committee, and even foreign agents from Allied countries.[105] While some of these individuals, like British intelligence officer Alexander, wanted information on German or Italian subversives,[106] many of them, having seen the July issues of the *News Letter* focusing on Japanese Americans, were interested in following up on this information. For example, on January 15, the Chinese consul stopped by to get information on P. D. Perkins, a University of Southern California expert on Japan and "distributor of pro-Japanese propaganda literature," whom he recalled reading about in one of the July *News Letter*s. Similarly, a January 19 entry notes, "McCarty (FBI) wants copy of Japanese book 'Japan-U.S. War,' referred to in NRS of July 16, 1941. He had a letter from Washington instructing him to get the book." A few days later, on January 23, Captain Murray, a naval intelligence officer, came by looking for the same book and was told to get it directly from Agent McCarty. On March 16, FBI agent Mason stopped by, wanting "further information on Japanese school books, story printed in NRS last July. Additional details, which were on hand when story was first written but not used, turned over to him. Also various other important Japanese matters discussed and brought to his attention."

The group kept a close eye on state-level investigations as well as federal ones. When Tom Cavitt of the Tenney Committee visited the NRS office on February 19 with news that Perkins had been "subpoenaed as a friendly witness to speak on Japanese ideology, etc." LAJCC/CRC officials "tipped him off as to Perkins being a registered Japanese agent and gave him background which was much appreciated." Two days later, they gave the same tip to British intelligence agent Alexander and discussed with him potential questions to put to Perkins during his testimony. On February 24, when a *Los Angeles Examiner* reporter called for "inside dope on the Tenney hearings," he was also given tips about Perkins.

Correspondence files further reveal contact with individuals within the Justice Department during the winter of 1942. For example, Leon Lewis sent a copy of the December 10, 1941, issue of the *News Letter* to William Cherin in the Special Defense Unit (SDU) at the Department of Justice. The unit, initially called the Neutrality Laws Unit, was established in the attorney general's office in 1940. In 1942, when the War Division within the Justice Department was established, the SDU became the Special War Policies Unit. The group dealt with subversive activities and the registration of foreign agents. Just before Pearl Harbor, Lewis had sent Cherin the run of *News Letter*s that began in July, noting that the publication "may be of interest in view of your present special assignment."[107] In sending the December 10 issue, Lewis explained that it had not been distributed in order to give "[the] benefit of every doubt . . . to those who had previously indicated a pro-Axis bias. We did not want to imply, by anything we published, that there was a possibility of continued disloyalty among these groups." Three months later, Lewis said, the group had concluded, "from the information which we have continued to gather, even though publication was suspended, we are convinced that there is almost as great a need for the *News Letter* today as there was before Pearl Harbor."[108] Correspondence also indicates that Lewis loaned the NRS material on Japanese language schools to FBI agent Richard Hood, who directed the FBI office in Los Angeles.[109] In a letter acknowledging receipt of the returned materials, Lewis expressed satisfaction that

"in his testimony before the Tenney Committee Togo Tanaka admitted that
the Japanese language columns of the RAFU SHIMPO did contain subversive material," as had been alleged by the NRS.[110]

While the flurry of attention to potential Japanese American subversion
subsided within a few months, as the Japanese American community was
forced out of the area and into concentration camps, communication with
authorities continued. Although the focus in 1942 and 1943 remained on potentially subversive Italian and German groups, Japanese Americans were occasionally referenced. In December 1942, for example, Roos wrote to Pat Horgan at the Los Angeles FBI office, apparently in response to a request for
information, to report that a local woman teaching at the Manzanar relocation camp was a conduit for communication between Japanese in the camp
and "former Nazis and Isolationists" in the area.[111] Both Lewis and Roos were
in touch with Victor W. Nielsen in the Office of Assistant Chief of Staff in the
Civil Affairs Division of the Western Defense Command at the Presidio in San
Francisco. In September 1943, Roos and Nielsen corresponded about the difficulties of coordinating information about Japanese Americans. While Roos's
letters make clear that he was primarily interested in discussing the case of an
alleged Nazi supporter, he did inquire of Nielsen, "I notice that you are not
Chief of the special Japanese research section. Does that mean you have nothing further to do with matters of the type which you handled before? If so,
who would be the person in your office with whom I should deal in the future, or would you prefer that I route everything through you so that you can
pass it on." In the same letter, Roos related that he had met the previous day
with James Steedman of the Dies Committee regarding a woman with alleged
ties to Japanese groups. "I would suggest that you write to him in care of the
Federal Building, Los Angeles, and ask for his cooperation, although I would
prefer that you do not indicate that you are doing so at my suggestion."[112]

Roos's desire to remain hidden is reflected in many LAJCC actions—most
obviously in the decision not to identify the organization as the home of
the News Research Service anywhere in the *News Letter*. Although the office
files make clear that many people, both from the government and from private organizations with whom they cooperated, knew exactly where to find
the News Research Service, the LAJCC/CRC succeeded in remaining hidden
from the public, even during Marcantonio's efforts in Congress to expose
the Dies Committee. Similarly, an investigator from the Japanese American
Evacuation and Resettlement Study sent to interview Roos in 1943 indicated that his "large Jewish law firm" operated the NRS.[113] Forty years later,
when Roos was interviewed for an oral history, he was remarkably candid
about many of these events but he repeatedly asked that the tape be turned
off when discussing others.[114]

The deployment of a behind-the-scenes strategy can be seen not only in
contacts concerning the group's investigations of potential subversives but

also in more straightforward defense work. For example, files from the winter of 1942 show that the group was involved in the effort to ensure that German Jewish immigrants—also classified as "enemy aliens" at the start of the war—would not be subject to undue restrictions or evacuation orders. Some Jewish individuals and organizations, like the Jewish Club of '33, testified at the Los Angeles hearings of the Tolan Committee that German Jews were misclassified as "enemy aliens."[115] In contrast, the LAJCC/CRC rejected this option and instead relied on personal contacts through private channels.

The LAJCC/CRC had contacts with groups like the Jewish Club of 1933 and was involved behind the scenes but refrained from public identification with their testimony. Both Leon Lewis and Dr. Maurice Karpf, who served on the LAJCC and was executive director of both the LA Jewish Welfare Federation and the Jewish Community Council,[116] were members of the newly formed Special Advisory Committee (also called the Special Service Committee) to the Los Angeles Émigré Service. Records of a February 16, 1942, meeting of the Special Advisory Committee show the efforts being made to coordinate testimony for the upcoming Tolan Committee hearings, as the group met with representatives of two German refugee groups, one led by Dr. Felix Guggenheim and the other, the Jewish Club of 33, led by Dr. Bernstein. They also indicated that they were coordinating with counterparts in San Francisco. At the meeting, "a difficult situation involving ex-patriotes [sic] was thoroughly explored in the light of intensified anti-Japanese agitation and prospective additional restrictions."[117] Ultimately, the two refugee groups agreed to present their position jointly before the Tolan Committee. In addition, the group learned that both the Beverly Hills Chamber of Commerce and the Los Angeles Realty Board had adopted resolutions demanding "the immediate removal of all enemy aliens." However, once they were informed of the implications of their resolutions for non-Japanese "enemy aliens," they changed their resolutions so that they would refer "only to Japs."[118]

While LAJCC/CRC leaders Lewis and Karpf worked with the Special Advisory Committee to coordinate testimony, they remained in the shadows. On February 27, 1942, just one week before the Tolan Hearings were to begin in Los Angeles, "Tolan Committee Investigating Enemy Alien Problems" was the first item of business on the agenda of the CRC's biweekly meeting.[119] Just a week earlier, an internal memo recounting a conversation with Jesse Steinhart of San Francisco's Survey Committee asserted that it "would be a mistake for any German Jewish refugee to approach General Dewitt [sic] with a view to special treatment and consideration." Instead, "Jesse undertook to see to it that someone who has frequent dealings with the General [DeWitt] would determine his attitude in regard to the refugees, so that at least (if he is not already) he would be informed of all the implications of such orders as may be issued."[120] At the February 27 meeting, the "general attitude of the Committee re the Tolan Committee request for a statement" was discussed.[121] The decision was made not to issue any public statement, with the group passing a motion that read, "The sense of this committee is that no article be given to the committee which purports to be the reply of the Jewish community of LA or any substantial part of it." The minutes do not indicate whether the discussion was limited to the issue of German Jewish refugees or touched also on Japanese Americans. However, in the aftermath of the vote, the focus of discussion was solely on the refugee question. Joseph Loeb, who cast the lone vote against the motion, expressed concern that "we commit a great injustice to the refugees by not doing something to prevent a repetition of the mistakes that were made by England, etc. It is a serious error to shelve it."[122] In response, a suggestion was made that "a couple of people call on Tolan and ask him not to raise this issue." Similarly, in an unsigned memo in the CRC's file on the Los Angeles Émigré Service Special Service Committee in March, it was suggested that "an outstanding American Jewish personality will arrange for an interview with General de Witt [sic] at his earliest convenience," in order to make the case that "the expatriated, expulsed and expropriated refugees don't belong to the enemy aliens."[123]

While these files are focused overwhelmingly on the German "enemy aliens," LAJCC/CRC leaders' tacit approval of removal and incarceration of Japanese aliens and Japanese American citizens can be discerned, although it was rarely stated directly—and never publicly. Indeed, given the role of the group in providing "evidence" against Japanese Americans, the lack of focus on their fate is striking. Occasionally it is touched on indirectly—when internal memos express concern that European "enemy aliens" had been inaccurately labeled, without mentioning Japanese American "enemy aliens." In such cases, the implication was that the label was inaccurate for the former and not for the latter. Although the group clearly followed the unfolding process of removal and incarceration,[124] the policy and its impact on the Japanese American community is barely mentioned in the records or mentioned only in passing. For example, the March memo suggesting a private approach to General DeWitt expresses concern that "after the elimination of the Japanese the majority of the 'enemy aliens' will be the 'refugees from Nazi oppression,'" which could create the "unfortunate" situation that "the population would more and more identify the 'enemy aliens' with the refugees. . . ."

The process of mass removal was also the context for the group's discussion of rumors that Jews were exploiting Japanese Americans who were forced by the removal order to sell their property. In a March 1942 letter to a Los Angeles County official, Leon Lewis detailed his efforts to investigate and refute such rumors. Lewis reported that he had heard such a rumor "repeated . . . a score of times" and asserted that "though there may have been cases of petty chiseling, apparently there is no foundation for many of the fantastic rumors that are circulating." Characteristically, rather than launching a public relations campaign to counter the rumors, Lewis laid out a plan for federal authorities and reputable liquidating companies to establish procedures "which would remove, in my opinion, once and for all any indiscriminate charges of exploitation by Jews." After suggesting that the rumors were "being circulated in exaggerated form by pro-Axis sympathizers," Lewis went on to offer the services of "competent attorneys of Jewish faith, to assist by legal and moral suasion, and without fee, any Japanese who claims he has been exploited by any Jewish purchaser."[125]

The subject of alleged exploitation was also broached in correspondence between David Coleman of the LAJCC/CRC and Eugene Block of San Franciso's Survey Committee. In May 1942, Block wrote to Coleman inquiring about the Los Angeles group's recent "exhaustive investigation of the rumors that certain individuals in whom we are interested as a group capitalized on the plight of evacuated Japanese by buying up merchandise and personal effects at ridiculously low prices," noting that "my understanding is that your inquiry found the reports unfounded." Block indicated that similar rumors "which do not altogether stand up" had been circulating in the Bay Area and asked Coleman to share with him information about the Los Angeles investigation. Several days later, Block again wrote to Coleman, thanking him for his prompt response and congratulating him on his work in this area. "The sum total of our inquiry up here amounts to about the same thing, and I agree fully with your conclusion on the basis of dignified silence," he wrote. Block had considered "some direct approach to the organized Japanese relief committee," but ultimately "decided to keep far away."[126]

While Block's preference for a "dignified silence" came in the context of the discussion of the exploitation rumors, it also aptly characterized the group's response to the entire removal and incarceration policy. Despite its contributions to the case against the Nikkei, discussion of the policy rarely appears in LAJCC/CRC documents, and the group made no public statement on the policy. As discussed in chapter 2, the *B'nai B'rith Messenger* made one brief editorial statement against mass removal, despite the fact that Lewis and LAJCC chairman Mendel Silberberg were on the paper's board of directors. When an investigator from the Japanese American Evacuation and Resettlement Study came to interview Roos in July 1943, Roos indicated that he "knew very little about the evacuation problems," and no interview took place. Shortly thereafter, the interviewer was contacted by Leon Lewis, eager to share "definitive proof . . . to refute the story that Jewish businessmen profited from the evacuation."[127] Although Lewis was happy to have the opportunity to counter the exploitation story, he did not offer information on the LAJCC/CRC and its connection to the *News Letter*. The investigator never uncovered the link and failed to realize the role that this Jewish organization had played in building the case for Japanese American removal.

One exception, a candid and direct, albeit private, engagement of the Japanese removal, does appear in correspondence between Leon Lewis and Maurice Karpf. In early April 1942, Lewis sent Karpf a copy of a Carey McWilliams's article from the *New Republic*, in which McWilliams argued that the Japanese should be given individual hearings to determine their loyalty, as was being done with European "enemy aliens." McWilliams refuted the notion that it was impossible to distinguish the loyal Japanese from the disloyal and stated that if Japanese Americans were "evacuated en masse, but no such action is taken involving citizens of German or Italian ancestry, then obviously one group of citizens will have been discriminated against solely on the basis of race." Lewis commented, "It strikes me as being rather superficial and his conclusions are certainly glib. I am surprised at the manner in which he has ignored certain elements of the problem, about which he should certainly know." Karpf responded, "I am reluctantly forced to agree with your judgment."[128]

Given the role that the LAJCC played in disseminating the "evidence" of alleged Japanese American subversion that contributed to the case for removal, this private endorsement of the policy of mass removal is hardly surprising. Yet, as with the decision not to participate in the public discussion of German refugees, the LAJCC/CRC fed information to those formulating policy and influencing public opinion but did not play a role in the public debate. Such secrecy was characteristic of its involvement from the outset, as when the group funneled some of the material provided to the Dies Committee through the American Legion rather than providing it directly to the committee.[129] Officials worked actively to discourage and condemn public disclosure of LAJCC/CRC involvement. When John Lechner of the Americanism Educational League implied in a March 1942 radio show that the organization had been an important source of information for the Dies Committee investigation, Lewis chastised him, writing, quite disingenuously, that he "doubted very much that Mr. Steedman of the Dies Committee had relied to any important degree upon the research facilities of either the AEL or the NRS."[130]

While the use of a behind-the-scenes strategy of personal contacts was common to a number of Jewish groups at the time, the level of secrecy practiced by the LAJCC in its engagement with this issue seems particularly strong. After all, mass removal was an extremely popular policy in California, and joining the many public officials and civic and patriotic groups who supported that policy was unlikely to result in negative repercussions. Taken together with their constant, overriding concern about anti-Semitism, it seems likely that, as with work in Hollywood, the LAJCC/CRC was concerned about the possible perception that a Jewish group was having an undue influence on policy.

In addition, despite its contributions to the case for mass exclusion, the LAJCC/CRC never focused on the Japanese issue. The Nikkei question was always a peripheral one to the organization: even in the winter of 1941–42 when they were most engaged in the issue, it remained very much a secondary concern to anti-Semitism and Nazism. Indeed, while the group had clearly come to believe that there were subversives among the Japanese American population, there is no evidence in their files of the sort of vitriolic racism that characterized the rhetoric of many of the groups arguing in favor of the exclusion policy. As with the information it publicized on pro-Nazi groups, its material on Japanese Americans focused on specific individuals and organizations and did not make allegations about "racial loyalties" of Nikkei in general. There is, in fact, no evidence that the LAJCC/CRC leadership engaged, even privately, in the kind of racist vitriol that was common among many supporters of the mass removal policy. Rather, when confronted with this kind of racism, the group disassociated itself. For example, as the Americanism Educational League (AEL), a group long associated with the LAJCC, became explicitly racist in the early years of the war, the LAJCC/CRC not only cut ties with the group but also began investigating it as a dangerous and subversive organization.

According to an AEL flyer, the group was founded in 1927 and aimed to "furnish, without charge, material, speakers and direction to civic leaders throughout the state in order to combat organized class and racial hatreds."[131] Given this focus, it is not surprising that the LAJCC later became one of the many AEL sponsoring groups and that Rabbi Magnin became a board member.[132] The group, led by Dr. John Lechner, appealed to the LAJCC not only on the basis of their shared commitment to fighting prejudice but also because it spoke out specifically against anti-Semitism as well as against fascism and Nazism. For example, early in the war, Lechner published a document titled "Who Caused the War" that countered efforts to blame the war on Jews. As Lechner explained to Leon Lewis in a cover letter accompanying the publication, there "is a move afoot, which is developing to overwhelming proportions, to blame the Jews for the war. I have been doing everything I can in my public addresses and in my contacts to stop that movement."[133] Ironically, given the vigorous efforts against Japanese Americans in which Lechner was already engaged, the pamphlet explained, "In order to circumvent the insidious campaign to place the blame for this war on the shoulders of an American minority group, these facts are given for careful study," and concluded that the root of the war was "Nazi totalitarianism" and "Japanism." Lechner argued that rather than blaming the Jews, Americans should "praise that group for its instinctive sensing of danger to America and for its endeavor to awaken the American to an attitude of realism. Americans dare not hunt for a scapegoat in the light of the foregoing truths, lest they themselves contribute to the enemy."

Like the LAJCC, the AEL had merged its fight against prejudice with the fight against fascism during the 1930s. By the early 1940s, it was chaired by Jack Tenney, the same California senator who chaired the state committee on un-American activities. Like the Dies Committee and the Tenney Committee, the AER's definition of "un-American" activity was quite broad and included anti-Semitic, fascist, and leftist movements. Yet the AEL did not espouse an exclusionist position until the spring of 1942. Even after Pearl Harbor, "Dr. Lechner, at the outset, could not make up his mind whether he opposed or favored mass evacuation of the Japanese from the Coast."[134] In January, Lechner made a speech in Los Angeles in which he argued against mass evacuation, saying it "would only cause hardship both to the Japanese and to other residents of the state."[135] However, Lechner soon embraced the policy and emerged as one of the leading anti-Nikkei spokespeople in the state. In the spring of 1942, the AEL touted its role in exposing alleged sabotage plans along the West Coast. By the fall, Lechner was working with the American Legion to paint the Japanese American Citizen's League as a front organization for a community rife with fifth column activity. That October, he published a thirty-three-page report titled "The Inside Story of our Domestic Japanese Problem" in which he reiterated charges about language schools, enumerated alleged subversive activities, and made a case for incarceration of all Japanese Americans including Hawaiians.[136] The following year, Lechner was the star witness in a series of hearings on the "Japanese problem" conducted in 1943 by the Tenney Committee at the urging of long-standing anti-Japanese groups like the American Legion. The committee's scathing report was used by the American Legion as ammunition in its campaign to urge deportation of Japanese Americans and to prevent their return to the state.[137]

Although LAJCC/CRC leaders had helped to build the case for mass exclusion and incarceration, they became increasingly uncomfortable with Lechner's campaign. In his letter following Lechner's March 29, 1942, radio appearance, Leon Lewis not only criticized Lechner's revelation of the NRS role in the Dies Committee report but also went on to call the broadcast "one of the most undignified and unseemly performances I have ever heard on the air . . . typical of the Fascist mentality that everybody who disagrees with you must, ipso facto, be a Communist."[138] As Lechner became increasingly identified with the most extreme form of exclusionism, the organization distanced itself. At the LAJCC/CRC office, where information on Lechner's group was once filed under "sponsored organizations," a file was opened on Lechner under "investigated groups."[139] The group ended its relationship with AEL and began actively monitoring Lechner's public appearances and publications, and Jewish leaders like Magnin resigned from the AEL board. LAJCC/CRC agents filed reports that used phrases like "a combination of Red and Jap baiting" to describe Lechner's speeches.[140] Several years later, when actor Eddie Cantor wrote to ask about the advisability of joining the AEL, Lewis responded, "I dropped all relationship with Dr. Lechner when I learned that he was soliciting funds from wholesale grocers to put on an anti-Japanese campaign following the Japanese exclusion in the early days of the war."[141]

The split with the AEL demonstrates that, although the LAJCC/CRC participated in the investigation of the Nikkei community, it would only go so far. The group proved quite willing to join forces with groups like the Dies and Tenney Committees, the AEL, and the American Legion in fighting anti-Semitism and fascism and became involved in the investigation of Japanese nationals and Japanese Americans in response to the Japanese alliance with Nazi Germany. Groups like the American Legion and Native Sons of the Golden West had been involved in a race-based anti-Japanese campaign for decades and were eager to use the wartime crisis to further their long-standing goal of ridding the state of the Nikkei community. By the middle of 1942, the AEL also embraced that goal. The LAJCC, however, had no long-standing interest in anti-Nikkei legislation and did not gravitate toward more extreme forms of exclusionism. As Lechner's statements became increasingly venomous and racial, the group came to see him as a threat rather than as an ally.

Similarly, while the LAJCC had cooperated with the American Legion in fighting domestic fascism since the 1930s,[142] it appears to have been allied with those within the organization who questioned its extreme position on the Japanese issue. For example, a lengthy, critical statement, written by an American Legion insider, appears in the LAJCC/CRC files on Intercultural Education. Dated June 25, 1942, it was most likely written by Louis Greenbaum, Los Angeles Legion legal adviser on public relations and general chairman.[143] The document charts his effort to shift the stance of the legion on the Japanese issue, explaining, "I could not approve of any program to rouse hate against any given racial or religious group." It then describes working with organizations including the Fair Play Committee to bring in speakers to sway the local legion, with regard to both the Japanese issue and Chinese exclusion. He recounts that after he contacted University of California President Robert Sproul, a woman came to see him at Sproul's request. She explained to him that "the group pushing the anti-Japanese question was a group inimical to the interests of all Americans" and showed him literature that led him to conclude that "the material was definitely anti-Semitic." She also explained to him the long history of exclusionist activism among legion members and provided documentation that the "same group of Legionnaires was raising the money and furnishing the means for the anti-Semitic group up North to put out their literature."[144] In tying extreme anti-Japanese sentiment to anti-Semitism, the statement reminded LAJCC/CRC officials of its own long-standing position: that the various forms of prejudice are linked and that discrimination against any one group represents a threat to all.

The evidence of the LAJCC/CRC break with the AEL, of its contact with moderates within the local American Legion, and of its continuing attention to and identification with civil rights issues more generally suggest that, although the LAJCC clearly contributed to the campaign to exclude Japanese Americans and uncritically published allegations against the Nikkei propagated by extremist groups, it differed in significant ways from long-standing anti-Nikkei organizations, like the American Legion or Native Sons of the Golden West. Clearly, their tactics were strikingly different, with the American Legion and Native Sons playing a public, vocal role in the debate while the LAJCC remained behind the scenes. However, the difference was not merely one of style or tactics but one of motives. The American Legion, the Native Sons, and local Granges had histories of vehement anti-Nikkei sentiment and activism going back several decades, which grew out of local politics based in economic and, more specifically, land competition during the decades prior to Pearl Harbor. In contrast, there is simply no evidence of long-standing hostility toward Japanese Americans among LAJCC activists or among Los Angeles Jews in general. Indeed, such anti-Japanese activism was something that the Jewish community had historically avoided. The LAJCC's involvement in anti-Nikkei propagandizing was primarily motivated not by historic anti-Asian sentiment but by Jewish anxieties about the Nazi-Japanese alliance in the larger context of the growth of anti-Semitic, pro-Nazi activity in the world and at home. The materials on Japanese nationals and Japanese Americans that the group developed and propagated were a small piece of a much larger anti-fascist effort. While not their central focus, these materials proved important because they were so valued by the very governmental bodies and "patriotic" groups that were in a position to further the LAJCC/CRC's central goal of exposing anti-Semites and Nazis as subversive and un-American.

Therefore, it was not economic or land competition, or even simple racism, that led this Jewish organization to lend support to the case against Japanese Americans but, rather, increasing insecurity combined with a belief in the conspiracy of world fascism. The signing of the Tripartite Pact led them to see members of the Nikkei community not as a beleaguered American minority ethnic group but as potential fascist sympathizers and subversives. This is not to say that race did not influence their actions. Indeed, like most Californians, LAJCC leaders appear to have tacitly accepted racist arguments that it was more difficult to distinguish the loyal from the disloyal among Japanese Americans—even among those who were citizens. Yet for these Jewish Angelinos, it was their own anxiety about domestic fascism and anti-Semitism that led them to set aside their avowed principles of justice for minorities and contribute to the case for the mass exclusion and incarceration of their Japanese American neighbors.

NOTES

1. Peter Irons, *Justice at War: The Story of the Japanese American Internment Cases* (Oxford: Oxford University Press, 1983), 214–15.

2. Morton Grodzins, *Americans Betrayed* (Chicago: University of Chicago Press, 1949), 329n14.

3. Irons, *Justice at War*, 214–15; *Hirabayashi v. United States*, majority opinion, quoted in Irons, *Justice Delayed: The Record of the Japanese American Internment Cases* (Middleton, Conn.: Wesleyan University Press, 1989), 60.

4. Irons, *Justice at War*, 215.

5. Irons, *Justice at War*, 215.

6. For most of the period covered in this discussion, the organization was still called the LAJCC and that name is used here. For discussion focusing on the period after the name change to Community Relations Council, LAJCC/CRC is used. The records of the organization under both of these names are archived as the Jewish Federation Council of Los Angeles' Community Relations Committee Collection (CRC2) at the Urban Archives Center, Oviatt Library, California State University, Northridge.

7. Karen Wilson, "Citizens of Los Angeles: Jewish Families and the Naissance of the Metropolis," M.A. thesis, Hebrew Union College, Los Angeles, 2003, 6.

8. Mike Davis, *City of Quartz: Excavating the Future in Los Angeles* (New York: Verso, 1990), 116. Karen Wilson notes that some elite clubs began to exclude Jews in the 1910s, and there are a few examples of exclusions as early as the 1890s. See Wilson, "Citizens of Los Angeles," 28n14. While Davis, who treats this issue only briefly, dates the problem to the turn of the century, both Wilson and Vorspan and Gartner point to a gradual increase, with these practices becoming particularly prominent in the 1920s and 1930s. Wilson's thesis documents the ways in which elite families weathered the dramatic changes in Los Angeles and maintained both their business interests and a level of influence in the city.

9. Max Vorspan and Lloyd Gartner, *History of the Jews of Los Angeles* (Philadelphia: Jewish Publication Society, 1970), 205. Karen Wilson's analysis of the officers and directors of the Chamber of Commerce from 1888 to 1921 suggests a policy of "token acceptance," with only one Jewish individual serving in most of these years. Wilson, "Citizens of Los Angeles," 50.

10. Vorspan and Gartner, *Jews of Los Angeles*, 200; see also Davis, *City of Quartz*, 102.

11. Henry Schwartz, "The Silver Shirts: Anti-Semitism in San Diego," *Western States Jewish History* 25, no. 1 (1992): 54–55; Michael E. Birdwell, *Celluloid Soldiers: The Warner Brothers Campaign against Nazism* (New York: New York University Press, 1999), 154–60. It is important to note that estimates of San Diego area members range wildly—from 17 to 2,000. The Special Committee was a precursor to the House Un-American Activities Committee, formed in 1938 and led by Congressman Martin Dies.

12. Daniel Geary, "Carey McWilliams and Antifascism, 1934–1943," *Journal of American History* 90, no. 3 (December 2003): 921. McWilliams's title referenced Sinclair Lewis's novel *It Can't Happen Here* (1935), which told the story of a fascist takeover of America.

13. Carey McWilliams, *It CAN Happen Here: Active Anti-Semitism in Los Angeles* (Los Angeles: American League against War and Fascism and Jewish Anti-Nazi League of Southern California, 1935), 3.

14. Bruce Phillips, "The Challenge of Family, Identity, and Affiliations," in *California Jews*, ed. Ava F. Kahn and Marc Dollinger (Hanover, N.H.: Brandeis University Press/University Press of New England, 2003), 20. It is also important to note that the Japanese American population in Los Angeles grew explosively. Indeed, the Japanese American population center, like that of the Jewish community, shifted from San Francisco to Los Angeles during this period.

15. Phillips, "The Challenge of Family, Identity, and Affiliations," 20–21.

16. See discussion of Boyle Heights in chapter 3.

17. Felicia Herman, "Jewish Leaders and the Motion Picture Industry," in *California Jews*, ed. Ava F. Kahn and Marc Dollinger (Hanover, N.H.: Brandeis University Press/University Press of New England, 2003), 96–97, 100.

18. Herman, "Jewish Leaders and the Motion Picture Industry," 100–101. For more on the formation of the group, see Shana Bernstein, *Building Bridges at Home in a Time of Global Conflict: Interracial Cooperation and the Fight for Civil Rights in Los Angeles, 1933–1954*, Ph.D. diss., Stanford University, 2003, chap. 2.

19. Herman, "Jewish Leaders and the Motion Picture Industry," 101–2.

20. Felicia Herman, "Hollywood, Nazism, and the Jews" *American Jewish History* 89, no. 1 (2001): 68n23.

21. Stuart Svonkin, *Jews against Prejudice: American Jews and the Fight for Civil Liberties* (New York: Columbia University Press, 1997), 15–16.

22. Records guide, Jewish Federation Council of Los Angeles' Community Relations Committee Collection (CRC2), Urban Archives Center, Oviatt Library, California State University, Northridge.

23. Herman, "Jewish Leaders and the Motion Picture Industry," 102. At the time, there was a division over strategy in the Jewish community, with the ADL and the American Jewish Committee, with a largely assimilated Reform constituency, relying on quiet persuasion in the halls of government and business, while the American Jewish Congress, led by Reform leader Stephen Wise but with a constituency drawn primarily from immigrant and second generation East European Jews, favoring more public methods such as protests and marches.

24. Records guide, CRC2, UAC.

25. "Memorandum on News Research Service," April 10, 1940, box 200, folder 17, page 1, Jewish Federation Council of Greater Los Angeles' Community Relations Committee Collection (CRC2), Urban Archives Center, Oviatt Library, California State University, Northridge.

26. Herman, "Jewish Leaders and the Motion Picture Industry," 102.

27. "Memorandum on News Research Service," April 10, 1940, box 200, folder 17, p. 61, CRC2, UAC.

28. Vorspan and Gartner, *History of the Jews of Los Angeles*, 201. According to Joseph Roos, Silberberg "had considerable political clout" and, later, was a key force behind Earl Warren's successful run for California's governorship. "Joseph Roos Oral History Interview," conducted by Leonard Pitt and Murray Wood, December 18, 1979, January 7 and 28, 1980, and February 14, 1980, pp. 8–10, Urban Archives Center, California State University, Northridge.

29. Box 110, folder 29, Jewish Federation Council of Greater Los Angeles' Community Relations Committee Collection (CRC2), Urban Archives Center, Oviatt Library, California State University, Northridge.

30. Box 196, folder 2, Jewish Federation Council of Greater Los Angeles' Community Relations Committee Collection (CRC2), Urban Archives Center, Oviatt Library, California State University, Northridge.

31. Bernstein, *Building Bridges*, 23. Bernstein refers to the LAJCC as the Community Relations Committee, the name that it would adopt in 1941.

32. In 1941, the *Messenger's* masthead listed forty-five individuals as members of its editorial board and advisory council. Among them were at least eight individuals who were part of the group that met to form the LAJCC in 1933. Among the eight members of the paper's Board of Directors were four from the original LAJCC group, including Lewis and Silberberg.

33. David Coleman, Report, February 18, 1941, box 132, folder 7, Jewish Federation Council of Greater Los Angeles' Community Relations Committee Collection (CRC2), Urban Archives Center, Oviatt Library, California State University, Northridge.

34. Eric Goldstein, *The Price of Whiteness: Jews, Race, and American Identity* (Princeton, N.J.: Princeton University Press, 2006), 58.

35. David Coleman, Report, February 18, 1941, box 132, folder 7, CRC2, UAC.

36. Herman, "Jewish Leaders and the Motion Picture Industry," 102.

37. The ADL's Fact Finding Committee and AJC's Survey Committee, like the LAJCC, "shared intelligence on American anti-Semites with the Federal Bureau of Investigation and the Dies Committee." Svonkin, *Jews against Prejudice*, 16.

38. Records guide, CRC2, UAC. See also "In Our Own Backyard: Resisting Nazi Propaganda in Southern California, 1933–1945," on-line exhibit, Special Collections, California State University, Northridge, part 8, introduction. Roos is identified as Lewis's law partner in "Interview with Joseph Roos," July 20, 1943, Japanese American Evacuation and Resettlement Study, section 2, reel 011, frame 0666, folder A 19.02, News Research Service, Inc., Los Angeles. Japanese American evacuation and resettlement records, BANC MSS 67/14 c, The Bancroft Library, University of California, Berkeley.

39. "Joseph Roos Oral History Interview," 4–5.

40. "Joseph Roos Oral History Interview," 9.

41. Copies of the *News Letter* and information about the NRS are included in the materials of the LAJCC.

42. "In Our Own Backyard," part 8, introduction.

43. "Memorandum on News Research Service," April 10, 1940, box 200, folder 17, p. 19, Jewish Federation Council of Greater Los Angeles' Community Relations Committee Collection (CRC2), Urban Archives Center, Oviatt Library, California State University, Northridge. Britt's book was *The Fifth Column Is Here* (New York: W. Funk, 1940).

44. Leon Lewis to William Cherin, March 11, 1942, box 209, folder 52, Jewish Federation Council of Greater Los Angeles' Community Relations Committee Collection (CRC2), Urban Archives Center, Oviatt Library, California State University, Northridge. Dennis was a well-known critic of the Roosevelt administration who was often labeled a fascist sympathizer in the press. He was charged with sedition under the Smith Act in 1944.

45. "Memorandum on News Research Service," April 10, 1940, box 200, folder 17, p. 7, CRC2, UAC.

46. "Update to Memorandum on News Research Service," February 1941, box 200, folder 27, p. 24, Jewish Federation Council of Greater Los Angeles' Community Relations Committee Collection (CRC2), Urban Archives Center, Oviatt Library, California State University, Northridge.

47. "Memorandum on News Research Service," April 10, 1940, box 200, folder 17, p. 68, CRC2, UAC. In August 1940, a letter was sent to leaders of the District IV B'nai B'rith (the western states) describing the *News Letter*, offering to add them to the mailing list, and asking them to share it with "an editor in your community of your acquaintance." Leon Lewis, draft of letter to B'nai B'rith District 4 leaders, August 9, 1940, box 197, folder 44, Jewish Federation Council of Greater Los Angeles' Community Relations Committee Collection (CRC2), Urban Archives Center, Oviatt Library, California State University, Northridge.

48. "Memorandum on News Research Service," April 10, 1940, box 200, folder 17, pp. 15–17, CRC2, UAC.

49. "Memorandum on News Research Service," April 10, 1940, box 200, folder 17, p. 22, CRC2, UAC.

50. "Update to Memorandum on News Research Service," February 1941, box 200, folder 27, p. 17, CRC2, UAC.

51. "Update to Memorandum on News Research Service," February 1941, box 200, folder 27, p. 19, CRC2, UAC.

52. Joseph Roos to M. A. McKavitt, Director of Libraries, U.S. Department of Justice, September 16, 1941, box 209, folder 52, Jewish Federation Council of Greater Los Angeles' Community Relations Committee Collection (CRC2), Urban Archives Center, Oviatt Library, California State University Northridge.

53. Warren Grover, *Nazis in Newark* (New Brunswick, N.J.: Transaction Publishers, 2003), 80–82.

54. Grover, *Nazis in Newark*, 104.

55. Grover, *Nazis in Newark*, 196.

56. "Memorandum on News Research Service," April 10, 1940, box 200, folder 17, 44–51, CRC2, UAC.

57. Telegram, Martin Dies to Leon Lewis, August 6, 1938. Reproduced in "Joseph Roos Oral History Interview," 72.

58. "Memorandum on News Research Service," April 10, 1940, box 200, folder 17, p. 44, CRC2, UAC.

59. Svonkin, *Jews against Prejudice*, 15–16.

60. *B'nai B'rith Messenger*, September 24, 1937, 4.

61. *B'nai B'rith Messenger*, September 24, 1937, 4.

62. "Joseph Roos Oral History Interview," 13, 33–34.

63. Box 84, folders 15–19, CRC2, UAC.

64. Los Angeles Jewish Community Center, records guide, CRC2, UAC.

65. Judy Kutulas, *The American Civil Liberties Union and the Making of Modern Liberalism, 1930–1960* (Chapel Hill: University of North Carolina Press, 2006), 35, 68–70.

66. Kutulas, *The American Civil Liberties Union*, 70. A copy of the ACLU press release, titled "Union Urges Defeat of Dies Committee" (January 18, 1941), was filed in the LAJCC papers. Box 196, folder 2, Jewish Federation Council of Greater Los Angeles' Community Relations Committee Collection (CRC2), Urban Archives Center, Oviatt Library, California State University, Northridge.

67. Kutulas, *The American Civil Liberties Union,* 26.

68. Lucille Milner to Joseph Roos, February 18, 1943 (Milner does not list the specific cases to which she refers); ACLU news release, October 19, 1942, box 196, folder 2, CRC2, UAC.

69. "Joseph Roos Oral History Interview," 26.

70. Request from James Steedman of the Dies Committee and lists of names, dated June 30, July 2, and July 11, 1941, box 171, folder 2, Jewish Federation Council of Greater Los Angeles' Community Relations Committee Collection (CRC2), Urban Archives Center, Oviatt Library, California State University, Northridge.

71. "Update to Memorandum on News Research Service," February 1941, box 200, folder 27, p. 20, CRC2, UAC.

72. Leon Lewis to Congressman Jerry Voorhis, January 15, 1940; Voorhis to Lewis, February 3, 1940; box 228, folder 6, Jewish Federation Council of Greater Los Angeles' Community Relations Committee Collection (CRC2), Urban Archives Center, Oviatt Library, California State University, Northridge.

73. Leon Lewis to Al Cohn, January 30, 1942, box 196, folder 2, Jewish Federation Council of Greater Los Angeles' Community Relations Committee Collection (CRC2), Urban Archives Center, Oviatt Library, California State University, Northridge.

74. Reinhold Niebuhr, "The Limits of Liberty," *The Nation* (January 24, 1942), clipping, box 196, folder 2, Jewish Federation Council of Greater Los Angeles' Community Relations Committee Collection (CRC2), Urban Archives Center, Oviatt Library, California State University, Northridge.

75. *News Letter,* May 10, 1939, as reproduced in the December 10, 1942, issue in the *News Letter,* box 204, Jewish Federation Council of Greater Los Angeles' Community Relations Committee Collection (CRC2), Urban Archives Center, Oviatt Library, California State University, Northridge.

76. *News Letter,* October 2, 1940, and October 9, 1940, box 204, Jewish Federation Council of Greater Los Angeles' Community Relations Committee Collection (CRC2), Urban Archives Center, Oviatt Library, California State University, Northridge. These two editions focus entirely on the alliance, emphasizing Japan and Germany's common goals, their collaboration on propaganda efforts, and Japan's efforts to cultivate nationalism among Japanese Americans, particularly in Hawaii.

77. *News Letter,* News Research Service, July 9, 1941, box 204, Jewish Federation Council of Greater Los Angeles' Community Relations Committee Collection (CRC2), Urban Archives Center, Oviatt Library, California State University, Northridge.

78. "Trojan Horse Brigade" was a phrase often used to suggest the potential for fifth-column activity. Congressman Martin Dies's book by this title describes the danger of subversive activity by both communists and fascists. Martin Dies, *Trojan Horse in America* (New York: Dodd, Mead & Company, 1940).

79. *News Letter,* News Research Service, July 16, 1941, box 204, pp. 1–3, Jewish Federation Council of Greater Los Angeles' Community Relations Committee Collection (CRC2), Urban Archives Center, Oviatt Library, California State University, Northridge.

80. *News Letter,* News Research Service, July 16, 1941, box 204, pp. 3–4, CRC2, UAC.

81. Letter to James Steedman, Dies Committee, July 10, 1941, box 25, folder 3, Jewish Federation Council of Greater Los Angeles' Community Relations Committee

Collection (CRC2), Urban Archives Center, Oviatt Library, California State University, Northridge. The copy in the file is a carbon and is not signed, but, like nearly all of the other outgoing correspondence in the file, it is most likely from Leon Lewis, or possibly from Joseph Roos.

82. Kilsoo Haan was a Korean nationalist and representative of the Sino-Korean People's League who resided in Washington, D.C., and worked with U.S. intelligence. He is known for his efforts to warn the United States of the impending attack on Pearl Harbor. "Biography," *Guide to the Kilsoo Haan Papers,* Online Archive of California http://content.cdlib.org/ark:/13030/kt7j49p87r/.

83. CRC2, UAC.

84. Bill Hosokawa, *JACL: In Quest of Justice* (New York: William Morrow, 1982), 140. Hosokawa attributes this information to an interview with George Knox Roth.

85. These materials likely came from Lt. Commander Kenneth D. Ringle, "one of the rare officers who could read Japanese." Roger Daniels, e-mail correspondence with the author, January 29, 2008. Joseph Roos indicates a close working relationship with Naval Intelligence; see "Joseph Roos Oral History Interview," 14.

86. "Joseph Roos Oral History Interview," 18.

87. Joseph Roos to Helen Loomis, Editor, Chinese Information Service, June 30, 1941; Loomis to Roos, July 11, 1941; box 197, folder 40, Jewish Federation Council of Greater Los Angeles' Community Relations Committee Collection (CRC2), Urban Archives Center, Oviatt Library, California State University, Northridge. Roos asks Loomis for more information for its upcoming *News Letter* focusing on Japan and Japanese Americans.

88. Joseph Roos to Dr. Maurice Williams, China Emergency Relief Committee, September 24, 1941; Joseph Roos to Chinese Ambassador (not named), August 13, 1941; box 197, folders 39, 42, Jewish Federation Council of Greater Los Angeles' Community Relations Committee Collection (CRC2), Urban Archives Center, Oviatt Library, California State University, Northridge.

89. Noriko Asato, *Teaching Mikadoism: The Attack on Japanese Language Schools in Hawaii, California and Washington, 1919–1972* (Honolulu: University of Hawaii Press, 2006), 42.

90. Asato, *Teaching Mikadoism,* 67.

91. Lewis to Senator Guy Gillette, October 7, 1941, box 209, folder 42, Jewish Federation Council of Greater Los Angeles' Community Relations Committee Collection (CRC2), Urban Archives Center, Oviatt Library, California State University, Northridge. Gillette's speech "Japanese Activities in the U.S." is also in this file. It is notable that, in 1943, Senator Gillette emerged as a key supporter of American intervention to save European Jewry.

92. For example, Leon Lewis sent a copy of that issue to William Cherin at the Department of Justice. Leon Lewis to William Cherin, March 11, 1942, box 209, folder 52, Jewish Federation Council of Greater Los Angeles' Community Relations Committee Collection (CRC2), Urban Archives Center, Oviatt Library, California State University, Northridge.

93. *News Letter,* News Research Service, December 10, 1941, box 205, CRC2, UAC.

94. Hosokawa, *JACL: In Quest of Justice,* 140–41.

95. Joseph Roos to James Steedman, January 4, 1942, box 25, folder 4, Jewish Federation Council of Greater Los Angeles' Community Relations Committee Col-

lection (CRC2), Urban Archives Center, Oviatt Library, California State University, Northridge.

96. "Office Contact, January-April, 1942," box 9, folder 8, Jewish Federation Council of Greater Los Angeles' Community Relations Committee Collection (CRC2), Urban Archives Center, Oviatt Library, California State University, Northridge.

97. Investigator note, "Interview with Joseph Roos."

98. U.S. House of Representatives, "Report on Japanese Activities," Special Committee on Un-American Activities, 77th Congress, First Session, 1942: 1886–89, 1938–39. *News Letter*, July 9 and 16, 1941, box 204, CRC2, UAC.

99. "Office Contact, January-April, 1942," February 5, 1942, box 9, folder 8, CRC2, UAC.

100. Grodzins, *Americans Betrayed*, 399. See also U.S. Department of Interior, War Relocation Authority, *Wartime Exile: The Exclusion of the Japanese Americans from the West Coast*, vol. 10 (New York: AMS Press, 1975[1946]): 116.

101. Tolan Committee Hearings, part 31: 11624.

102. When Magnin received an inquiry from the Chicago ADL in 1940 about the *News Letter's* reliability, he responded by telegram, "News Research Service Thoroughly Reliable." Rabbi E. Magnin, telegram, October 7, 1940, box 164, Jewish Federation Council of Greater Los Angeles' Community Relations Committee Collection (CRC2), Urban Archives Center, Oviatt Library, California State University, Northridge.

103. George Gleason is mentioned as a key contact in Los Angeles in Fair Play Committee correspondence and corresponded personally with Galen Fisher during the summer of 1942. Fisher to Gleason, August 17, 1942. Pacific Coast Committee for National Security and Fair Play, Bancroft Library, Berkeley, Box 1, correspondence.

104. Naval Intelligence was centrally involved in assessing the potential threat of the Japanese American community on the West Coast. See Klancy Clark de Nevers, *The Colonel and the Pacifist: Karl Bendetsen—Perry Saito and the Incarceration of Japanese Americans during World War II* (Salt Lake City: University of Utah Press, 2004), 96–97.

105. "Office Contact, January-April, 1942," box 9, folder 8, CRC2, UAC.

106. "Office Contact, January-April, 1942," box 9, folder 8, CRC2, UAC. Alexander's visit was on January 24, 1942.

107. Lewis to Cherin, December 1, 1941, box 209, folder 52, Jewish Federation Council of Greater Los Angeles' Community Relations Committee Collection (CRC2), Urban Archives Center, Oviatt Library, California State University, Northridge.

108. Box 209, folder 52, CRC2, UAC.

109. Lewis to R. B. Hood, U.S. Department of Justice, Los Angeles, March 25, 1942, box 228, folder 23, Jewish Federation Council of Greater Los Angeles' Community Relations Committee Collection (CRC2), Urban Archives Center, Oviatt Library, California State University, Northridge. Peter Irons identifies Richard B. Hood as the director of the FBI Los Angeles office. Irons, *Justice at War*, 79. Roos later had the occasion to correspond with Hood on a more personal matter: his sister, a bookstore owner in St. Louis, was being investigated by the FBI after "someone denounced her" for allegedly selling "pro-Nazi or pro-Communist literature." Asking for Hood's help in exonerating his sister, Roos explained, "If my sister is a Nazi or a Communist, then I am one too. My sister's political thinking is congruent with mine," and speculated that the report must have come "from some 'zealous patriot'

(with questionable patriotism). You know the kind I mean." Roos to R. B. Hood, FBI Los Angeles office, April 2, 1942, box 228, folder 23, Jewish Federation Council of Greater Los Angeles' Community Relations Committee Collection (CRC2), Urban Archives Center, Oviatt Library, California State University, Northridge.

110. Tanaka, a Portland-born Nisei, edited the English section of the *Rafu Shimpo*. He testified before the Tenney Committee that the Japanese section, under separate editorship, did publish "pro-Axis" materials. California Joint Fact-Finding Committee on Un-American Activities, Senator John Tenney, Chair, "Report," 1943, on-line, http://www.archive.org/details/reportofjointfac00calirich.

111. Joseph Roos to Pat Horgan, FBI, Los Angeles office, December 14, 1942, box 228, folder 23, Jewish Federation Council of Greater Los Angeles' Community Relations Committee Collection (CRC2), Urban Archives Center, Oviatt Library, California State University, Northridge.

112. Box 299, folder 32, CRC2, UAC.

113. Investigator note, "Interview with Joseph Roos."

114. For example, when he was asked to identify certain investigators for the Dies Committee or asked about details regarding some NRS operations, Roos had the interviewer turn the tape off. "Joseph Roos Oral History Interview," 73, 76.

115. Tolan Committee Hearings, Los Angeles, March 6, 1942: 11733–37.

116. Vorspan and Gartner, *History of the Jews of Los Angeles*, appendix II, 293.

117. Special Advisory Committee, Los Angeles Émigré Service, February 16, 1942, box 144, folder 19, Jewish Federation Council of Greater Los Angeles' Community Relations Committee Collection (CRC2), Urban Archives Center, Oviatt Library, California State University, Northridge.

118. Box 144, folder 19, CRC2, UAC.

119. Agenda, February 27, 1942, box 1, Jewish Federation Council of Greater Los Angeles' Community Relations Committee Collection (CRC2), Urban Archives Center, Oviatt Library, California State University, Northridge.

120. Memo, February 19, 1942. LAJCC/CRC papers, Urban Archives, CSUN, CRC 2, box 144, folder 19.

121. Minutes, February 27, 1942. LAJCC/CRC papers, Urban Archives, CSUN, CRC 2, box 1. Shorthand transcribed by Dorothy Roberts.

122. This refers to Britain's policy of interning all resident aliens from enemy countries, even those who had arrived as refugees fleeing these regimes.

123. Box 144, folder 20, CRC2, UAC. Joseph Loeb's dissenting vote is intriguing. Although the minutes of the meeting suggest that the discussion referred only to the German "enemy alien" issue and not to Japanese Americans, Loeb, as discussed in chapter 3, was considered by the Berkeley-based Fair Play Committee an individual who was sympathetic to Japanese Americans.

124. A copy of the Tolan Committee report was kept in the committee's files. Box 42, folder 15, Jewish Federation Council of Greater Los Angeles' Community Relations Committee Collection (CRC2), Urban Archives Center, Oviatt Library, California State University, Northridge.

125. Leon Lewis to H. U. M. Higgins, March 20, 1942, box 223, folder 42, Jewish Federation Council of Greater Los Angeles' Community Relations Committee Collection (CRC2), Urban Archives Center, Oviatt Library, California State University, Northridge.

126. Eugene Block to David Coleman, May 18, 1942, and May 21, 1942, box 132, folder 8, Jewish Federation Council of Greater Los Angeles' Community Relations Committee Collection (CRC2), Urban Archives Center, Oviatt Library, California State University, Northridge.

127. Investigator note, "Interview with Joseph Roos."

128. Lewis to Karpf, April 7, 1942; Karpf to Lewis, April 14, 1942, box 42, folder 15, Jewish Federation Council of Greater Los Angeles' Community Relations Committee Collection (CRC2), Urban Archives Center, Oviatt Library, California State University, Northridge.

129. Series description, box 9, folder 8, Jewish Federation Council of Greater Los Angeles' Community Relations Committee Collection (CRC2), Urban Archives Center, Oviatt Library, California State University, Northridge.

130. Leon Lewis to John Lechner, March 30, 1942, box 9, folder 25, Jewish Federation Council of Greater Los Angeles' Community Relations Committee Collection (CRC2), Urban Archives Center, Oviatt Library, California State University, Northridge.

131. Americanism Educational League (AEL) flyer, box 9, folder 25, Jewish Federation Council of Greater Los Angeles' Community Relations Committee Collection (CRC2), Urban Archives Center, Oviatt Library, California State University, Northridge.

132. Joseph Roos alleged in an interview that the relationship between the LAJCC and the AEL was even closer: that the AEL was, in fact, a front organization set up by the LAJCC to work with veterans' groups. No independent confirmation of this has been found. "Joseph Roos Oral History Interview," 23.

133. Lechner to Lewis, April 24, 1942, and Americanism Educational League (AEL) flyer, box 9, folder 25, CRC2, UAC.

134. Carey McWilliams, *Prejudice: Japanese Americans: Symbol of Racial Intolerance* (Hamdon, Conn.: Archon Books 1971 [1941]), 236.

135. Lechner, quoted in McWilliams, *Prejudice*, 236.

136. Box 10, folder 8, CRC2, UAC.

137. McWilliams, *Prejudice*, 243. California Joint Fact-Finding Committee on Un-American Activities, Senator John Tenney, Chair, "Report," 1943.

138. Lewis to Lechner, March 30, 1942, box 9, folder 25, CRC2, UAC.

139. There is a file for Lechner under "investigated groups" that begins in 1944; box 75, folder 25, Jewish Federation Council of Greater Los Angeles' Community Relations Committee Collection (CRC2), Urban Archives Center, Oviatt Library, California State University, Northridge.

140. Report on Lechner speech to the Hollywood Taxpayer's Association, November 28, 1944, box 75, folder 25, Jewish Federation Council of Greater Los Angeles' Community Relations Committee Collection (CRC2), Urban Archives Center, Oviatt Library, California State University, Northridge.

141. Leon Lewis to Eddie Cantor, April 29, 1946, box 75, folder 25, Jewish Federation Council of Greater Los Angeles' Community Relations Committee Collection (CRC2), Urban Archives Center, Oviatt Library, California State University, Northridge.

142. It should be noted that Leon Lewis was identified by an investigator for the Japanese American Evacuation and Resettlement Study as a "prominent Legionaire." Investigator note, "Interview with Joseph Roos."

143. The document is unsigned, but Greenbaum's name is penciled at the top of page 1; box 111, folder 15, Jewish Federation Council of Greater Los Angeles' Community Relations Committee Collection (CRC2), Urban Archives Center, Oviatt Library, California State University, Northridge.

144. June 25, 1943, letter; box 111, folder 15, Jewish Federation Council of Greater Los Angeles' Community Relations Committee Collection (CRC2), Urban Archives Center, Oviatt Library, California State University, Northridge.

Epilogue

By 1943, with Japanese Americans no longer present in the region and American progress in the war in the Pacific easing concerns about an attack on the West Coast, the hysteria had eased. Although communities and organizations with a long history of anti-Nikkei sentiment continued to express hostility, groups and individuals oriented toward defending civil liberties began to find their voices. As was the case throughout this episode, western Jews' responses were shaped by their identities both as westerners and as Jews and reflected the broader trends both in the region and in the larger American Jewish community.

In some quarters, the vitriol continued throughout the war. In California, a group calling itself the California Citizens Council for the Adoption of a Japanese Exclusion Law formed in 1943. California State Treasurer Charles Johnson, who would run for the Senate in 1944, gave a speech urging that Japanese Americans not be allowed to return to California.[1] General De Witt himself, testifying before a House subcommittee in April 1943, strongly opposed the return of Japanese Americans to the West Coast, stating, "I don't want any of them here. They are a dangerous element. There is no way to determine their loyalty. . . . There is a feeling developing, I think, in certain sections of the country that the Japanese should be allowed to return. I am opposing it with every proper means at my disposal."[2] His *Final Report*, released the same year, repeated many of the charges contained first in the NRS *News Letter* and later in the Dies Yellow Paper. Even after the decision was made to close the camps in 1945, vigilantes in several California communities openly threatened to prevent the return of the Nikkei.[3]

Similarly, in Oregon a 1943 state senate resolution called for the cancellation of Nisei citizenship and the deportation of all Japanese Americans after

147

the war. It was justified by the argument that "there has been and will be no method of determining which American born Japanese are loyal to the land of their birth and which are loyal to the pagan ideology of their ancestors."[4] A later measure, passed in 1945, strengthened Oregon's Alien Land Law, making it illegal for the Issei to live on farms owned by their Nisei relatives.[5] In Hood River, Oregon, the American Legion Post removed the names of Nisei servicemen from its honor roll, provoking national condemnation.[6]

Parallel groups operated in Washington. Two of the most active were the Seattle-based Remember Pearl Harbor League (RPHL) and the Japanese Exclusion League (JEL). Both focused their efforts in 1944 and 1945 on public campaigns to oppose the return of Japanese Americans. According to a recent analysis, "the groups' leadership and members came mainly from organized labor, veteran's organizations, and agricultural interests who felt threatened by competition with Japanese and Japanese-Americans," and included "many leading Seattle citizens from organizations such as Native Sons of the Golden West, the American Legion, farm leaders, and women's clubs." The RPHL characterized all Japanese Americans as "a menace" that threatened to form colonies in the United States and favored the deportation of "all Japanese." Both the RPHL and the JEL advocated the adoption of a constitutional amendment to deny citizenship to the Nisei.[7]

Those who endeavored to lend their support to Japanese Americans and encourage their return to the Pacific West were clearly cognizant of the limits of what was possible in this climate and of the potential dangers of speaking out. Fair Play Committee correspondence shows that, even as the committee quietly explored the possibility of a lawsuit aimed at "determining the right of evacuees to return to the coast" in 1944, its spokespeople publicly stated that the group did not favor their return until such a time as the War Relocation Authority (WRA) deemed it appropriate. When the Pasadena chapter learned that a change in this position was being considered, it objected strongly and several members threatened to resign.[8] Individuals who had spoken in defense of Japanese Americans sometimes faced sanctions, formal or informal. For example, when George Knox Roth, who strongly defended Japanese Americans on his radio program, refused to reveal to the Tenney Committee the sources of funding for the show, he was found in contempt.[9] When Gus Solomon's expression of support for the lifting of the Exclusion Order was reported in the *Oregonian* in December 1944, he was threatened repeatedly and called "a Communist, anarchist and traitor."[10]

Yet the hostility was not as pervasive as it had been in 1942 and, by 1943–44, there were far more voices, particularly within the government and the press, that spoke out with sympathy for Japanese Americans. Noted California Progressive and CCIH commissioner Carey McWilliams, who had earlier "supported mass evacuation of Japanese aliens and was ambivalent about citizens," became "an important defender of Japanese Americans" during this period.[11] Just a year after signing EO 9066, President Roosevelt supported the creation of a Nisei army unit, writing, "No loyal citizen of the United States should be denied the democratic right to exercise the rights of citizenship. . . . Americanism is a matter of the mind and heart; Americanism is not, and never was, a matter of race or ancestry."[12] By 1943, Dillon Myer, the director of the War Relocation Authority (WRA), was actively supporting the idea of allowing Japanese Americans to return to the West Coast. He wrote to Assistant Secretary of War John McCloy in October of that year, urging him to review the problem with WRA officials.[13] Myer and others on his staff communicated regularly with members of the Fair Play Committee during this period, exchanging ideas for public relations campaigns aimed at countering anti-Nikkei sentiment. Myer himself spoke publicly on the issue to civic groups.[14] Although the Supreme Court upheld the conviction of Gordon Hirabayashi, a Nisei, for violating the curfew order in 1943, it ruled the following year in the case of Mitzuye Endo that "a citizen of unquestioned loyalty could not be incarcerated or prevented from returning to a West Coast home." In anticipation of that ruling (shared with the administration in advance of its announcement), the army announced in December 1944 an end to the exclusion, effective just after the new year.[15] Newspapers that had earlier outspokenly called for mass removal and incarceration now urged sympathy for the prospective returnees.[16]

At the same time, groups like the ACLU also began to speak out in support of the Nikkei. Although it had voted not to oppose the policy in 1942 and had shied away from the early court cases challenging restrictions, the ACLU position gradually shifted and the organization filed an amicus brief in the Korematsu case in late 1944.[17] In the same year, the ACLU contacted Portland lawyer Gus Solomon, asking him to identify a local attorney to file a constitutional test of the exclusion in Oregon. Ultimately, Solomon took on the case himself when several other lawyers declined. Al Wirin of the Southern California ACLU prepared the parallel California test case, although the ruling in the Endo case and the decision to close the camps rendered both cases moot.[18] As a result of this work, Solomon became aware of a local group, organized by the Portland branch of the National Conference of Christians and Jews and the Portland Council of Churches, focused on aiding returning Nikkei. Whereas earlier Solomon had found no outlet for his opposition to the incarceration policy, he now marveled that "there were literally thousands of people who felt as I did. Among them were some of the outstanding leaders in the community." Soon Solomon was serving as secretary of the Portland Committee to Aid Relocation and was in charge of its employment division. By early 1945, the Portland group, with seventy-five members, had counterparts in other Oregon towns as well as in Washington and California.[19]

Solomon's experience was mirrored in many other West Coast communities. With American and Allied progress in the Pacific War, fears of an attack faded and some who had earlier endorsed mass removal softened their opinions. At the same time, those, like Solomon, who had always been in sympathy with the Nikkei became more vocal and organized. The Fair Play Committee's records reflect this activity. The group enjoyed a period of expansion beginning in 1943, creating new chapters in various western cities, including Seattle, Portland, Sacramento, Pasadena, and Fresno. New contacts were established throughout the region, even in places as remote as Pendleton, Oregon. Student branches were operating not only at Berkeley but also at UCLA, Stockton, Mills College, San Jose State, Washington University, the College of Puget Sound, and Pomona.[20]

Reflecting these broader trends, it was during this period of expansion that an increasing number of Jewish community leaders joined the organization's campaign. In March 1943, for example, San Francisco's Rabbi Reichert assisted in efforts to recruit Rabbi Edgar Magin, Judges Benjamin Scheinman and Harry Hollzer, and Mr. Sol Lesser, all of the Los Angeles area, to the Fair Play Board. By April, both Scheinman and Magnin had joined (Hollzer, while declining the invitation, expressed sympathy with the group). In September, San Jose's Rabbi Iser L. Freund wrote to Galen Fisher, "I am heartily in favor of the endeavors of the Committee of American Principles and Fair Play and will be happy to be of service when a Branch will be organized in San Jose." The Fair Play Committee's executive secretary, Ruth Kingman, also corresponded with Eugene Block, leader of San Francisco's Survey Committee, the leading Jewish civil rights organization in that city.[21] Records from the Los Angeles Fair Play Committee chapter indicate contact with Ben Meyer, a Jewish welfare leader and president of Union Bank and Trust Company and Lugwig Schiff, a member of the Jewish Welfare Federation, among others.[22]

Although their actions did reflect more general trends, evidence suggests that a number of the Jews who became involved with the Fair Play Committee in 1943 and 1944 saw their activities as rooted in their Jewish identity. Portland's Gus Solomon, like his counterpart Al Wirin from Los Angeles, was a lawyer with deep roots in the Jewish community. In later interviews, Solomon made clear connections between his commitment to civil liberties and civil rights and his own experiences with discrimination. At the time, he reached out to other Jewish lawyers, like Gilbert Sussman, in his work with the Portland Committee to Aid Relocation. His employment subcommittee tapped leading merchant and B'nai B'rith leader Harry Gevurtz, along with other, non-Jewish, civic, business, and labor leaders in their work to end a boycott of Japanese farmers.[23]

Some of these individuals were motivated by a sense of "outsider status" as Jews. According to his biographer, the employment discrimination that

Solomon experienced as a young lawyer in Portland was a "raw and defining experience" that shaped his later efforts.[24] Similarly, historian Eric Muller, in explaining why Judge Louis E. Goodman distinguished himself as the only federal judge to dismiss charges against Nisei draft resisters in the summer of 1944, points to Goodman's background as the child of East European Jewish immigrants, arguing that "Goodman undoubtedly had some sense, as both a Jew and a child of immigrants, of what it meant to be an outsider in America."[25] Goodman's conclusion at the trial that "it is shocking to the conscience that an American citizen be confined on the ground of disloyalty, and then, while so under duress and restraint, be compelled to serve in the armed forces, or be prosecuted for not yielding to such compulsion," certainly suggests the kind of "outsider status" that historians like Michael Alexander have argued are central to Jewish identification with groups like Japanese Americans.[26]

Yet in Goodman's case, as in Solomon's, it appears that sympathy for and action in support of Japanese Americans was influenced not only by an outsider identification but also by personal contacts. Although there is no clear evidence of Goodman's engagement with the issue prior to hearing the Nisei draft resistors' cases, his connection to San Francisco's Temple Emanu-El, where he was a lifelong member and taught Sunday school, is suggestive. At Emanu-El, Goodman had contact with congregational leaders like Rabbi Reichert and Monroe Deutsch, who had been involved in Fair Play Committee activities from the beginning, and others who were active in 1943 and 1944. In 1947, Goodman would deliver a Yom Kippur sermon focusing on the importance of "[cherishing] the cause of the oppressed or the disenfranchised" and warning the congregation not to qualify their Americanism.[27]

Indeed, personal contacts appear to link many of the individuals who became part of the Fair Play Committee or shared its cause. For example, Deutsch used his connections, both inside and outside the Jewish community, to aid the committee. As president of San Francisco's prestigious Commonwealth Club, Deutsch, at the suggestions of Ruth Kingman, arranged for Nisei Air Force tail gunner Ben Kuroki, who had flown over two dozen missions in Europe, to speak to the club. Kuroki addressed a full house at the Palace Hotel, describing his service in the military, and received a standing ovation. Members of the audience wept openly. Ruth Kingman, who described the scene years later in an interview, credited the Kuroki speech with turning the tide in California with regard to attitudes toward Japanese Americans.[28] Moved by the speech, Deutsch wrote to Secretary of War Henry Stimson:

As one of those who believes that the fundamental rights of American citizens must be safeguarded whatever their ancestry, their color or their religion, I have been keenly interested in the status of the Japanese in this country, particularly the American-Japanese. While their removal from this coast area occurred on the basis of military necessity, I feel firmly that as soon as danger has ceased they should be restored to every right that every other American citizen has. I believe that our whole democratic process is menaced when we fail to observe the principles on which our government rests, in the case of any one group. . . .

As Abraham Lincoln pointed out that our nation cannot exist half slave and half free, so it cannot exist with various classes of citizens whose rights fall into different categories.

If we are fighting for democracy, we must see to it that democracy is maintained here.[29]

Deutsch urged others, both from the Commonwealth Club and the Jewish community, to join his appeal to Stimson, asking them to "[comment] on Sergeant Kuroki's speech, if you heard it, and your belief that all Americans regardless of ancestry, including those of Japanese descent, should as promptly as the military situation permits be granted their full rights as citizens."[30]

Among those contacted by Deutsch was Daniel Koshland, a well-known Levi Strauss executive and San Francisco philanthropist, vice president of Temple Emanu-El, and a fellow anti-Zionist activist. Koshland obliged, writing to Stimson,

The recent visit here of Sergeant Ben Kuroki of the U.S. Army made a profound impression on his hearers, of whom I was one.

The forces of bigotry and racial hysteria are so vocal on the Pacific Coast that I cannot refrain from expressing my views. If we win the war and fail to preserve the rights of our own citizens, irrespective of race, creed, or ancestry, we will only have brought forth a monster which may destroy us all.

May I therefore respectfully request that the War Department do its utmost to grant full rights to all American citizens as soon as the military situation permits such action?[31]

Although Koshland made his appeal in universal terms, his other activities suggest that he saw his civil rights work as a Jewish activity. Indeed Koshland, whose generous financial support was critical to the civil rights coalition that formed in San Francisco in the 1930s, was a founding member of the Survey Committee, "a 1930s Jewish defense association that supported African American, Asian, and Mexican American civil rights during and after World War II." When activists like Koshland and Eugene Block, who served as the director of the Survey Committee, participated in broad, Bay Area civil rights activities they did so as representatives of a Jewish organization. The pattern of individual Jews participating in broad interracial coalitions through specifically Jewish organizations was one that would become quite common during the war years and afterward and is suggestive of an ideological mindset that connected "the defense of Jewish freedom, the struggle of the Allies against the Axis powers, and the campaign for civil rights."[32]

Likewise, Joseph Loeb, who was active in similar circles in Los Angeles, saw his involvement in Nikkei defense as tied closely to his Jewish identity. When a Fair Play Committee activist approached him in 1943, he indicated that "as a Jew [he] was especially concerned at the hypocrisy the West Coast is showing in the 'handling' of the Japanese minority." The Fair Play Committee Pasadena representative, William Carr, reported to Kingman that Loeb "should be a good man for your Los Angeles committee."[33] Like many Jewish leaders who became involved in Nikkei defense in this period, Carr perceived a common thread between anti-Japanese prejudice and anti-Semitism. When reporting on an anti-Nikkei speech by Americanism Educational League (AEL) leader Lechner, Carr observed, "I feel the crowd would have booed 'kikes' and 'niggers.'"[34]

Loeb not only was a well-known lawyer and a Jewish community leader but also, like Deutsch, Reichert, and Koshland, was involved with the anti-Zionist American Council for Judaism. In addition, he was closely connected to the LAJCC (by this time known as the CRC). And Loeb was not the only CRC activist to become involved in Fair Play Committee efforts. Rabbi Magnin and Judges Scheinman and Hollzer had both been among the LAJCC's founders. Mendel Silberberg, chair of the LAJCC/CRC since its founding a decade earlier, joined the Los Angeles Fair Play Committee group in the summer of 1944 and was listed on the letterhead as a member of the board by August of that year.[35]

The involvement of these LAJCC founders and leaders in Fair Play Committee activities seems ironic given the organization's contribution, through the News Research Service, to the case for Japanese American mass removal and incarceration. It was reflective of the shift in the organization during the war, as the group's focus changed from the monitoring of pro-Nazi and fascist groups to an emphasis on intergroup relations. The federal government's expanded activity in monitoring subversives after the American entry into the war "freed [the CRC] to morph into the public and community relations branch of the organized Jewish community."[36] As Joseph Roos explained,

> A change came about because, once America entered into World War Two, the need to watch over the Nazis and their allies, like for instance the America First Committee, no longer existed because by then our own governmental agencies, the intelligence agencies, the FBI, the Office of Strategic Services, all of those were watching. So, while we continue accepting and filing information, we paid rather relatively little attention to it.[37]

As early as the summer of 1942, Leon Lewis began to focus his attention on reaching out to other Los Angeles minority groups in work referred to as "building bridges." He sent letters to Jewish leaders in other cities, "seeking models for ways to improve relations among and to increase contacts with other minority groups, as well as to help convince local Jews they must also 'champion the rights of other minority groups.'"[38] While it continued to be active in sharing information with authorities during the early war years, the CRC shifted its attention to coalition building."[39] With Japanese Americans now incarcerated in inland camps, these efforts focused primarily on African Americans and Mexican Americans and were reflective of both national Jewish civil rights efforts and governmental initiatives at the national and local level to promote wartime unity.

The urgent need for such campaigns in Los Angeles became more apparent in the wake of the 1943 Zoot Suit Riots, which dramatically exposed the strength of anti-Chicano prejudice and resulted in the creation by both the city and the county of groups dedicated to improving intergroup relations. Jews and African Americans, due to their strong organizational structures, often took the lead in these efforts, with Mexican American and Asian American groups becoming more involved in the postwar era.[40] Thus, the shifting focus of the CRC toward intergroup relations coincided in Los Angeles with vastly increased opportunities for involvement. The result was that "the CRC became one of the most active catalysts for civil rights coalition building in Los Angeles during the World War II and postwar decade."[41] By the end of the war, "community relations [was] a greater concern than fighting the organized anti-Semites."[42] More precisely, as historian Shana Bernstein points out, the CRC came to understand that "fighting anti-Semitism meant protecting all minorities." As Roos explained in a 1944 letter, the way to fight anti-Semitism was "to foster through public education the integration and adjustment of all racial and religious groups, and thereby break down the agitatory [sic] propaganda of those who would create internal dissention and confusion."[43] In just a few years, the group's primary activities had shifted dramatically, from secretive intelligence gathering motivated by anxiety about anti-Semitism and fascism to intergroup work and public education campaigns that defined prejudice more broadly.

Although the LAJCC/CRC had contributed to the anti-Nikkei campaign in 1941–42, this shift toward "building bridges" became apparent in its posture toward the Nikkei community even during the war. As early as the spring of 1942, the group had volunteered its services to counter exploitation of Japanese Americans. Certainly, this activity was self-interested, motivated by concern that accusations of exploitation could fuel anti-Semitism.[44] Yet it also contained elements of the new approach: by arranging for Jewish lawyers to work with members of the Nikkei community they hoped to build trust. The new emphasis on intergroup relations is also evident in Mendel Silberberg's decision to become a member of the Los Angeles Fair Play Committee board in 1944. By 1946, the Japanese American Citizens League (JACL) was included in CRC files on "cooperating groups." The CRC and the JACL corresponded that year, strategizing about ways to fight Proposition 15, which would have extended some of the alien exclusions.[45]

This shift toward intergroup relations was not confined to Los Angeles. In San Francisco, the Survey Committee played a similar role as an integral component of the city's civil rights/intergroup relations movement that coalesced as the Bay Area Council Against Discrimination during the war.[46] In Seattle and Portland, the local sections of the Council of Jewish Women used their settlement houses to become incubators of intergroup, neighborhood-based coalitions and activities. At the same time, the Pacific Northwest branches of national groups like the ADL and the AJC joined with African American and other groups to work on issues like employment discrimination.[47] Nationally, the three major Jewish defense groups, the ADL, the AJC, and the AJCong were in the "vanguard" of the movement.[48] Whereas earlier, the Jewish community had "pursued a bifurcated program of social action, working to protect the rights and liberties of others through nonsectarian organizations while restricting their own communal agencies to more narrowly Jewish objectives," by the mid-1940s Jewish defense groups increasingly worked through interfaith and interracial coalitions to achieve broader goals.[49] During the next two decades, the American Jewish community "focused outwardly," according to historian Jonathan Sarna. American Jews embraced a plethora of universal causes, including civil rights, which "became a central religious issue for American Jews in the postwar era."[50]

Although a series of events and issues, ranging from the Six Day War to disputes over affirmative action, led to a more inward focus by the 1970s,[51] the strong association of Jews with civil rights, civil liberties, and liberal causes generally continued. In the 1980s, it seemed natural to many in the American Jewish community that organizations like the ADL would play a supportive role in the campaign for redress for Japanese Americans who had been subject to removal and incarceration.[52] Indeed, to many American Jews, support for redress seemed so obviously "right" that they mistakenly "remember" that groups like the ADL (and the ACLU) took a supportive position toward the Nikkei during the war.[53]

This moral clarity makes the actual response of the American Jewish community seem, in retrospect, surprising and disappointing. But neither western Jews nor any other group had quite that clarity of vision in 1942. This was particularly true for those living in the Pacific West. Fearing an attack and suspicious of potential enemies, Californians, Oregonians, and Washingtonians focused their fears on a group whose members had long been

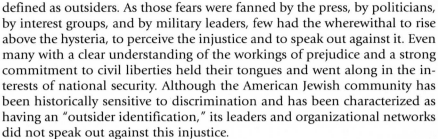

defined as outsiders. As those fears were fanned by the press, by politicians, by interest groups, and by military leaders, few had the wherewithal to rise above the hysteria, to perceive the injustice and to speak out against it. Even many with a clear understanding of the workings of prejudice and a strong commitment to civil liberties held their tongues and went along in the interests of national security. Although the American Jewish community has been historically sensitive to discrimination and has been characterized as having an "outsider identification," its leaders and organizational networks did not speak out against this injustice.

For those on the East Coast, the issue provoked not even a ripple: it was remote and outweighed by the much more real and immediate crisis of European Jewry and the need to support the war effort. The immediacy of the crisis on the West Coast and the personal relationships involved made this issue, and the responses to it, more complicated. While silence proved the most frequent response, it was a silence fraught with contradictions and laden with the baggage of western ethnic identities and relationships. As the shared concerns of American Jewry, to fight prejudice and to support the war effort, pulled western Jews in competing directions, their responses were informed by their identities and histories as American Jews and as westerners.

NOTES

1. Reports on all of these activities are found in the Pacific Coast Committee on National Security and Fair Play, Bancroft Library, University of California, Berkeley, carton 2, folder 3.

2. Quoted in U.S. Department of the Interior, War Relocation Authority, *Wartime Exile: The Exclusion of the Japanese Americans from the West Coast*, vol. 10 (New York: AMS Press, 1975 [1946]), 153–54.

3. Linda Tamura, *Hood River Issei: An Oral History of Japanese Settlers in Oregon's Hood River Valley* (Urbana: University of Illinois Press, 1933), chap. 33.

4. Senate Joint Memorial, number 9, February 17, 1943, Pacific Coast Committee on National Security and Fair Play, Bancroft Library, Berkeley, carton 1, folder 62.

5. Harry Stein, *Gus J. Solomon: Liberal Politics, Jews, and the Federal Courts* (Portland: Oregon Historical Society Press, 2006), 79–80.

6. Tamura, *Hood River Issei*, chap. 33.

7. Jennifer Speidel, "After Internment: Seattle's Debate over Japanese Americans' Right to Return Home," *Seattle Civil Rights and Labor History Project*, on-line, www.depts.washington.edu/civilr/.

8. Pacific Coast Committee on National Security and Fair Play, Bancroft Library, Berkeley, box 6.

9. Shizue Seigel, *In Good Conscience: Supporting Japanese Americans during the Internment* (San Mateo, Calif.: AACP, 2006), 27–35.

10. Stein, *Gus J. Solomon*, 79. Solomon was later appointed a federal judge by President Truman. The federal courthouse in Portland is named for him.

11. Quoted in Roger Daniels, "The Japanese American Cases, 1942–2004: A Social History," *Law and Contemporary Problems* 68, no. 159 (2005): 163.

12. Daniels, "The Japanese American Cases, 1942–2004," 160. An all-Nisei unit, the 442nd, became the most decorated unit in United States military history.

13. Peter Irons, *Justice at War: The Story of the Japanese American Internment Cases* (Oxford: Oxford University Press, 1983), 269–70.

14. Pacific Coast Committee on National Security and Fair Play, Bancroft Library, Berkeley, box 1.

15. Daniels, "The Japanese American Cases, 1942–2004," 161.

16. For example, the *Oregonian*, which had strongly advocated mass removal and incarceration called for sympathy for the returnees. See Stein, *Gus J. Solomon*, 80.

17. Daniels, "The Japanese American Cases, 1942–2004," 163.

18. Stein, *Gus J. Solomon*, 78–79.

19. Stein, *Gus J. Solomon*, 80.

20. Pacific Coast Committee on National Security and Fair Play, Bancroft Library, Berkeley, box 1, correspondence, March 1942—September 1943.

21. Iser to Fisher, September, 27, 1943. All correspondence from Pacific Coast Committee on National Security and Fair Play, Bancroft Library, Berkeley, box 1, "Correspondence," March 1942–September 1943.

22. Pacific Coast Committee on National Security and Fair Play, Bancroft Library, Berkeley, carton 1, folders 36, 42, and 43. Schiff declined an invitation to join the board.

23. Stein, *Gus J. Solomon*, 80, 82.

24. Stein, *Gus J. Solomon*, 23.

25. Eric Muller, *Free to Die for Their Country: The Story of the Japanese American Draft Resisters in World War II* (Chicago: University of Chicago Press, 2001), 132–33. Just over three hundred Nisei who were incarcerated at ten different camps refused induction into the U.S. Army. Their cases were heard in various federal district courts during the summer of 1944. All except for those whose cases were heard by Judge Goodman were convicted and served sentences averaging two years.

26. Muller, *Free to Die for Their Country*, 143. Michael Alexander, *Jazz Age Jews* (Princeton, N.J.: Princeton University Press, 2001).

27. Muller, *Free to Die for Their Country*, 133.

28. Ruth Kingman, "The Fair Play Committee and Citizen Participation," an interview conducted in 1971 by Rosemary Levinson in *Japanese-American Relocation Reviewed, Volume II: The Internment*, Regional Oral History Office, Bancroft Library, University of California, Berkeley, 1976.

29. Monroe Deutsch to Secretary of War Stimson, March 27, 1944, Pacific Coast Committee on National Security and Fair Play, Bancroft Library, Berkeley, box 2.

30. Monroe Deutsch, March 17, 1944, Pacific Coast Committee on National Security and Fair Play, Bancroft Library, Berkeley, box 2.

31. Daniel Koshland to Secretary of War Stimson, March 22, 1944. Pacific Coast Committee on National Security and Fair Play, Bancroft Library, Berkeley, box 2.

32. William Issel, "Jews and Catholics against Prejudice," in *California Jews*, edited by Ava F. Kahn and Marc Dollinger (Hanover, N.H.: Brandeis University Press/University Press of New Englad, 2003), 124–27.

33. William Carr to Ruth Kingman, June 13, 1943, Pacific Coast Committee on National Security and Fair Play Records, Bancroft Library, Berkeley, box 6.

34. William Carr to Ruth Kingman, July 6, 1943, Pacific Coast Committee on National Security and Fair Play Records, Bancroft Library, Berkeley, box 6.

35. Pacific Coast Committee on National Security and Fair Play Records, Bancroft Library, Berkeley, carton 1, folder 36.

36. Shana Bernstein, *Building Bridges at Home in a Time of Global Conflict: Interracial Cooperation and the Fight for Civil Rights in Los Angeles, 1933–1954*, Ph.D. diss., Stanford University, 2003, 154.

37. "Interview with Joseph Roos," July 20, 1943, Japanese American Evacuation and Resettlement Study, section 2, reel 011, frame 0666, folder A 19.02, News Research Service, Inc., Los Angeles, Japanese American Evacuation and Resettlement Records (BANC MSS 67/14 c), Bancroft Library, University of California, Berkeley, 41.

38. Bernstein, *Building Bridges at Home*, 109.

39. Bernstein, *Building Bridges at Home*, 94, 155.

40. Bernstein, *Building Bridges at Home*, chap. 3.

41. Bernstein, *Building Bridges at Home*, 155.

42. Joseph Roos oral history, quoted in Bernstein, *Building Bridges at Home*, 156.

43. Joseph Roos, January 6, 1944, quoted in Bernstein, *Building Bridges at Home*, 157.

44. See discussion in chapter 4.

45. Jewish Federation Council of Los Angeles' Community Relations Committee Collection (CRC2), Urban Archives Center, Oviatt Library, California State University, Northridge, box 223.

46. Issel, "Jews and Catholics against Prejudice," 123.

47. Cone, Droker, and Williams, *Family of Strangers*, 254.

48. Stuart Svonkin, *Jews against Prejudice: American Jews and the Fight for Civil Liberties* (New York: Columbia University Press, 1997), 17.

49. Svonkin, *Jews against Prejudice*, 13, 17–18.

50. Sarna, *American Judaism: A History* (New Haven, Conn.: Yale University Press, 2004), 307–9.

51. Sarna, *American Judaism*, 306–23.

52. The Redress Movement resulted in a detailed investigation of the policy, a repudiation of it as racist, a full presidential apology, and restitution payments for surviving Japanese Americans who had been incarcerated.

53. It has been my experience when speaking about Jewish silence on wartime policies to community groups that many people not only express surprise but also assert that groups like the ADL or the ACLU actually did act to support Japanese Americans and fight against the removal and incarceration policy. Among those who have made such assertions are people who have extensive experience in these organizations.

Bibliography

PERIODICALS

The B'nai B'rith Messenger, Los Angeles, California.
Emanu-El and the *Jewish Journal*, San Francisco, California.
Garfield Messenger, Seattle Public School Archives, Seattle, Washington.
News Letter, News Research Service, Los Angeles, California.
Oregon Native Son, volume I, 1899.
The Oregonian, Portland, Oregon.
Oregon Voter, Portland, Oregon.
The Scribe, Portland, Oregon.
Seattle Jewish Transcript, Seattle, Washington.
Temple Emanu-El Chronicle, Temple Emanu-El, San Francisco, California.
Temple Tidings, Temple de Hirsch, Seattle, Washington.
"A Walk through Japantown—1935," *Hokubei Mainichi*, Sunday, January 1, 1989, Supplement.

GOVERNMENT DOCUMENTS

California Joint Fact-Finding Committee on Un-American Activities, "Report," 1943. Online, http://www.archive.org/details/reportofjointfac00calirich.
California Commission on Immigration and Housing. *Second Annual Report.* January 1916.
Oregon State Immigration Commission. *Biennial Report.* 1913–1914.
U.S. Department of the Interior. *Wartime Exile: The Exclusion of the Japanese Americans from the West Coast.* New York: AMS Press, 1975 [reprint; originally published 1946].

U.S. House of Representatives. Hearings before the Select Committee Investigating National Defense Migration (Tolan Committee). 77th Congress, Second Session, parts 29, 30, 31, 1942.

U.S. House of Representatives, Special Committee on Un-American Activities. "Report on Japanese Activities." House of Representatives, 77th Congress, First Session, 1942.

ARCHIVAL COLLECTIONS

The Bancroft Library, University of California, Berkeley.
"Interview with Joseph Roos." July 20, 1943. Japanese American Evacuation and Resettlement Study, section 2, reel 011, frame 0666, folder A 19.02. News Research Service, Inc., Los Angeles. Japanese American evacuation and resettlement records (BANC MSS 67/14 c).
Pacific Coast Committee for National Security and Fair Play records (BANC MSS C-A 171).
Japanese American National Museum, Los Angeles.
Boyle Heights Oral History Project, transcripts.
Oregon Jewish Museum, Portland, Oregon.
Jewish Service Association minutes, January–March, 1942.
Neighborhood House, Board minutes.
Oregon Émigré Committee, minutes.
Portland Jewish Oral History Project.
Portland Section, National Council of Jewish Women, minutes.
Seattle Public Schools Archives, Seattle, Washington.
Special Collections, University of Washington Library, Seattle, Washington.
Mary Farquharson papers.
Washington State Jewish Historical Society archives.
Congregation Bikur Cholim papers.
Rabbi Samuel Koch Papers.
Seattle Section, National Council of Jewish Women.
Temple de Hirsch papers.
Urban Archives Center, Oviatt Library, California State University, Northridge.
Jewish Federation Council of Greater Los Angeles' Community Relations Committee Collection (CRC2) records.
"Joseph Roos Oral History Interview." Conducted by Leonard Pitt and Murray Wood, December 18, 1979; January 7 and 28, 1980; and February 14, 1980.
Western Jewish History Center, Berkeley, California.
Irving Reichert papers.
Temple Emanu-El collection.

SECONDARY SOURCES

Agresti, Olivia Rossett. *David Lubin: A Study in Practical Idealism.* Berkeley: University of California Press, 1922.

Alexander, Michael. *Jazz Age Jews.* Princeton, N.J.: Princeton University Press, 2001.

Almaguer, Tomas. *Racial Fault Lines: The Historical Origins of White Supremacy in California.* Berkeley: University of California Press, 1994.

Asato, Noriko. *Teaching Mikadoism: The Attack on Japanese Language Schools in Hawaii, California, and Washington, 1919–1927.* Honolulu: University of Hawaii Press, 2006.

Austin, Allan W. *From Concentration Camp to Campus: Japanese American Students and World War II.* Urbana: University of Illinois Press, 2004.

Berner, Richard. *Seattle Transformed: World War II to Cold War.* Seattle: Charles Press, 1999.

Bernstein, Shana. "Building Bridges at Home in a Time of Global Conflict: Interracial Cooperation and the Fight for Civil Rights in Los Angeles, 1933–1954." Ph.D. diss., Stanford University, 2003.

"Biography," *Guide to the Kilsoo Haan Papers,* Online Archive of California http://content.cdlib.org/ark:/13030/kt7j49p87r/.

Birdwell, Michael E. *Celluloid Soldiers: The Warner Brothers Campaign against Nazism.* New York: New York University Press, 1999.

Blair, Doug. "The 1920 Anti-Japanese Crusade and Congressional Hearings." Seattle Civil Rights and Labor History Project, http://depts.washington.edu/civilr/research_reports.htm.

Boxerman, Alan. "Kahn of California." *California Historical Quarterly* 55, no. 4 (1976): 340–51.

Britt, George. *The Fifth Column Is Here.* New York: W. Funk, 1940.

Buerge, David, and Junius Rochester. *Roots and Branches: The Religious Heritage of Washington State.* Seattle: Church Council of Greater Seattle, 1988.

Burgers, Jan Herman. "The Road to San Francisco: The Revival of the Human Rights Idea in the Twentieth Century." *Human Rights Quarterly* 14, no. 4 (November 1992): 447–77.

Chiasson, Lloyd. "Japanese American Relocation during World War II: A Study of California Editorial Reaction." *Journalism Quarterly* 68, nos. 1 & 2 (1991): 263–68.

Clar, Reva. "Samuel Sussman Snow: A Pioneer Finds El Dorado." *Western States Jewish Historical Quarterly* 3, no. 1 (1970): 3–25.

Clar, Reva, and William Kramer. "Chinese-Jewish Relations in the Far West: 1850–1950" part I. *Western States Jewish History* 21, no. 1 (1988): 12–35.

Clar, Reva, and William Kramer. "Chinese-Jewish Relations in the Far West: 1850–1950" part II. *Western States Jewish History* 21, no. 2 (1989): 132–53.

Cone, Molly, Howard Droker, and Jacqueline Williams. *Family of Strangers: Building a Jewish Community in Washington State.* Seattle: University of Washington Press/Washington State Jewish Historical Society, 2003.

Daniels, Roger. *Asian America: Chinese and Japanese in the United States since 1850.* Seattle: University of Washington Press, 1988.

———. *Concentration Camps: North America: Japanese in the United States and Canada during World War II.* Malabar, Fla.: R. E. Krieger, 1981.

———. *Guarding the Golden Door: American Immigration Policy and Immigrants Since 1882.* New York: Hill and Wang, 2004.

———. "The Japanese American Cases, 1942–2004: A Social History." *Law and Contemporary Problems* 68, no. 159 (2005): 159–71.

——. *Not Like Us: Immigrants and Minorities in America, 1890–1924*. Chicago: Ivan R. Dee, 1997.

——. *The Politics of Prejudice*. Berkeley: University of California Press, 1962.

——. *Prisoners without Trial*. New York: Hill and Wang, 1993.

——. "Words Do Matter: A Note on Inappropriate Terminology and the Incarceration of the Japanese Americans." Pp. 190–214 in *Nikkei in the Pacific Northwest*, edited by Louis Fiset and Gail M. Nomura. Seattle: University of Washington Press, 2005.

Daniels, Roger, Sandra C. Taylor, and Harry H. L. Kitano. *Japanese Americans from Relocation to Redress*. Salt Lake City: University of Utah Press, 1986.

Davis, Mike. *City of Quartz: Excavating the Future in Los Angeles*. New York: Verso, 1990.

Degginger, Craig. "Washington's Jewish Heritage. Jewish Geneological Society of Washington State, www.members.tripod.com/~JGSWS/history.htm.

de Nevers, Klancy Clark. *The Colonel and the Pacifist: Karl Bendetsen, Perry Saito and the Incarceration of Japanese Americans during World War II*. Salt Lake City: University of Utah Press, 2004.

Devine, Jean Porter. *From Settlement House to Neighborhood House*. Seattle: Neighborhood House, 1976.

Dickson, Lenore. "Social Distance in Two Seattle High Schools." M.A. thesis, University of Washington, 1951.

Dies, Martin. *Trojan Horse in America*. New York: Dodd, Mead & Company, 1940.

Diner, Hasia. *In the Almost Promised Land: American Jews and Blacks, 1915–1935*. Baltimore: Johns Hopkins University Press, 1977, 1995.

Dollinger, Marc. *Quest for Inclusion: Jews and Liberalism in Modern America*. Princeton, N.J.: Princeton University Press, 2000.

Dye, Douglas M. *The Soul of the City: The Work of the Seattle Council of Churches during World War II*. Ph.D. diss., Washington State University, 1997.

Eisenberg, Ellen. "As Truly American as Your Son: Voicing Opposition to Internment in Three West Coast Cities." *Oregon Historical Quarterly* 104, no. 4 (2004): 542–65.

——. "Civil Rights and Japanese American Incarceration." Pp. 110–22 in *California Jews*, edited by Ava F. Kahn and Marc Dollinger. Hanover, N.H.: Brandeis University Press/University Press of New England, 2003.

Eisenberg, Ellen, Ava F. Kahn, and Bill Toll. *Jews of the Pacific West: Creating a Regional Society* (tentative title). Seattle: University of Washington Press, forthcoming, 2009.

Elliott, Wendy. "The Jews of Boyle Heights, 1900–1950." *Southern California Quarterly* 78, no. 1 (1996): 1–10.

Elliot-Scheinberg, Wendy. *Boyle Heights: Jewish Ambiance in a Multicultural Neighborhood*. Ph.D. diss., Claremont Graduate University, 2001.

Flamm, Jerry. *Good Life in Hard Times: San Francisco in the 1920s and 1930s*. San Francisco: Chronicle Books, 1999.

Geary, Daniel. "Carey McWilliams and Antifascism, 1934–1943." *Journal of American History* 90, no. 3 (December 2003): 912–34.

Glanz, Rudolph. "Jews and Chinese in America." *Jewish Social Studies* 16, no. 3 (1954): 219–34.

Glassberg, David. "Making Places in California." Pp. 167–202 in *Sense of History: The Place of the Past in American Life.* Amherst: University of Massachusetts Press, 2001.

"A Glimpse of Portland's Japantown, 1940." Portland: Oregon Nikkei Legacy Center, undated.

Goldstein, Eric. *The Price of Whiteness: Jews, Race and American Identity.* Princeton, N.J.: Princeton University Press, 2006.

Gordon, Linda. *The Great Arizona Orphan Abduction.* Cambridge, Mass.: Harvard University Press, 2001.

Greenberg, Cheryl. "Black and Jewish Responses to Japanese Internment." *Journal of American Ethnic History* 14, no. 2 (Winter 1995): 3–37.

Greenstein, Howard. *Turning Point: Zionism and Reform Judaism.* Chico, Calif.: Scholars Press, 1981.

Grodzins, Morton. *Americans Betrayed.* Chicago: University of Chicago Press, 1949.

Grover, Warren. *Nazis in Newark.* New Brunswick, N.J.: Transaction Publishers, 2003.

Herman, Felicia. "Hollywood, Nazism, and the Jews." *American Jewish History* 89, no. 1 (2001).

———. "Jewish Leaders and the Motion Picture Industry." Pp. 95–109 in *California Jews*, edited by Ava Kahn and Marc Dollinger. Hanover, N.H.: Brandeis University Press/University Press of New England, 2003.

Higham, John. *Strangers in the Land: Patterns of American Nativism, 1860–1925.* New York: Atheneum, 1985 [1963].

Hosokawa, Bill. *JACL: In Quest of Justice.* New York: William Morrow and Company, 1982.

"In Our Own Backyard: Resisting Nazi Propaganda in Southern California, 1933–1945." Online exhibit, Special Collections, California State University, Northridge.

Irons, Peter. *Justice Delayed: The Record of the Japanese American Internment Cases.* Middleton, Conn.: Wesleyan University Press, 1989.

———. *Justice at War: The Story of the Japanese American Internment Cases.* Oxford: Oxford University Press, 1983.

Issel, William. "Jews and Catholics against Prejudice." Pp. 123–34 in *California Jews*, edited by Ava F. Kahn and Marc Dollinger. Hanover, N.H.: Brandeis University Press/University Press of New England, 2003.

Jacobson, Matthew Frye. *Whiteness of a Different Color.* Cambridge, Mass.: Harvard University Press, 1988.

Jameson, Elizabeth. *All That Glitters: Class, Conflict, and Community in Cripple Creek.* Urbana: University of Illinois, 1998.

Japanese American National Museum. *Los Angeles's Boyle Heights.* Images of America Series. Charleston, S.C.: Arcadia Publishing, 2005.

"The 'Japanese Question' Confronts the State." *Oregon Responds to World War II*, web exhibit, Oregon State Archives, http://arcweb.sos.state.or.us/exhibits/ww2/threat/question.htm.

The Jewish Immigration Bulletin. Report of the 6th annual meeting of the Hebrew Sheltering and Immigrant Aid Society of America, 5, no. 30 (March 1915).

Johnston, Robert. *The Radical Middle Class.* Princeton, N.J.: Princeton University Press, 2003.

Katagiri, Doug, ed. *Nihonmachi: Portland's Japantown Remembered.* Portland: Oregon Nikkei Legacy Center, 2002.

Kessler, Lauren. *Stubborn Twig.* New York: Penguin, 1993.

King, Desmond. *Making Americans: Immigration, Race and the Origins of the Diverse Democracy.* Cambridge, Mass.: Harvard University Press, 2000.

Kingman, Ruth. "The Fair Play Committee and Citizen Participation." Oral history conducted in 1974 by Rosemary Levenson. *Japanese-American Relocation Reviewed, Volume II: The Internment,* Regional Oral History Office, The Bancroft Library, University of California, Berkeley, 1976. Online, http://ia331334.us.archive.org/1/items/japaneseamerican01leverich/japaneseamerican01leverich.pdf.

Koepplin, Leslie. *A Relationship of Reform: Immigrants and Progressives in the Far West.* New York: Garland Press, 1990.

Kolsky, Thomas. *Jews against Zionism: The American Council for Judaism, 1942–1948.* Philadelphia: Temple University Press, 1990.

Kramer, William, and Reva Clar. "Rabbi Edgar F. Magnin and the Modernization of Los Angeles Jewry," part I. *Western States Jewish History* 19, no. 3 (1987): 233–51.

Kutulas, Judy. *The American Civil Liberties Union and the Making of Modern Liberalism, 1930–1960.* Chapel Hill: University of North Carolina Press, 2006.

———. "In Quest of Autonomy: The Northern California Affiliate of the American Civil Liberties Union and World War II." *Pacific Historical Review* 67, no. 2 (1998): 201–31.

Lehman, Benjamin. "Homage to Monroe Deutsch: Three Addresses Delivered at a Gathering in His Memory." Berkeley: University of California, 1955.

Limerick, Patricia. *Legacy of Conquest.* New York: Norton, 1987.

Lowenstein, Steven. *The Jews of Oregon.* Portland: Jewish Historical Society of Oregon, 1987.

Margolis, Ben. "Law and Social Conscience." Oral History interview by Michael Balter, 1984–85, University of California, Los Angeles, Oral History Program, Department of Special Collections, Charles E. Young Research Library, U.C. Los Angeles. Online: http://content.cdlib.org/ark:/13030/hb6c6010vb/.

Matthews, Fred H. "White Community and 'Yellow Peril.'" *The Mississippi Valley Historical Review* 50, no. 4 (March 1964): 612–33.

McKay, Floyd. "Pacific Northwest Newspapers and Executive Order 9066." Paper presented at The Nikkei Experience in the Northwest conference, Seattle, 2000.

McWilliams, Carey. *It CAN Happen Here: Active Anti-Semitism in Los Angeles.* Los Angeles: American League against War and Fascism and Jewish Anti-Nazi League of Southern California, 1935.

———. *Prejudice: Japanese Americans: Symbol of Racial Intolerance.* Hamdon, Conn.: Archon Books, 1971 [1944].

Morris, Benjamin. "True American: The Media Battle on Private Schools and the Oregon Compulsory Education Bill, 1922–1925." M.A. Thesis, University of Portland, 2005.

Muller, Eric. *Free to Die for Their Country: The Story of the Japanese American Draft Resisters in World War II.* Chicago: University of Chicago Press, 2001.

"Neighborhood Profile." The Boyle Heights Oral History Project, Japanese American National Museum, Los Angeles.

Okihiro, Gary. "The Press, Japanese Americans, and the Concentration Camps." *Phylon* 44, no. 1 (1983): 66–83.

Olin, Spencer C., Jr. "European Immigrant and Oriental Alien: Acceptance and Rejection by the California Legislature of 1913." *Pacific Historical Review* 35 (1966): 303–15.

Olmstead, Timothy. "Nikkei Internment: The Perspective of Two Oregon Weekly Newspapers." *Oregon Historical Quarterly* (Spring 1984): 5–32.

Pak, Yoon K. *Wherever I Go, I Will Always be a Loyal American: Schooling Seattle's Japanese Americans during World War II*. New York: Routledge Falmer, 2002.

Phillips, Bruce. "The Challenge of Family, Identity and Affiliations." Pp. 17–28 in *California Jews*, edited by Ava F. Kahn and Marc Dollinger. Hanover, N.H.: Brandeis University Press/University Press of New England, 2003.

Proceedings of the Asiatic Exclusion League, 1907–1913. New York, Arno Press, 1977.

Roedigger, David. *Working Toward Whiteness*. New York: Basic Books, 2005.

Rogoff, Leonard. "Is the Jew White? The Racial Place of the Southern Jew." *American Jewish History*, Special issue on Directions in Southern Jewish History 85, no. 3 (September 1997), 195–230.

Rosenbaum, Fred. *Architects of Reform: Congregational and Community Leadership Emanu-El of San Francisco, 1849–1980*. Berkeley: Judah L. Magnes Museum, 1980.

———. *Free to Choose: The Making of a Jewish Community in the American West*. Berkeley, Calif.: Judah L. Magnes Museum, 1976.

———. *Visions of Reform: Congregation Emanu-El and the Jews of San Francisco, 1849–1999*. Berkeley, Calif.: Judah L. Magnes Museum, 2000.

Saalfeld, Lawrence J. *Forces of Prejudice in Oregon, 1920–1925*. Portland, Ore.: Archdiocesan Historical Commission, 1984.

Sanchez, George. "Roundtable on Regionalism: The Significance of Place in American Jewish Life." Plenary remarks, American Jewish History Biennial Scholars' Conference, Charleston, June 2006.

———. "What's Good for Boyle Heights Is Good for the Jews: Creating Multiracialism on the Eastside during the 1950s." *American Quarterly* 56, no. 3 (September 2004): 633–61.

Sarna, Jonathan. *American Judaism: A History*. New Haven, Conn.: Yale University Press, 2004.

Schmid, Calvin. *Social Trends in Seattle*. University of Washington Publications in the Social Sciences, vol. 14. Seattle: University of Washington Press, 1944.

Schmoe, Floyd. "Seattle's Peace Churches and Relocation." In *Japanese Americans: From Relocation to Redress*, ed. Roger Daniels, Sandra C. Taylor, and Harry H. L. Kitano. Salt Lake City: University of Utah Press, 1986.

Schwartz, Henry. "The Silver Shirts: Anti-Semitism in San Diego." *Western States Jewish History* 25, no. 1 (1992): 52–60.

Seigel, Shizue. *In Good Conscience: Supporting Japanese Americans during the Internment*. San Mateo, Calif.: AACP, 2006.

Shaffer, Robert. "Cracks in the Consensus: Defending the Rights of Japanese Americans during World War II." *Radical History Review* 72 (1998): 84–120.

———. "Opposition to Internment: Defending Japanese American Rights during World War II." *The Historian* 61, no. 3 (Spring 1999): 597–619.

Simon, James. *The Antagonists: Hugo Black, Felix Frankfurter and Civil Liberties in Modern America*. New York: Simon and Schuster, 1989.

Speidel, Jennifer. "After Internment: Seattle's Debate over Japanese Americans' Right to Return Home." *Seattle Civil Rights and Labor History Project*. Online, www.depts.washington.edu/civilr/.

Stein, Harry. *Gus J. Solomon: Liberal Politics, Jews, and the Federal Courts*. Portland: Oregon Historical Society Press, 2006.

Steiner, Jesse F. *The Japanese Invasion*. Chicago: A.C. McClurg, 1917; reprint, New York: Arno Press, 1978.

Stern, Alexandra Minna. *Eugenic Nation: Faults and Frontiers of Better Breeding in America*. Berkeley: University of California, 2005.

Stuppy, Laurence. "Henry H. Lissner, M.D., Los Angeles Physician." *Western States Jewish Historical Quarterly* 8, no. 3 (1976): 209–16.

Svonkin, Stuart. *Jews against Prejudice: American Jews and the Fight for Civil Liberties*. New York: Columbia University Press, 1997.

Tamura, Linda. *Hood River Issei: An Oral History of Japanese Settlers in Oregon's Hood River Valley*. Urbana: University of Illinois Press, 1993.

Taylor, Sandra. *Jewel of the Desert: Japanese American Internment at Topaz*. Berkeley: University of California Press, 1993.

Toll, William. *The Making of an Ethnic Middle Class*. Albany: SUNY Press, 1982.

———. "Permanent Settlement: Japanese Families in Portland in 1920." *Western Historical Quarterly* 28, no. 1 (Spring 1997): 18–43.

Toy, Eckard. "Whose Frontier? The Survey of Race Relations on the Pacific Coast in the 1920s." *Oregon Historical Quarterly* 107, no. 1 (Spring 2006): 36–63.

Van Nuys, Frank. *Americanizing the West Race, Immigrants, and Citizenship, 1890–1930*. Lawrence: University Press of Kansas, 2002.

———. "A Progressive Confronts the Race Question: Chester Rowell, the California Alien Land Act of 1913, and the Contradictions of Early Twentieth Century Racial Thought." *California History* 73 (Spring 1994): 2–13.

———. "Sowing the Seeds of Internment: James D. Phelan's Anti-Japanese Crusade, 1919–1920." Pp. 1–11 in *Remembering Heart Mountain: Essays on Japanese American Internment in Wyoming*, edited by Mike Mackey. Powell, Wyo.: Western History Publications, 1998.

Varzally, Allison. *Ethnic Crossings: The Making of a Non-White America in the Second Quarter of Twentieth Century California*. Ph.D. diss., University of California, Los Angeles, 2002.

———. "Romantic Crossings: Making Love, Family and Non-Whiteness in California, 1925–1950." *Journal of American Ethnic History* 23, no. 1 (Fall 2003): 3–54.

Vorspan, Max, and Lloyd Gartner. *History of the Jews of Los Angeles*. Philadelphia: Jewish Publication Society, 1970.

Weill, Irma. "Alphonse Weill of Bakersfield." *Western States Jewish Historical Quarterly* 4, no. 1 (1971): 1–10.

Wild, Mark. *Street Meeting: Multiethnic Neighborhoods in Early Twentieth Century Los Angeles*. Berkeley: University of California Press, 2005.

Wilson, Karen. "Citizens of Los Angeles: Jewish Families and the Naissance of the Metropolis." M.A. thesis, Hebrew Union College, Los Angeles, 2003.

Wong, Marie Rose. *Sweet Cakes, Long Journey: The Chinatowns of Portland Oregon.* Seattle: University of Washington Press, 2004.

Woo-Sam, Anne. "Americanizing Californians: Americanization in California from the Progressive Era through the Red Scare." *PART: An On-Line Journal of Art Histories and Visuality* 9 (2003). http://dsc.gc.cuny.edu/part/part9/identities/articles/woosa.html.

Yoo, David. *Growing Up Nisei: Race, Generation and Culture among Japanese Americans of California, 1924–1949.* Urbana: University of Illinois Press, 2000.

Index

About the Author

Ellen Eisenberg has taught at Willamette University since 1990, and was appointed to the Dwight and Margaret Lear Professorship in American History in 2003. She holds a BA from Carleton College and a Ph.D. from the University of Pennsylvania, and is the author of *Jewish Agricultural Colonies in New Jersey, 1882–1920* (Syracuse, 1995). Her work on western Jewish communities has appeared in *American Jewish History* and *Journal of American Ethnic History* as well as in the anthologies *California Jews* (Brandeis University Press, 2003) and *Jewish Life in the American West* (Autry Museum/ Heyday Books, 2002). Her current projects include a monograph coauthored with Ava Kahn and William Toll on the history of Jews in the Pacific West, to be published by University of Washington Press in 2009. She lives in Salem, Oregon, with her husband Ami Korsunsky and sons Alex and Ben.